BODY, HEART, AND TEXT IN THE *PEARL*-POET

Kevin Marti

Studies in Mediaeval Literature
Volume 12

The Edwin Mellen Press
Lewiston/Queenston/Lampeter

Library of Congress Cataloging-in-Publication Data

Marti, Kevin.
   Body, heart, and text in the "Pearl"-poet / Kevin Marti.
     p. cm. -- (Studies in mediaeval literature ; v. 12)
   Includes bibliographical references and index.
   ISBN 0-7734-9764-1
   1. Pearl (Middle English poem) 2. Gawain and the Grene Knight.
3. Patience (Middle English poem) 4. English poetry--Middle
English, 1100-1500--History and criticism. 5. Body, Human, in
literature. 6. Heart in literature. I. Title. II. Series.
PR1972.G353M37 1991
821'.1--dc20.   91-29879
                                                                                CIP

This is volume 12 in the continuing series
Studies in Mediaeval Literature
Volume 12   ISBN 0-7734-9764-1
SML Series   ISBN 0-88946-314-X

A CIP catalog record for this book
is available from the British Library.

Copyright © 1991 Kevin Marti

All rights reserved. For information contact

   The Edwin Mellen Press   The Edwin Mellen Press
          Box 450   Box 67
    Lewiston, New York   Queenston, Ontario
       USA 14092   CANADA, L0S 1L0

The Edwin Mellen Press, Ltd.
Lampeter, Dyfed, Wales
UNITED KINGDOM SA48 7DY

Printed in the United States of America

For Paul Amago

CONTENTS

Acknowledgments   i

1. Interpretive Framework   1
2. The Gothic Cathedral   27
3. Body, Space, and Microcosm in Medieval Literature   51
4. Preliminary Textual Examples   63
5. *Pearl*'s Vineyard Parable as a Textual Center   83
6. "To Clanly Clos": *Pearl*'s Concentric Settings   101
7. The Spatiality of the Heart in *Pearl*   131
8. "Ayquere Hit Is Endelez": Pentangle and Text in *Sir Gawain and the Green Knight*   157
9. "Hellen Wombe": The Heart of *Patience*   171

BIBLIOGRAPHY   183

INDEX   205

ACKNOWLEDGMENTS

At each stage of this project I have benefited from others' advice and support. Giuseppe Mazzotta first suggested the topic during a lecture on Dante; I am deeply indebted to him for his encouragement and counsel at critical junctures in my research. The late R. E. Kaske gave me the necessary orientation for my wanderings within the labyrinth of patristic lore, and read my early manuscripts with care. Others who were especially supportive at an early stage include Thomas Hill, Alice Colby-Hall, and Arthur Groos.

I did most of my research at the Bayerische Staatsbibliothek in Munich; I am grateful to the librarians there for their patience. My colleagues at the University of Munich provided a much-needed sounding board; Elisabeth Bronfen, Volker Hoffmann, Elisabeth Donaldson, and Mark Osborne supplied encouragement and bibliography. Helmut Gneuss and Johannes Gottwald took great pains to provide me with research facilities and information about Munich's maze of libraries. Jutta Hillebrand, Gaby Knappe, Evelyn Wirth, and Michael Banneck contributed to my project in many practical ways.

The structure of my argument took definitive shape during two years of daily conversations with Paul Amago, who taught me how to read buildings and worked hundreds of hours building the research file; my greatest debt is to him.

My colleagues at the University of New Orleans have supported my work in many ways. John Hazlett and Inge Fink read the manuscript with care and helped me avoid a number of blunders. Brenton Steele also read the manuscript and, more importantly, provided a judicious mix of prodding and support that helped me bring the project to its conclusion. Robert Sturges and Rima Reck contributed excellent advice on a number of matters. Sean Sperry, William Middleton, and David Swords provided considerable help with technical problems.

Much credit is due to Harriette Whiteman and Elva McAllaster, whose interest in my work spans many years, and to the Danforth Foundation for its generous financial assistance. I am also grateful to the editors at the Edwin Mellen Press, especially Andrea Laese and John Rupnow, for their patient cooperation at various stages of manuscript preparation.

Finally I must thank my parents for calmly resolving many long-distance emergencies while I wrote abroad, and for supporting my work in countless other ways.

Chapter One

INTERPRETIVE FRAMEWORK

For some time now it has been possible to speak of a "modern rediscovery of the body," a contemporary revalidation of man's oldest matrix for understanding his world. This current fashion, embraced in both academic and nonacademic circles, has found its way into published explorations of the most disparate topics. The symbolic primacy of phallus and womb in Freud, for example, and the consequent reinterpretation of man's environment as projected layers of his own corporeal space, prompted C. G. Jung to hail "the rediscovery of the body after its long depreciation in the name of the spirit."[1]

Elaine Scarry sees an analogous spatial paradigm in the field of history and economics, noting Marx's understanding of human labor "in successive circles of self-extension" around the shape of the hand and back.[2] Mircea Eliade's works on comparative religion urge modern man to rediscover the forgotten microcosmic symbolism of his body, to retreat from the prevailing Cartesian framework of homogenous, relative space,[3] and Alan W. Watts' more popular writings make a similar plea.[4] Philosophers in the wake of Edmund Husserl have devoted considerable attention to the phenomenological relation of body and space,[5] and the especially wide-ranging interests by anthropologists in this area have borne fruit in a large volume of published work, in particular four anthologies edited by Dietmar Kamper.[6] The heightened body consciousness in popular culture which has accompanied this academic movement has also been documented in several studies.[7] Whatever their academic or popular orientation, writers in this tradition return consistently to the same theme: the body as a lost principle of unity, a meaning-laden spatial center, a microcosm.[8]

Scholarly and critical writings on the arts have, to some extent, adapted the concerns of this movement to their own purposes. The close interdependence between the human body and its built environment is, of course, nothing new in architecture theory, but even here many critics find that the governing corporeal matrix has been abandoned; the rational, Cartesian order governing modernist building design ignores, they claim, the organic proportion and symbolic framework of body-centered space. Kent Bloomer and Charles Moore's *Body, Memory and Architecture*, a brilliant critique of modernism, has established itself as the starting-place for studies of the body in the other arts as well.[9] Writings on the human body in painting, for example, often presuppose an understanding of the body's relation to architectural form.[10]

Joseph Frank is often credited with having inaugurated the self-conscious use of "spatiality" as a critical term, and most studies in his wake have confined themselves primarily to the novel and modern literature.[11] Always somewhat controversial, these studies have nonetheless by now acquired sufficient respectability that one may encounter glancing references to literary space in many publications whose principal concerns lie elsewhere.[12] As is so often the case with relatively recent (and even not so recent) developments in literary scholarship, detailed analyses of the body and space in individual texts have largely ignored the Middle Ages.[13]

The result is both ironic and a bit comical: as contributors to a research tradition claiming to have resurrected an organizing principle lost since the Middle Ages, scholars have nonetheless systematically ignored the very texts where, by their own argument, that principle should be most explicitly operative. The post-medieval "repression" of the body, the migration of the body's perceived center from the heart up to the head accompanying Western man's growing trust in reason, continues to govern the work of its discoverers.[14] Medieval literature is still relegated to the philologists (no one else can read all the languages, anyway).

Gaston Bachelard's seminal work in literary space acknowledges its debt to Freudian and phenomenological tradition, and Bloomer and Moore write with a similar awareness of both Freud and anthropological theories of space and perception. But, unfortunately, more recent studies of literature have sometimes been inclined to work in something of a theoretical vacuum—a trend that is likely to increase as the notion of literary space gains respectability.[15] As a response to this tendency, the present study begins by stressing the eclecticism of any really satisfying research of this kind: all attempts to come to terms with the body in literature—especially medieval literature—must *by definition* be interdisciplinary, because by reasserting the body's epistemological centrality we reclaim for it its status as a nexus for all ways of knowing in all disciplines. That it held this status in the Middle Ages can hardly be doubted, and it is with the unearthing of this lost status and all of its consequences that the vast collection of research on the body concerns itself. Scholars undertaking studies without knowledge of the goals of the entire cross-disciplinary enterprise often fail simply because they do not know what they are trying to prove. The simultaneous growth of interest during recent decades in both interdisciplinary studies and the epistemological unity of the body is surely no coincidence.

Lest the preceding paragraphs mislead anyone, I must stress from the outset my intent to restrict my inquiry as much as possible to the most traditional, time-honored methods of medieval literary scholarship. This study is primarily only interdisciplinary in ways that many excellent studies have been before it: it takes as a starting point minute examination of extensive theological traditions written in Latin, and applies its findings to the interpretation of vernacular texts. The comparison here between the structure and symbolism of literature and that of both the Gothic cathedral and medieval iconography is also nothing new to medieval studies, though the impressionistic and fragmentary nature of some such studies has made many scholars wary of them; I hope to overcome these common shortcomings via detailed textual analysis and support from a broad range of sources.

This study aims to be theoretical, but proceeds in a manner uncharacteristic of most of the scholarship which juxtaposes texts with current theories of literature. Recent innovations in the ways scholars read texts have a demonstrable affinity to the contours of my argument, but my conclusions in no way presuppose acceptance of (or even familiarity with) these trends. Rather than imposing a twentieth-century critical framework on the texts at hand, this study proposes a medieval theory of reading/writing based on medieval sources. The last few decades' interest in the body and textual spatiality is relevant here only to the extent that it constitutes a rediscovery—but to this extent it is enormously relevant. For if, as is claimed, medieval man's body constituted his single most important aesthetic and perceptual framework, we may consequently expect it to provide a demonstrably sustained and consistent structure in the full range of his artistic production. The following chapters concern themselves with the elucidation of corporeal structures in the *Pearl*-Poet's opus—especially the *Pearl* poem itself—via disclosure of parallel structural concerns in theology, other vernacular literature, and medieval iconography and architecture. But these latter areas of inquiry do not fully subordinate themselves to my interpretation of the *Pearl*-Poet. In most of them I attempt to make a substantial, original contribution whose validity is independent of any other chapter.

The microcosm/macrocosm matrix that so clearly dominated medieval spatial perception implies a structural and semantic equivalence of part and whole, the capacity for meaning to reside as fully in a detail as in an overarching design. Hence we may expect literary research taking the body as its theme to confront the tiniest textual cruxes at the same time that it seeks to define the most comprehensive infra- and intertextual patterns. Many studies consider the individual spaces described within a poem without coming to terms with the space created by the text's own body of words itself, not to mention its relation to other texts and to nonliterary aesthetic products. Here the issue of thematic and structural unity in a text—an issue that reasserts itself in every attempt to interpret a work of literature—is revealed as a question of layers of unity, of concentric clusters of unities. The implications for scholarship, of course, are as daunting as they are alluring, because in an aesthetic world of microcosms the only literary interpretations which can claim validity at one level are those that work at all literary and extra-literary levels. I have written the chapters that follow as a rough indication of what shape such a research project might take, a trial run in book form. *Pearl* constitutes its expository centerpiece; the other works briefly discussed are considered as microcosmic structures whose resemblence to the *Pearl* varies as a measure of their proximity to it: at the nearest level, two of the poet's other three poems, then other medieval texts, and finally architectural and iconographic influences. My most meticulous grappling with textual cruxes and other problems similarly restricted to tiny stretches of text confines itself to the chapters on *Pearl*; in my consideration of other texts, I focus more exclusively on broader structural similarities (in particular, the role of the structural and thematic "center"), though even in them unravelling a structurally central crux often provides the cornerstone of my interpretation.

The first chapters of this study broadly outline the theological foundations of microcosmic spatial and temporal organization, discussing its appearance in cathedral design and, in general, its literary manifestations. Here I begin by looking at the social and doctrinal basis for the organizing nexus of the body in the Middle Ages, clarifying the status of medieval thinking within the longer tradition of microcosmic speculation, aligning microcosmic theory with the related doctrines of plenitude and recapitulation, and mentioning a few of the almost endless variety of spatial "centers" that this cluster of doctrines recognized.

Edward T. Hall's classic sociological study of space, *The Hidden Dimension*, finds that the complex configurations of entire cultures often can be reduced to extremely simple matrices governing social and material organization at every level. He writes: "long experience with different patterns of culture has taught me that the same basic threads tend to be woven throughout the entire fabric of a society."[16] He contrasts, for example, the "grid" pattern of Asia Minor, the Roman empire, and modern-day England with the "star" pattern dominant in France and Spain. Thus, he explains, the French highway network links each city with the cluster of smaller cities nearby via a star pattern, whereby travellers from one minor city to another must follow routes to and from the nearest major city rather than a more direct course; at the highest level, Paris constitutes the hub of a star linking it with the most important cities all over France.

Anyone who has had to come to terms with a foreign culture during an extended stay abroad must be especially struck by the enormous usefulness of Hall's key idea here; he defines cultural coherence according to the specific character of its microcosmic hierarchy.[17] Surely, too, Hall provides an analytical *modus operandi* whose applicability to medieval theological organization should particularly impress students of the Middle Ages—though I am aware of no scholar who has made the connection. At every level, medieval culture derives its shape from the body of Christ much as French culture finds its ruling matrix in the star; spatially, temporally, and doctrinally, Christ's body constitutes the center. And this notion of "centrality" amounted to quite a bit more than the familiar affirmation of the pivotal position of Christology in medieval theology. It was not only an important doctrine in its own right; it also provided the doctrinal kernel for the medieval understanding of geometry, geography, and history. In the course of this discussion I will show the extraordinary precision with which Hall's formulation may guide us, like travellers looking for Paris on a road map, to the structural and thematic center of works of art microcosmically displaying medieval culture in its wholeness; following the structural lineaments of buildings, drawings, and texts until they converge, we will consistently encounter the body (or heart) of Christ at the center—or the microcosmic body represented by one or more of its figural equivalents: the pearl, pentangle, altar vessel, rose, wheel, or chain.

Beginning with the human body and tracing the extensions it creates around itself via unions with other people, we can easily understand the corporeal character of the medieval family, guild ("corporation"), kingdom ("body politic"), and church ("mystical body"); each of these social unions, like their counterparts in modern religious and political organization, functioned as a relatively self-contained organism whose members' different roles conjoined to provide for the group what no individual could obtain on his own. Architecturally and geographically, this arrangement manifested itself, then much as now, in family structures clustered into communities, communities grouped into cities or castles, and cities gathered into kingdoms—with prominent "head" or "heart" structures denoting dominance at each concentric level: the highest stories of a dwelling, churches and royal dwellings within cities, major cities within kingdoms.[18] Even human language, spoken and written, and human artistic expression have since long before the Middle Ages ranked among these other bodily "extensions."[19]

The dominant, central locus of Christ's body in medieval spatial perception receives attention in Josef Sauer's well-known study of cathedral symbolism in the Middle Ages, and in the work of Hugo Rahner.[20] Christ's body as the center of medieval time and history has commanded an especially broad range of scholarly attention.[21] And from an even larger perspective, a plethora of publications in recent decades, spearheaded by the work of Émile Mersch, have firmly established the doctrine of the mystical body as a center and *summa* of patristic theology as a whole—a *nexus mysteriorum* from which all truth emanates and in which all teachings converge.[22] All of these notions of centrality manifest themselves in the patristic understanding of corporeal textuality, whereby the Bible resides as a body at the microcosmic core of the physical and symbolic universe: "Daß das Bibelwort ein beseelter Leib ist, der als Monade das Ganze der sichtbaren und gewußten Welt umfaßt, steht am Anfang der Tradition."[23] Hence the literary confluence of such a vast network of related teachings in the poetic works at hand will come as no surprise.

A general awareness of medieval culture's body matrix is not hard to come by in the scholarship of several fields. Kamper writes:

> Die Wissenschaften, die sich bisher mit dem Schicksal des Körpers befaßt haben, gehen fast übereinstimmend davon aus, daß der historische Fortschritt europäischer Prägung seit dem Mittelalter aufgrund einer spezifisch abendländischen Trennung von Körper und Geist ermöglicht wurde. . . .[24]

Students of art have undoubtedly shared this general awareness with scholars in other disciplines; one of Gerhart B. Ladner's well-known essays on pictorial art begins with this categorical statement: "In the Middle Ages the central tenet of Christian theology was also the greatest justification of Christian art. It was the Incarnation which made religious art legitimate."[25] Marshall McLuhan's main thesis is the similarity of medieval and modern worlds via a shared corporeal sense in poetry and painting, and David L. Jeffrey's work on textual referentiality warns against the popular conception of "unembodied" medieval spirituality.[26] But the studies accompanying such statements often offer little more than hazy first impressions where literary interpretation is concerned; either their subject is something other than textual interpretation itself, or they are undertaken by nonmedievalists poorly equipped to enter the labyrinth of exegetical learning. We will require a very precise understanding of the "embodiedness" of medieval culture before proceeding to the "embodiedness" of medieval texts.

Of first importance is the doctrine of the microcosm itself, a philosophical tradition whose Western roots extend to the Greeks and beyond, and whose influence remains strong in twentieth-century atomic theory. The point of departure for any treatment of this tradition is the work of Adolf Meyer, G. P. Conger, and Rudolf Allers; these long studies, though somewhat uneven in quality, nonetheless provide a historical overview of the topic as outlined in philosophical and, to a lesser extent, theological treatises. What they do not study—and what is generally missing in scholarship—is the broader cultural impact that intensive analysis of aesthetic form reveals.[27]

Meyer credits Plato with the first systematic expression of microcosmic theory, though one does not find the generic labels *microcosmus* and *macrocosmus* (or *megacosmus*, as in Bernardus Silvestris) until much later.[28] The notion was well-known to the Greek fathers via Neoplatonism, and to Latin authors through Chalcidius' commentary on the *Timaeus*, Macrobius, and Isidore's *Etymologiae*.[29] Entire medieval works dedicated to the concept include that by Bernardus Silvestris, *De mundi universitate, sive Megacosmus et Microcosmus*,[30] a work entitled "Microkosmus" by Joseph Ibn Zaddik which Bernardus apparently inspired,[31] and another with the same title authored by Geoffrey of St. Victor,[32] all three written in the twelfth century. The doctrine reappears in the writings of many major medieval thinkers. Aquinas, for example, states: "In homine est quaedam similitudo ordinis universi, unde et minor mundus dicitur quia mones naturae quasi in homine confluunt," and again "Omnis creatura corporalis in assimilationem hominis tendit, in quantum per hoc summae bonitati assimilatur";[33] Meyer also finds the term mentioned in Johannes Scotus, Hugh of St. Victor, and Nicolas of Cusa.[34] Medieval literary references include a line from Theseus' speech in Chaucer's *Knight's Tale*: "Wel may men knowe, but it be a fool, / That every part dirryveth from his hool" (ll. 3005-06).

Research on the microcosm in the history of ideas often underscores its political manifestation at the expense of more theological ramifications; hence a king constitutes the state's head and, at another metaphorical level, the kingdom's sun, around which lesser powers revolve.[35] The notion of the "body politic" makes its most conspicuous early appearance with Plato and survives into the fourteenth century through the writings of John of Salisbury, Marsilius of Padua and Nicolas of Cusa, providing the key matrix for the educational institution as microcosm (*universitas*).[36] But Greek corporational theory entered the religious sphere as early as St. Paul, and in the Middle Ages exercised an equal, if not greater, influence via theological and mystical teachings.[37] Thus Mersch dedicates an entire book to the relations between microcosmic theory and the patristic understanding of the mystical body.[38]

The idea of the Logos, "der Mittler zwischen Gott und Welt,"[39] provides a basis for Greek microcosmic speculation in Philo of Alexandria and Heraclitus long before New Testament writers adopted it for their own purposes.[40] Man's own position as God's image at the center of creation, standing between divine and animal existence and containing within him elements of all creatures superior and inferior, thus found expression first among Greek writers and later, repeatedly, in medieval theology. The human position as *nodus et vinculum, medietas et catena* of the entire universe constitutes what one scholar considers the "profoundest intuition" in Greek thinking, and the impact on the Middle Ages is unmistakeable.[41] Augustine writes that man is "medium quoddam; sed inter pecora et angelos . . . medius homo . . . infra angelis sed super pecoribus; homini cum pecoribus mortalitatem, rationem vero cum angelis," and his formulation reappears frequently elsewhere.[42] Albertus Magnus assigns to man this same position in the middle of creation, as does Dante.[43]

A precise understanding of the medieval conception of centeredness is thus indispensible to any treatment of microcosmic theory and, as we shall see, to any attempt to interpret artistic structures displaying a well-defined "middle." The doctrine of the microcosm also helps provide a basis for medieval symbolism, in particular, the spatial matrix of multi-levelled scriptural exegesis. Allers writes: "Symbolism becomes particularly complicated when envisioned on the background of a world conception which admits several levels of being. Then, anything on a lower level may be a symbolic representative of something pertaining to a higher level."[44] Thus, he explains, the way is paved for a microcosmic hierarchy of four symbolic levels in Ps.-Rabanus Maurus' famous comparison with architecture:

> In nostrae ergo animae domo historia fundamentum ponit, allegoria paries erigit, anagogia tectum opponit, tropologia vera tam interius

per affectum quam exterius per effectum boni operis, variis ornatibus dependit.[45]

Allers also cites Hildegard of Bingen's reliance on the body as a key to the macrocosmic symbolism of sun, moon, and stars.[46] And he sees the well-known doctrine of the Book of Nature in the same light; the entire created world points us spatially outwards, towards the highest spiritual truths, and inwards, towards the center of Nature's microcosm in our own bodies.[47]

One of the strengths of Allers' survey is its recognition of microcosmic theory as a basis for already familiar medieval ways of thinking. Here he appears to differ with Meyer and Conger, both of whom claim to find only relatively scarce and uninfluential traces of the doctrine in the Middle Ages. Meyer justifies the brevity of his discussion of medieval microcosmic speculation thus:

> Was aus jenen Zeiten an mikro- und makrokosmischen Anklängen sich kundgiebt, trägt keinen eigentümlichen Charakter an sich, sondern ist bestenfalls Reminiscenz an Plato, Aristoteles und den Neuplatonismus.[48]

Conger writes:

> Thus some of the microcosmic theories persisted in later times in something of the form given them by the medieval Christian thinkers; but they were not of great importance for the Christian system. The data from the microcosmic theories may be said, like the evidence from so many other fields, to indicate that the interests of Christianity at this time were chiefly other-worldly, and concerned more with escaping from the world than with picturing men as members of it.[49]

And even Allers does not give as much weight to medieval handling of his topic as he does to that of other periods. As so often happens in surveys for which medieval thought only constitutes a small part, these scholars have erroneously equated innovation with importance, not realizing that medieval culture preferred subtle rearrangements of traditional forms to more radical breaks with the past. Had they followed their line of inquiry through the theology of the body into the close texture of related doctrines, or looked for microcosmic structure in artistic

Interpretive Framework

form, they would have found the *minor mundus* as inherent to the warp and woof of medieval thinking as to that of any other era.

One of the most striking aspects of medieval microcosmic theory is its appearance in geometrical mysticism, especially in the geometry of circles and spheres; in the Middle Ages, as in the classical period, the geometry of the circle is the basic principle of microcosmic proportion.[50] The vast system of concentric spheres constituting the Ptolemaic world picture is familiar to everyone, but its ultimate basis in the spatiality of the body probably requires some clarification. All space in the universe was contained by these spheres, and all spheres found their origin in the shape, mystically conceived, of God: "Deus est sphaera infinita, cuius centrum ubique est et circumferentia nusquam."[51] This famous definition of God can be traced at least to the Orphic poets, and is essential in the cosmology of the *Timaeus*. Following this definition, the Neoplatonists held that creation proceeded from the innermost sphere outwards, and likewise, that God the Father's power entered his created world through its innermost center in Christ. Geometrically, this center of all centers attains the greatest possible spatial contraction simultaneous with the widest conceivable circumference: it is at once a point and the largest possible sphere.[52] The Incarnation imposes a paradoxical spatial organization on creation whereby God, who in himself contains all things, allows himself in turn to be contained by his entire creation; when Christ enters the innermost space of Mary's womb, Mary is said to contain that which contains her and everything else: "illum continens, a quo tu et omnia continentur."[53] The radical transformation of this one central act leaves no part of the universe unchanged. Christ's coming brings with it a new and universal conception of centeredness; now every point within the space of creation may itself constitute the center of all space: "in jedem kleinsten Stückchen der Welt [ist] die ganze göttliche Sphäre, ihr Mittelpunkt und ihr unendlicher Umfang zugleich enthalten. . . ."[54] Through a mystical union with Christ, each Christian's own body becomes a new center of the universe.[55] These formulations find their way, under different guises, into the writings of Boethius, Chalcidius, Augustine, Alanus de Insulis, Meister Eckhart, Bonaventure, Thomas Aquinas, and Nicolas of Cusa, among others.

Medieval geometrical mysticism, then, presupposes a structure of time and space quite foreign to the Newtonian framework, though akin in many ways to a modern physics of relativity (once again, a "rediscovery" spanning several fields).[56] Instead of the "endlose Neben- und Nacheinander des Raumes und der Zeit," the Incarnation effects the "wahrhaft unendliche Ineinander der raum- und zeitlosen Ewigkeit."[57] At the center of spatial and temporal reality lies a point where all space and time converges—where, paradoxically, both *all* space and time and *no* space or time can be found. Dante calls this "il punto / a cui tutti li tempi son presenti" (*Paradiso* 17.18), and again: "là 've s'appunta ogni ubi e ogni quando" (*Paradiso* 29.12).[58] Beginning with this point, time acquires a spatial dimension and space a temporal continuity. And all other points in the universe, through the Incarnation, share this same quality with the central one. One can see an analogous connection between space and time in numerous modern writings as well; in the Middle Ages it was termed the doctrine of the *plenitudo*.[59]

Christian space centers itself on several points, but all of these points converge mystically upon the same physical location. Adam's grave, Eden's Tree of Life, and the Cross on Golgotha together constitute both a geographic center and a theological core; Christian history's most important events—Adam's sin and death, and Christ's Atonement and death—occur in the same place. Both universal sin and universal salvation begin within the space of the Old and New Adam's body.[60] By extension, Mount Sinai (or Mount Zion), Jerusalem, and the heavenly New Jerusalem are also considered to occupy the same central location.[61] Christian time centers on the same point and the same body: "to find the true meaning of history is to find the bodily meaning."[62] Augustine saw the origin of time in form, in created bodies.[63] The ages of the world parallel the ages of man, and when truth becomes history, history becomes a body (*carnaliter adimpleri*).[64] This spatialization of time took very specific forms in the Middle Ages; Hugh of St. Victor and Hildegard of Bingen, for example, allegorize the feet-to-head sequence of Christ's body as time's progression from pre-Creation formlessness to Judgment.[65] By participation in the *persona mystica*, time's one body perpetuates itself through a long progression of bodies; the body occupies one time and all times.[66]

Interpretive Framework 13

Christ's body, a microcosm for the entire body of history, stands exactly at the center of history; all historical meaning derives from that one point. Like the space of the Ptolemaic universe, all of time is "konzentrisch und symmetrisch um Christus geordnet."[67] Jeffrey writes: "the chief effect of 'in the beginning God created' on medieval thought is its construal of human perspective as inextricably middled."[68] Christ's body provides a vortex, a historical nodal point, an umbilical connection with the atemporal; Frye calls the resurrection "strictly speaking a leap out of time altogether."[69] Christian time is, following Eliade's formulation, "reversible."[70] The end of time begins in the middle of historical time, and on the last Day the meaning of all the ages will be gathered together; the first week of history, too, figures forth in microcosm each world age to come.[71] The center of history replicates itself at its edges, at each point of its circumference; time is circular.[72]

A concomitant of incarnated time is the Middle Ages' figural conception of history, ably presented in essays by Erich Auerbach and Elizabeth Salter.[73] Auerbach writes: "Figural interpretation establishes a connection between two events or persons, the first of which signifies not only itself but also the second, while the second encompasses or fulfills the first."[74] The *figura*, unlike allegory as most commonly understood, defines relationships between two concrete historical realities, or between historical and post-historical (eschatalogical) realities; unlike most allegory, the events or persons involved are real. Such an understanding of history only becomes possible when time is corporeal and each segment of time constitutes a microcosm. The *figura* establishes a relation between what is eternally and transcendently present and transitory events within the flux of time which bear the image of the former. Hence the Flood "prefigures" Christian baptism, and both find their fulfillment at Judgment, since both partake microcosmically in the plenitude of time enacted in the gathering up of history on that Day. Figural time confers the ability to be both image and reality, *umbra* and *corpus*, signifier and signified: the eucharist constitutes the prototypical *figura*.[75]

The notion of plenitude implicit in the microcosmic configuration of space and time finds its doctrinal justification in the Middle Ages' understanding of corporeal *recapitulatio*. The head recapitulates the body; all parts and functions of the bodily macrocosm find their counterpart in the head's microcosm. A modern "rediscoverer" calls the head "ein Staat im Staate in Klein- und Keimform, ein Embryo, der dem Leib aufsitzt, und seinerseits bereits alle lebenswichtigen Funktionen in sich vereint."[76] Just as all men derive from Adam, as members of the same body, so too all believers share membership in the mystical body of Christ; man fell and is raised again as one body (*tanquam membra unius corpori*).[77] As the head provides a structural nexus for all of the body's members, so Christ contains all Christians within himself. Thus Emmeran Scharl, in *Recapitulatio Mundi*, equates "Behauptung" with "Zusammenfassung."[78]

We have noticed the sphericity of God in mystical geometry ("Deus est sphaera infinita"); man's body, fashioned microcosmically in God's image, also bears a precise traditional relation to the circle and sphere.[79] And the roundness of man's head provides the key to its structural predominance: it is a body within a body, and—because the universe is round as well—a cosmos within a body. Christ rules the members of his body as a small, dense sphere within a larger one.[80] Extending this principle, the doctrine of recapitulation provides the basis for an ordering of all of creation into concentric spheres: "Alles ausnahmslos, auch die sichtbaren und körperlichen Dinge, ist im Leibe Christi, des Gottmenschen, wie in einem 'Kompendium' sinnerfüllt, zusammengefaßt, verjüngt und vollendet."[81] As a microcosm/member of Christ, man shares this special relation to the physical and spiritual world. Scharl writes: "So wurde im Menschen, dem Mikrokosmos, das All 'wiederhergestellt.'"[82] And Christ's work recapitulates time as well as space; the *plenitudo temporis*, whether at the beginning, middle, or end of history is a recapitulation of all time.[83] The relation of each day of creation week to the six (or seven) ages of the world constitutes an especially painstaking and detailed elaboration of the *recapitulatio*.[84]

The body as microcosm, then, is in itself a succinct resume of the broadest contours of medieval theology. This idea hovers in the background of quite a few secondary sources, as I have indicated, and occasionally receives particular emphasis (as in the work of Mersch). But no scholar to date has adequately gathered together the main structural principles in such a way that they can be confidently exploited to interpret both texts spanning several medieval literatures and nonliterary aesthetic structures. Only when we have the broad doctrinal picture firmly in mind can we begin to tackle the minute textual problems at hand, problems rendered especially complex where their solution requires access to recondite exegetical knowledge.

A few strands of the preceding analysis require emphasis and elaboration before we commence the present interpretive task. At the core of this discussion is the paradox of containment: Christ, the *verbum breviatum*, both contains the world within himself and allows himself in turn to be contained by the world.[85] As we wander the labyrinths of aesthetic space, we will repeatedly find ourselves closest to the spatial perimeter precisely at that point where we feel most confident of having discovered the center. Medieval architects and poets quite deliberately designed their works inside out. The structure of the human body itself, of course, furnishes the most immediate analogy: while we normally consider the skin to be the mediator between the body's interior and its environment, the gastrointestinal tract also constitutes the outer world's intrusion into the most intimate center of corporeal space. Thus our most compelling sense of interiority, "gut feelings," base themselves on a metaphor that paradoxically describes an external relation. The structure of the body reflects the paradox of Christian temporal and spatial understanding; the geographic and historical edges make their most prominent appearance in the middle.

The governing metaphor here is not only a body, but an inside out body, or a body in the process of turning itself inside out. Northrop Frye calls this the "decentralizing approach to Christian metaphors," saying:

> Instead of an individual finding his fulfillment within a social body, however sacrosanct, the metaphor is reversed from a metaphor of integration into a wholly decentralized one, in which the total body is complete within each individual. The individual acquires the internal authority of the unity of the Logos, and it is this unity which makes him an individual.[86]

Hence Christianity requires that its adherents turn themselves inside out, as Scarry explains:

> The failure of belief is, in its many forms, a failure to remake one's own interior in the image of God, to allow God to enter and to alter one's self. Or to phrase it in a slightly different form, it is the refusal or inability to turn oneself inside out, devoting one's physical interior to something outside itself, calling it by another name. Disobedience or disbelief or doubt in the scriptures is habitually described as a withholding of the body, which in its resistance to an external referent is perceived as covered, or hard, or stiff. . . .[87]

A new convert must be born again, must again begin at the womb and journey to the body's exterior: "a baby not only emerges out of the interior of the body but itself represents the interior of the parental body."[88] Related here, of course, is the image of the wound—"the most extreme and literal" turning inside out of the body—through which the crucified Christ gives birth to his church.[89] After conversion, God's "habitation" within the believer's body reflects this inside out spirituality; Augustine describes God as "interior intimo meo et superior summo meo."[90] In medieval art, this inside out quality is doubtless responsible for what McLuhan terms "the feeling of looking in," a quality akin to Hopkins' conception of "inscape."[91]

The predominance of center and edge in Christian space can seem bewildering to twentieth-century man, accustomed as he is to homogeneous, Cartesian space stretching to infinity in a rigidly uniform grid. Medieval space is not homogeneous; although any given point may represent a microcosm, not all places are equal. Meaning becomes denser at center and edge, and all other points acquire meaning by their microcosmic relation to those denser areas. Eliade calls these areas "kraftgeladener, bedeutungsvoller Raum," and a number of German scholars apply the term *Verdichtung*; I will refer frequently to spatial and temporal "thickening."[92] Hence a cathedral's altar, though it constitutes only one of many structural microcosms within the building's symbolism, nonetheless possesses a symbolic compactness that other parts lack.

The "thickening" that creates inside out aesthetic structures is responsible, finally, for each aesthetic microcosm's "self-recreation" or self-reflexivity—in short, for its ability to reproduce itself from within, as one body gives birth to another. On a macrocosmic level, Christian time and space (as well as new

Christians themselves) are generated from Christ's central body outwards. A Gothic cathedral's entire complex symbolism of space and time also originates in and regenerates itself from the body of Christ on the altar; the eucharistic host is at once a symbolic *summa* and an inexhaustible source of new hosts.

The doctrine of the monad is crucial here, and I will return to it repeatedly; though the twentieth century most commonly traces the notion to Leibnitz, it was already current in the Middle Ages. The first of twenty-four definitions of God listed in the twelfth-century *Liber XXIV Philosophorum* states: "Deus est monas monadem gignens et in se reflectens suum ardorem."[93] The principle of self-recreation evident in this definition extends itself to the mystical understanding of center and edge in the second definition: "Deus est sphaera cujus centrum ubique, circumferentia nusquam." Dietrich Mahnke, whose work on concentric circles we have already noticed, writes in his related book on monadology: "Jede Monade ist ein Mikrokosmus, ein *Spiegel des ganzen Universums*, und damit zugleich ein zweiter Weltschöpfer."[94] Each monad is a "Verkörperung Gottes," an entity whose existence stands outside of time and has neither beginning nor end; each constitutes by itself both subject and object, signifier and signified.[95] Applying Hall's construct, the monad of Christ's body furnishes a source and structure of meaning for medieval culture like the pattern of the star in modern France.

Not only does the body provide a nodal point for the numerous geographic and historical constructs that constitute its extensions; the body itself also contains several "interior centers" in medieval tradition. This complex spatial order *inside* the body provides a rough analogue to the perceived congruence of disparate axes of the world in Christian geography. Scholars occasionally take note of one or the other of these centers, but no detailed consideration of the multiplicity of such centers is, to my knowledge, available.

The womb is the most obvious bodily center, in light of the foregoing discussion of spatial self-reflexivity and self-recreation. The body reproduces itself from the womb; a new circumference emerges from the center. Here Christ first enters the world in human form, and when his body is laid in a tomb/womb at death, he simultaneously harrows hell's womb.[96] The womb thus constitutes the innermost center of the body and of the earth's sphere, and it provides a spatial coordinate for the *plenitudo temporis*. Christ emerges from timelessness into the womb, recapitulating the long geneaology of David; when he enters hell's womb, he endows history with a new center, an abrupt transition from old to new represented in the tearing of the temple curtain. At the Incarnation and Harrowing, God's all-encompassing sphere of time and space submits to containment within the earth-body's smallest and most central temporal and spatial frame. The geometric centrality of the womb is represented in a long tradition of drawings showing the body inscribed within a circle whose center is the genitalia.[97] In addition, Hildegard of Bingen's many representations of the earth's globe emerging from the womb and of the universe depicted as a mammoth vagina are particularly striking.[98]

Medieval tradition locates a second site of birth-giving and regeneration in the heart. Christ's heart gives birth to the church, which emerges from his side in the form of the water and blood of the afterbirth, the wound itself finding its correlate in the vagina.[99] Individual Christians, in turn, are said to give birth to Christ in their own hearts. Thus the heart appropriates from the tradition of the womb a spatial and temporal focus that is equally paradoxical: individual believers bear the one who once bore all of them collectively; the contained is greater than the container. Christ's heart, located traditionally at the juncture of the cross's two beams, marks the convergence of north, south, east and west, and yet Christ's body extends into all the ends of the earth as it is reborn in the hearts of his followers. Christ's death at the center of time makes new life possible at all points of future and (thanks to the Harrowing) past time. The Harrowing penetrates into a hell which is not only a womb but a heart, the *cor terrae*.[100] As twin centers representing in microcosm the world-body's multiple centers, both heart and womb resonate with the traditional symbolism of garden and tomb;[101] the heart, like the womb, constitutes the center of the circle in a separate tradition of drawings showing geometrically-inscribed bodies.[102]

Recapitulatio, then, does not confine itself to the *caput*; the head resumes the entire body in itself, but so do the heart and womb. And the genitals bear a special relation to the head: genital organization recapitulates capital organization. "The head in the crown is the penis in the vagina."[103] Coitus reenacts at the center of the body the Harrowing which penetrates to the center of all space and time. Displacement from below implies the *plenitudo temporis*: the last shall be first and the first shall be last.

Other, less important, corporeal centers receive attention in the Middle Ages as well. Medieval Europe shares a widespread belief that the navel is the body's nucleus and that holy sites constitute the navel(s) of the earth.[104] The navel coincides with the center of the circle in a separate strand of the tradition of geometrically-inscribed bodies.[105] And even the eye acts as a perceptual center. McLuhan writes: "In Medieval and primitive times the mode of seeing came from the use of the center of the eye."[106]

As a consequence of the *plenitudo temporis* and microcosmic space, then, Christian conceptions of centeredness often juxtapose centrifugal structures against centripetal ones. Frye observes that in Christianity "a central sacred place could no longer exist."[107] The center of sacred space is less a geographic one and more a psychological one: each believer's body is a temple. P. Idiart addresses this paradox under the heading "La dialectique chrétienne de l'un et du multiple," saying, "En vérité, c'est que le Centre chrétien n'est plus un *lieu*, mais une *personne*"; each believer has access to this person.[108] He writes further:

> Le Centre du Monde est le lieu privilégié où peut s'opérer la rencontre des hommes, des esprits, des dieux, souvent parce qu'il est le point d'origine des uns et des autres, quelquefois parce que arbre, montagne, poteau ou pyramide, il est fonctionellement en rapport avec tous.[109]

Christ's coming effects a cosmic salvation, a universal restructuring of time and space.[110] The idea that each man constitutes a universal center, then, becomes a commonplace. Gerard Paré writes: "Tous, depuis Origène et saint Augustin jusqu'à saint Albert le Grand et saint Thomas, traitent longuement de l'*imago Dei* et font de l'homme le centre de l'Universe."[111] De Bruyne summarizes his discussion of microcosmic theory similarly: "L'homme est la 'conclusion' de l'évolution, le 'centre' de l'Univers."[112] The eucharist is the sign and seal of each Christian's new relation to the cosmos: a daily reenclosure of the container by the contained, an infinitely repeated reenactment of both the Incarnation and the Harrowing of hell.[113]

Notes

1. *Modern Man in Search of a Soul*, trans. W. S. Dell and Cary F. Baynes (New York: Harcourt, 1933) 219.
2. Scarry, Elaine, *The Body in Pain: The Making and Unmaking of the World* (New York: Oxford UP, 1985) 284.
3. "Ebenso wie die Behausung des modernen Menschen ihre kosmologischen Werte verloren hat, ist auch sein Körper jeder religiösen oder geistigen Bedeutung beraubt. Man könnte summarisch sagen: für die modernen, nicht religiösen Menschen ist der Kosmos undurchsichtig, unbewegt und stumm geworden." *Das Heilige und das Profane: Vom Wesen des Religiösen*, Rowohlts deutsche Enzyclopädie 31 (Reinbek bei Hamburg: Rowohlt, 1957) 104. Elsewhere Eliade writes: "Toujours à l'aide de l'histoire des religions, l'homme moderne pourrait retrouver le symbolisme de son corps, qui est un anthropo-cosmos." "Le symbolisme du centre," *Images et Symboles* (Paris: Gallimard, 1952) 44-45. Originally appeared as "Psychologie et histoire des religions: À propos du symbolisme du centre," *Eranos-Jahrbuch* 19 (1950): 252-82.
4. See especially "The World is Your Body," *The Book: On the Taboo Against Knowing Who You Are* (New York: Collier, 1967) 80-100.
5. See, for example: Martin Heidegger, *Sein und Zeit* (Tübingen: Niemeyer, 1953), and "Bauen Wohnen Denken," *Vorträge und Aufsätze* (Pfullingen: Neske, 1954) 145-62; Ludwig Binswanger, "Das Raumproblem in der Psychopathologie," *Ausgewählte Vorträge und Aufsätze* 2 (Bern: Francke, 1955) 174-225; Walter Götz, *Dasein und Raum: Philosophische Untersuchungen zum Verhältnis von Raumerlebnis, Raumtheorie und gelebtem Dasein* (Tübingen: Niemeyer, 1970); Elisabeth Ströker, *Philosophische Untersuchungen zum Raum* (Frankfurt: Klostermann, 1977); Hermann Schmitz, *Der Leib* and *Der leibliche Raum*, vol. 2-3 of *System der Philosophie* (Bonn: Bouvier, 1965-67), 3 vols.
6. With co-ed. Volker Rittner, *Zur Geschichte des Körpers* (München: Hanser, 1976); with Christoph Wulf, *Die Wiederkehr des Körpers* (Frankfurt: Suhrkamp, 1982); *Der andere Körper*, Edition Corpus: Alltagswissen, Körpersprache, Ethnomedizin 1 (Berlin: Mensch und Leben, 1984); *Das Schwinden der Sinne* (Frankfurt: Suhrkamp, 1984). The opening of the introduction to *Die Wiederkehr* summarizes the basic presupposition underlying these studies: "Von einer Wiederkehr des Körpers zu sprechen, unterstellt bereits ein Verschwinden, eine Spaltung, eine verlorene Einheit. Es geht mithin um die Trennung von Körper und Geist, um den Abstraktionsprozeß des Lebens mit seiner Distanzierung, Disziplinierung, Instrumentalisierung des Körperlichen als Grundlage des historischen Fortschritts, um die damit einhergehende Entfernung und Ersetzung der menschlichen Natur durch ein vermitteltes gesellschaftliches Konstrukt, mit einem Wort: um Rationalisierung im weitesten Sinn—also um zivilisationstheoretische und geschichtsphilosophische Prämissenz" (9).
7. E.g., Reinhard Kloos and Thomas Reuter, *Kraft und Schönheit: Die Geschichte der Körperkultur-Bewegung in Deutschland* (Frankfurt: Syndikat, forthcoming); Stephan Oettermann, *Zeichen auf der Haut: Die Geschichte der Tätowierung in Europa* (Frankfurt: Syndikat, 1979).

8. In addition to the Eliade and Watts references above, two more examples of recent interest in the body's microcosmic significance are Kamper and Wulf's discussion in *Der andere Körper* 5, and the key notion of the "holon" in Arthur Koestler, *Janus: A Summing Up* (London: Pan, 1979) 264ff. and passim.

9. *Body, Memory and Architecture* (New Haven: Yale UP, 1977); see also Bernard Rudofsky, *Architecture without Architects: A Short Introduction to Non-Pedigreed Architecture*, 5th ed. (New York: Museum of Modern Art, 1964); Joseph Rykwert, *On Adam's House in Paradise: The Idea of the Primitive Hut in Architectural History* (New York: Museum of Modern Art, 1972).

10. See Edward T. Hall, "Art as a Clue to Perception," *The Hidden Dimension: Man's Use of Space in Public and Private* (London: Bodley Head, 1969) 71-83; Marshall McLuhan and Harley Parker, *Through the Vanishing Point: Space in Poetry and Painting* (New York: Harper, 1969); Hermann Schmitz, *Der Leib im Spiegel der Kunst*.

11. "Spatial Form in Modern Literature," *Sewanee Review* 53 (1945). Rpt. (revised) in *The Widening Gyre* (New Brunswick: Rutgers UP, 1963). See also "Spatial Form: An Answer to the Critics," *Critical Inquiry* 4 (1977): 231-52. Another important early treatment is Gaston Bachelard's *La poétique de l'espace* (Paris: PU de France, 1957).

12. Here is a sampling of the scholarship on literary space: J. J. van Baak, *The Place of Space in Narration: A Semiotic Approach to the Problem of Literary Space*, Studies in Slavic Literature and Poetics 3 (Amsterdam: Rodopi, 1983); Maurice Blanchot, *L'espace litteraire*, 4th ed. (Paris: Gallimard, 1955); Elisabeth Bronfen, *Der literarische Raum: Eine Untersuchung am Beispiel von Dorothy M. Richardsons Romanzyklus Pilgrimage*, Studien zur englischen Philologie N.F. 25 (Tübingen: Niemeyer, 1986); Alexander Gelley, "Metonymy, Schematism and the Space of Literature," *New Literary History* 11 (1980): 469-87; William Holtz, "A Reconsideration of Spatial Form," *Critical Inquiry* 4 (1977): 271-83; Joseph Kestner, *The Spatiality of the Novel* (Detroit: Wayne State UP, 1978); Herman Meyer, "Raumgestaltung und Raumsymbolik in der Erzählkunst," *Studium Generale* 10 (1957): 620-30; Cary Nelson, *The Incarnate Word: Literature as Verbal Space* (Urbana: U of Illinois P, 1973); A. Ritter, ed., *Landschaft und Raum in der Erzählkunst* (Darmstadt: Wissenschaftliche, 1975); Christian Sappok, *Die Bedeutung des Raumes für die Struktur des Erzählwerks* (München: Sagner, 1970); Jeffrey R. Smitten and Ann Daghistany, eds., *Spatial Form in Narrative* (Cornell UP, 1981); Sharon Spencer, *Space, Time and Structure in the Modern Novel* (New York: New York UP, 1971).

13. Exceptions are the first chapter of Nelson and several articles by S. L. Clark and J. N. Wasserman; I will discuss these scholars' work in the following chapters.

14. For the corporeal center's migration from heart to head, see Kamper, *Wiederkehr* 13.

15. The thorough theoretical underpinning of Bronfen's work is a notable exception.

16. Hall 137-38.

17. He does not use the word "microcosm," however.

18. Bloomer and Moore 51ff., 77ff.

19. For representations in Greek literature of the body as art, speech, history, the state, and an army, see E. Schweizer's discussion, *Theologisches Wörterbuch zum Neuen Testament* (1964) 7: 1024-42.

20. Josef Sauer, *Symbolik des Kirchengebäudes und seiner Ausstattung in der Auffassung des Mittelalters*, 2nd ed. (1924; Münster: Mehren, 1964). Sauer calls the equivalence of the church with the body of Christ "den tiefsten Gedanken mittelalterlicher Symbolik wie überhaupt der ganzen damaligen Weltanschauung" (36). Hugo Rahner, *Griechische Mythen in christlicher Deutung*, 3rd ed. (Zürich: Rhein, 1966); see especially "Das Mysterium des Kreuzes" 55-73.

21. The following studies of this topic rank among the best: Oscar Cullmann. *Christus und die Zeit: Die urchristliche Zeit- und Geschichtsauffassung* (Zürich: Evangelischer. 1946): Erich Frank, *St. Augustine and Greek Thought* (Cambridge: Augustinian Society. 1942); Karl Löwith, *Meaning in History* (Chicago: U of Chicago P, 1949); John Marsh, *The Fulness of Time* (London:

Nisbet, 1952); Reinhold Niebuhr, *Faith and History* (New York: Scribner's, 1951); Henri-Charles Puech, "La gnose et le temps," *Eranos Jahrbuch* 20 (1951): 57-113; Gilles Quispel, "Zeit und Geschichte im antiken Christentum," *Eranos Jahrbuch* 20 (1951): 115-40; E. C. Rust, *The Christian Understanding of History* (London: Lutterworth, 1947); Paul Tillich, *The Interpretation of History* (New York: Scribner's, 1936).

22. Émile Mersch's publications all take this thesis as their starting point; the following are especially worth noting: *Le corps mystique du Christ, études de théologie historique*, 2 vols. (Louvain: Museum Lessianum, 1933), whose third edition (Paris: Museum Lessianum, 1951) was unavailable to me; *Le Christ, l'homme et l'univers: Prolégomènes à la théologie du corps mystique*, Museum Lessianum section théologique 57 (Brussels: Desclée, 1962), see 126-27 for the idea of the *nexus mysteriorum*; *Morale et corps mystique*, 4th ed., Museum Lessianum section théologique 34 and 47 (Paris: Desclée, 1955); *Theology of the Mystical Body*, trans. C. Follert (St. Louis: Herder, 1951). Somewhat less useful but nonetheless important is the work of Sebastian Tromp, who like Mersch has made research on the mystical body his life's work: *Corpus Christi quod est Ecclesia*, 4 vols. (Roma: U Gregoriana, 1946-60). Vol. 1, *Introductio generalis*, trans. by A. Condit as *The Body of Christ Which is the Church* (New York: Vantage, 1960); vol. 2, *De Christo capite mystici corporis*; vol. 3, *De spiritu Christi anima*; vol. 4, *De virgine deipara Maria corde Mystici*. See also Joseph Anger, *La doctrine du Corps Mystique de Jesus Christ d'après les principes de la théologie de Saint-Thomas* (Paris: Beauchesne, 1946); Ernest Mura, *Le corps mystique du Christ: sa nature et sa vie divine* (Paris: Blot, 1947).

23. Hans Jörg Spitz, *Die Metaphorik des geistigen Schriftsinns: Ein Beitrag zur allegorischen Bibelauslegung des ersten christlichen Jahrtausends*, Münstersche Mittelalter-Schriften 12 (München: Fink, 1972) 247.

24. *Wiederkehr des Körpers* 12. Eliade clarifies this historical change in terms of man's loss of microcosmic awareness: "Das Christentum der industriellen Gesellschaft . . . hat seit langem seine kosmischen Werte, die es noch im Mittelalter hatte, eingebüßt. Damit soll das Christentum der Städte nicht als 'abgesunken' oder 'minderwertig' bezeichnet, sondern nur gesagt werden, daß die religiöse Empfindungsfähigkeit der Städter stark verarmt ist. Zu der kosmischen Liturgie, zu dem Mysterium der Teilnahme der Natur am christologischen Drama haben die Christen einer modernen Stadt keinen Zugang mehr. Ihr religiöses Erleben ist nicht mehr dem Kosmos 'offen.'" *Das Heilige und das Profane* 104-05.

25. *Ad Imaginem Dei: The Image of Man in Medieval Art*, Wimmer Lecture 16 (Latrobe, PA: Archabbey, 1965) 1.

26. See McLuhan 7-8. David L. Jeffrey, "The Self and the Book: Reference and Recognition in Medieval Thought," *By Things Seen: Reference and Recognition in Medieval Thought*, ed. David L. Jeffrey (Ottawa: U of Ottawa P, 1979) 13.

27. Adolf Meyer, *Wesen und Geschichte der Theorie vom Mikro- und Makrokosmus*, Berner Studien zur Philosophie und ihrer Geschichte 25 (Bern: Sturzenegger, 1901); G. P. Conger, *Theories of Macrocosms and Microcosms in the History of Philosophy* (1922; New York: Russell, 1967); Rudolf Allers, "Microcosmus: From Anaximandros to Paracelsus," *Traditio* 2 (1944): 319-407. Meyer's work is especially weak, neglecting a good deal of published information already available at the time of his writing. Conger's monograph is more helpful, but may have had the effect of discouraging studies like the present one by its skepticism concerning the importance and impact of the whole tradition. Allers' article proves useful in a number of ways, although it was written without knowledge of Conger's work (see Allers 399ff.). Studies of microcosmic tradition in literature are rare and generally restrict themselves to isolated texts or portions of text; exceptions are James Edwin Cross, "Aspects of the Macrocosm and Microcosm in Old English Literature," *Comparative Literature* 14 (1962): 1-22; Janet Gilligan, "Neoplatonic Cosmology and the Middle English *Patience*," diss., Northern Illinois U, 1986; and C. S. Lewis, *The Discarded*

Image: An Introduction to Medieval and Renaissance Literature (Cambridge: Cambridge UP, 1964).
   28. Meyer 24.
   29. Allers 320-21.
   30. Allers 359; Meyers 49.
   31. Meyer 50.
   32. Conger 33.
   33. *Summa*, 2^a, d. 1, q. 2, a. 3; d. 2, q. 2, a. 3, ad 3. Cf. 2^a, d. 1, q. 2, a. 3; 1^a, q. 91, a. 1, c; q. 96, a. 1, c.
   34. Meyer 97.
   35. Allers 323, 367-68.
   36. Allers 368-69; Meyer 22.
   37. See Ernst H. Kantorowicz, *The King's Two Bodies: A Study in Medieval Political Theology* (1957; Princeton: Princeton UP, 1970) 505-06.
   38. *Le Christ, l'homme et l'univers: Prolégomènes à la theologie du corps mystique*, Museum Lessianum section théologique 57 (Brussels: Desclée, 1962).
   39. Meyer 38-39.
   40. Congers 3, 54.
   41. W. Jaeger, cited in Allers 355.
   42. *De civ. Dei* 9.13 (*PL* 44.267), cited in Allers 362, along with a similar quote from Hugh of St. Victor ("homo quasi in medio collocatus, habet super se Deum, sub se mundum"), and references to other writers who repeat Augustine's idea (e.g., William of St. Thierry and Petrus Lombardus).
   43. Albertus Magnus, *Summa Theologiae* 2, tr. 11, q. 4, m. 2; Dante, *De monarchia* 1.3.
   44. Allers 370.
   45. *Alleg. in Script. Sanct.* (*PL* 112.850); discussed in Allers 330. The work is now doubtfully attributed to Garner of Rochefort (d. early 13th century).
   46. Allers 378.
   47. Allers 327.
   48. Meyer 46.
   49. Conger 36. On 30 he states that microcosmic theories were "latent or recessive throughout the Christian medieval period."
   50. See Ernst Moessel, *Die Proportion in Antike und Mittelalter*, 2 vols. (München: Beck, 1926-31); Conger, passim.
   51. For an admirably thorough study of the mystical conception of concentric rings, traced from its Greek origins through its appearance in German romanticism, see Dietrich Mahnke, *Unendliche Sphäre und Allmittelpunkt: Beiträge zur Genealogie der mathematischen Mystik*, Deutsche Vierteljahrsschrift für Literaturwissenschaft und Geistesgeschichte 23 (Halle: Niemeyer, 1937). The following page references in Mahnke indicate only a few examples of the ideas discussed; to understand the scope of these traditions, one must consult his entire chapter on medieval sources (144-215).
   52. Mahnke, *Unendliche Sphäre* 19-20, 151.
   53. *The Legends and Writings of Saint Clare of Assisi*, trans. Ignatius Brady, (St. Bonaventure, NY: Franciscan Institute, 1953) 94.
   54. Mahnke, *Unendliche Sphäre* 150.
   55. Mahnke, *Unendliche Sphäre* 156, 168.
   56. See McLuhan 257; Mircea Eliade, *Le mythe de l'éternel retour: archétypes et répétition*, 3rd ed. (Paris: Gallimard, 1949) 129.
   57. Mahnke, *Unendliche Sphäre* 12. For the relation of space to time in Augustine, see Quispel 132.

58. Cf. Aquinas, *Summa contra Gentiles* 1.66. For this idea in Bonaventure, see Mahnke, *Unendliche Sphäre* 176.

59. Max Bense writes that there is "in Wirklichkeit kein Nacheinander der Dinge, nur ein Nebeneinander." *Raum und Ich: Eine Philosophie über den Raum* (München: Oldenbourg, 1943) 25. Cf. discussion of Bergson in Gerardus van der Leeuw, "In dem Himmel ist ein Tanz": *Über die religiöse Bedeutung des Tanzes und des Festunges*, trans. Clercq van Weel, Der Tempel des Leibes 1 (München: Dornverlag, 1931) 13-14. Bachelard writes: "Dans ses mille alvéoles, l'espace tient du temps comprimé. L'espace sert à ca" (27).

60. Rahner, *Griechische Mythen* 64-71. Eliade provides an especially good overview of the idea of a center in Christianity and other religions in "Symbolisme du Centre," *Images et Symboles* 2-72. In *Das Heilige und das Profane*, Eliade calls this center the place "wo man den Göttern am nächsten ist" (39).

61. In Eliade's chapter, see especially 60. Cf. Sauer 160.

62. Norman O. Brown, *Love's Body* (New York: Random, 1966) 222, cf. 203. In general, see also *Life Against Death: The Psychoanalytic Meaning of History* (London: Routledge, 1959).

63. *Confessions* 12.8.8, 9.9.

64. Tertullian, *De resurrectione* 20. See Cross 2; Erich Auerbach, "Figura," *Scenes from the Drama of European Literature* (New York: Meridian, 1959) 11-76; Edgar de Bruyne, *Études d'esthétique médiévale* (Brussels: De Tempel, 1946) 276; Northrop Frye, *The Great Code: The Bible and Literature* (New York: Harcourt, 1982) 224-25.

65. Friedrich Ohly, "Die Kathedrale als Zeitenraum," *Schriften zur mittelalterlichen Bedeutungsforschung* (Darmstadt: Wissenschaftliche, 1977) 182-83.

66. Ernst H. Kantorowicz, *The King's Two Bodies: A Study in Medieval Political Theology* (Princeton: Princeton UP, 1957) 310-11; Frank Kermode, *The Sense of an Ending: Studies in the Theory of Fiction* (New York: Oxford UP, 1967) 73-74.

67. Ohly, "Die Kathedrale als Zeitenraum" 324.

68. Jeffrey 2.

69. *The Great Code* 98. For more on Christ's body as a historical center, see the works already cited in van der Leeuw, Niebuhr, Quispel, etc.

70. *Das Heilige und das Profane* 40.

71. Rust 67; Alois Dempf, *Sacrum Imperium: Geschichts- und Staatsphilosophie des Mittelalters und der politischen Renaissance* (München: Oldenbourg, 1929) 232. Cf. the opening lines of T. S. Eliot's "Burnt Norton": "Time present and time past / Are both perhaps present in time future, / and time future is contained in time past."

72. For more discussion of linear versus cyclical conceptions of time in the Middle Ages, see Donald R. Howard, *The Three Temptations: Medieval Man in Search of the World* (Princeton: Princeton UP, 1966) 265-67.

73. Auerbach, "Figura"; E. Salter, "Medieval Poetry and the Figural View of Reality," *Proceedings of the British Academy* 54 (1970, for 1968): 73-92.

74. Auerbach, "Figura" 53-54.

75. See Auerbach, "Figura" 60; Brown, *Love's Body* 200-01, 221-22. R. Graber writes: "Die Eucharistie ist Symbol des mystischen Leibes und sogar der mystische Leib selbst." *Christus in seinen heiligen Sakramenten* (München: Kösel, 1940) 107. Cf. the *persona geminata* of the king, the *Rex imago Christi*, in Kantorowicz 59.

76. Kamper, *Schwinden der Sinne* 186.

77. See discussion of Aquinas in O. Gierke, *Political Theories of the Middle Age*, trans. F. W. Maitland (Boston: Beacon, 1958) 103ff.

78. *Recapitulatio mundi*, Freiburger Theologische Studien 60 (Freiburg: Herder, 1941) 21, 50-51.

Interpretive Framework

79. The tradition of the body as a sphere, complete with innumerable diagrams showing figures with outstretched limbs inscribed in circles, is discussed further in my treatment of *Pearl*.

80. "Sed et in rotunditate capitis hominis rotunditas firmamenti ostenditur et in recta aequalique mensura ejusdem capitis recta et aequalis mensura firmamenti demonstratur, quia idem caput rectam mensuram ubique habet, ut etiam firmamentum aequali mensura constitutum est quatenus ex omni parte rectum circuitum habere possit et ne ulla pars ejus partem alteram injusto modo excedat." Hildegard of Bingen, *Liber divinorum operum* 15, quoted in de Bruyne 354. Conger finds the same principle in Zeno (14) and John of Salisbury, restating the latter's view as follows: "In obeying a prince we follow the leading of nature which has placed all the senses of man, the microcosm, in the head, and subjected the other members to it" (35-36). Alastair Fowler discusses the circularity of the head in the context of bodies inscribed within circles in *Spenser and the Numbers of Time* (London: Routledge, 1964) 263-65. For the idea of the cosmos-shaped head in Plato, see the *Timaeus*, trans. Benjamin Jowett, *The Collected Dialogues of Plato*, ed. Edith Hamilton and Huntington Cairns (Princeton: Princeton UP, 1961) 44. Cf. also Robert Jordan, *Chaucer and the Shape of Creation* (Cambridge: Harvard UP, 1967) 13.

81. Scharl viii. Scharl orders his discussion according to the successive spheres which Christ recapitulates: "wir [sprechen] erst vom Fleische Christi, weil in ihm wie in einem 'Kompendium' die übrige Körperwelt vom Logos angenommen und verklärt ist, und gehen dann wie in konzentrischen Kreisen auf das Fleisch des Gesamtmenschen über und in Kapitel IV auf die übrige Körperwelt." Cf. Mersch, *Le Christ* 37.

82. Scharl 113.

83. Scharl 9, 12-13, 19, 28-31, 79-81; Brown, *Love's Body* 207-08.

84. Scharl 13-14, 16-17, 38; Dempf 232; van der Leeuw 39-40; Sauer 73.

85. See discussion of this Augustinian formulation in Henri de Lubac, *Histoire et esprit: l'intelligence de l'Écriture d'après Origène* (Paris: Montaigne, 1950) 446.

86. *The Great Code* 100-01. His continuation of this idea on 167 clarifies its microcosmic implications: "Once again, my interest is not in doctrines of faith as such but in the expanding of vision through language. In particular, I am interested in seeing what happens if we follow a suggestion made earlier in this book and turn the traditional form of the metaphorical structure inside out. Instead of a metaphor of unity and integration we should have a metaphor of particularity, the kind of vision Blake expressed in the phrase 'minute particulars' and in such lines as 'To see the world in a grain of sand.'"

87. *Body in Pain* 202-03.

88. Scarry, *Body in Pain* 188; cf. 192, 203-04, 216.

89. Scarry, *Body in Pain* 349.

90. Quoted and discussed in Quispel 126.

91. McLuhan 24.

92. E.g., Bronfen 112. Cf. "wasabi," a concept from Japanese pictorial composition designating the compression of meaning into select zones of space.

93. Clemens Baeumker, ed., *Beiträge zur Geschichte der Philosophie des Mittelalters* (1928): 207-14, cited in Georges Poulet, *Les métamorphoses du cercle* (Paris: Plon, 1961) xxv.

94. *Eine neue Monadologie* (Berlin: Reuther, 1917) 58.

95. Mahnke, *Monadologie* 9, 16-18, 59.

96. Cf. "hellen wombe," *Patience*, l. 306, and the discussion of the Harrowing in chapter nine. See Eliade, *Images et Symboles* passim for the womb/tomb equation. For the cave as the first home, understood as the womb, see Alexander Tzonis and Liane Lefairre, "The Mechanical vs. the Divine Body," *Journal of Architectural Education* 29 (1975): 4-7.

97. The tradition is older than the Middle Ages; several such medieval drawings are available, in addition to the better-known Renaissance representations. See Otto von Simson, *The Gothic Cathedral: Origins of Gothic Architecture and the Medieval Concept of Order* (New York:

Pantheon, 1956) fig. 10; Rudolf Wittkower, *Architectural Principles in the Age of Humanism*, Columbia University Studies in Art History and Archaeology 1 (New York: Random, 1965); Alastair Fowler, *Spenser and the Numbers of Time* (London: Routledge, 1964) 263-64; Michael Bayback, Paul Delany, and A. Kent Hieatt, "Placement 'in the middest,' in *The Faerie Queen*," *Silent Poetry: Essays in Numerological Analysis*, ed. Alastair Fowler (New York: Barnes, 1970) 142-43.

98. Charles J. Singer, "The Scientific Views and Visions of St. Hildegard," *Studies in the History and Method of Science*, ed. Charles J. Singer, 2 vols. (New York: Arno, 1975) 1: 9 and passim.

99. See, in general, Carolyn Bynum, *Jesus as Mother: Studies in the Spirituality of the High Middle Ages* (Berkeley: U of California P, 1982).

100. See Matt. 12:40: "sicut enim fuit Ionas in ventre ceti tribus diebus et tribus noctibus, sic erit Filius hominis in corde terrae tribus diebus et tribus noctibus."

101. See Gerhard Bauer, *Entstehungsgeschichte* (München: Fink, 1973), vol. 1 of *Claustrum animae: Untersuchungen zur Geschichte der Metapher vom Herzen als Kloster*, 1 vol. to date.

102. See especially the figures in Wittkower, *Architectural Principles*, and in Richard Salomon, ed., *Opicinus de Canistris: Weltbild und Bekenntnisse eines avignonesischen Klerikers des 14. Jahrhunderts*, Studies of the Warburg Institute 1ab (London: Warburg Institute, 1936).

103. G. Roheim, *Animism, Magic and the Divine King* (London: Knopf, 1930) 230, quoted in Brown, *Love's Body* 134-35. See also Brown 128.

104. In general, see W. W. Roscher, *Neue Omphalosstudien*, Abhandlungen der königlichen Sächsischen Gesellschaft der Wissenschaften, Philologische-historische Klasse 31.1 (Leipzig: Teubner, 1915).

105. Again see diagrams in Wittkower, *Architectural Principles*; also Singer fig. 7.

106. McLuhan 18.

107. *The Great Code* 159.

108. "Prêtre paien et prêtre chrétien," *Études sur le Sacrement de l'Ordre* (Paris: du Cert, 1957) 360.

109. Idiart 357.

110. Idiart 363-64.

111. *Le Roman de la Rose et la scholastique courtoise*, Publications de l'Institut d'Études Médiévales d'Ottawa 10 (Paris: Vrin, 1941) 116.

112. De Bruyne 275. Mersch writes: "Chaque homme donc, par l'imagination, est constitué, pour toute l'humanité, réceptacle suffisant et, en quelque sorte, centre de réunion, comme chaque homme déjà, par rapport à l'ensemble de générations humaines, peut etre considéré comme un centre d'aboutissement et de diffusion" (*Le Christ* 58; cf. 20). Also see Dante, *De monarchia* 1.3 for man's position "in the middle."

113. For more information on the question of a multiplicity of centers in microcosmic Christian space see Eliade, *Images et Symboles* 49-50, and *Das Heilige und das Profane* 26-27, 34-35; Spitz 19-22. In art criticism, Hall's comparison between the single point perspective of Renaissance and Baroque painters and the multiple perspective of Japanese gardens might also be applied to distinguish medieval and post-medieval notions of perspective.

Chapter Two

THE GOTHIC CATHEDRAL

Any conscientious examination of medieval textual space in the High Middle Ages must presuppose some knowledge of Gothic architecture. Whatever other resonances we derive from its complex symbolic texture, the Gothic cathedral is clearly a body, a book, and a microcosm. But the history of aesthetic criticism is littered with unsatisfying attempts to bring nonliterary forms to bear on literature, so I begin this chapter with a few qualifiers.[1] First, like the studies of individual texts and of iconography here, this analysis of microcosmic cathedral structure is intended as an original contribution independent of whatever light it may shed on my other studies. Though the cathedral's general structural affiliations with the human body and its status as a microcosmic *summa* are commonplaces, I have as yet uncovered no research which applies microcosmic theory to Gothic architecture in any detail. This lacuna in the history of architecture probably results from an even larger one in the history of ideas, the consistent undervaluation of the role of microcosmic speculation in medieval culture.

It is often both unnecessary and misleading to argue, as some scholars have, that a given poet "modeled" his text on Gothic architecture. It is more appropriate to argue that the text is modeled on the structure of the universe.[2] Within a cultural matrix that found the whole residing in all parts, structural parallels among the most varied art forms are expected and should be of considerable interest, but do not necessarily imply the influence of one art form on another. What we need as scholars is more of a cultural "big picture": interdisciplinary studies that begin with broad assessments of an idea's theological foundation, then move from one aesthetic dimension to another, occasionally applying a magnifying lens to render details more clearly. Only against that broad background can we really begin to ascertain the horizontal influence between art forms—as I believe I can show in the architectural structures of *Pearl*. And only then can we begin to understand the difference between "influence," in the usual sense, and what it means for a number of different works of art to partake of the same cultural pattern (like the French star). Given the coherence of European medieval culture, thanks in part to the unifying matrix of the body, medieval art poses an especially promising subject for this kind of scholarly enterprise. The doctrine of the Word made flesh is precisely what tempts us to seek space in texts and textuality in "spatial" art forms.

One encounters, of course, frequent mention of the symbolism of the body in Gothic architecture. Sauer, as I have noted, calls the equation of the church with Christ's body the "tiefste[n] Gedanke[n] mittelalterlicher Symbolik."[3] George Lesser writes: "The church building signifies nothing less than the body of the Lord."[4] Medieval sources stress the idea no less than modern ones; one writes: "Dispositio autem materialis ecclesiae modum humani corporis tenet."[5] The two axes of a cathedral, meeting at the center, symbolize both the cross and the body on the cross. The eucharist at the center is the source of meaning for the entire building, a fact made more evident with the rising importance of the mystery of the eucharist in the thirteenth century.[6] By extension, then, the church is equated with the body of Mary, who herself represents the entire mystical body of believers.[7] Modern sources claiming to have rediscovered this somatization of built space essentially echo medieval ones, yet each scholar stops short of an analysis that would order individual structural layers of the Gothic church into a systematic understanding of corporeal theology.[8]

The body as microcosm undoubtedly constitutes a major organizing principle at all levels of Gothic architecture.[9] The tiny, round host at the center is both a miniature cosmos and a miniature cathedral; deriving their meaning from this central source, all of the church's other structures provide either macrocosmic extensions that enclose the eucharist or patterned repetitions of the eucharist's informing shape at other points within the plenitude of built space. Thus the altar vessels become a first layer of enclosure, followed by the shape of the altar and baldachin themselves, then the nave, the successive enclosures created by one or more aisles, and finally the exterior wall of the cathedral. Side altars repeat the same principle at the structural edge, each a miniature cathedral at the hub of successive, concentric arches; thus individual points on the building's circumference recapitulate the spatial dynamics of the center.[10]

Medieval allegorical interpretation of concentric architectural structure confirms this general appearance of "plenitude." Allegorists identify the church with Eden, Noah's ark, the ark of the covenant, the tabernacle, Solomon's Temple and the Heavenly Jerusalem, all in the same breath.[11] In the church all holy sites converge and each site both contains and is contained by all others. Spatial plenitude in the cathedral presupposes a multiplicity of both meanings and levels of meaning, and all meanings are operant at all levels. The cruciform design unites north, south, east, and west at the altar, where Christ's body emblemizes both the center of the world and the point of greatest spatial density. The cross, "gehaltvollstes und tiefsinnigstes Motiv der ganzen mittelalterlichen Symbolik," gathers into the middle of the church the tree of Paradise, Abraham's sacrifice, Moses' staff, and the serpent in the wilderness—many places into one.[12]

Less obvious than its microcosmic spatial organization is the cathedral's analogous time configuration; as in architectural symbolism generally, time manifests itself spatially.[13] The *plenitudo temporis* is a necessary corollary of spatial plenitude, as the holy sites evoked range from salvation history's first garden to its final, triumphant city. The temporal all-inclusiveness of cathedral symbolism—the representation of all periods of history within one building—is correctly attributed by several scholars to Christ's position at the center of history, but usually only with relation to a limited aspect of cathedral ornamentation.[14] Most helpful is Friedrich Ohly's extended analysis of the Cathedral of Siena in "Die Kathedrale als Zeitenraum," where he links the *plenitudo temporis* of the building as a whole firmly with the theology of the body:

> Das Ganze stellt sich dort als Körper dar, und der Einklang des Einzelnen wird darin deutlich (*Ibi quoddam universitatis corpus effingitur, et concordia singulorum explicatur*). Da wird wie eine zweite Welt dieser vorübergehenden und vergänglichen entgegengestellt gefunden, weil, was in dieser Welt in Zeitaltern

> vorübergeht, in jener Welt wie in einem Stand der Ewigkeit zu gleicher Zeit besteht. Dort folgt nicht dem Vergänglichen das Gegenwärtige, löst nicht das Kommende das Gegenwärtige ab, sondern was immer dort ist, ist gegenwärtig.[15]

He compares the sacramental centrality of the altar, in particular, with the Christ-event in the middle of history, saying that time is "verdichtet" around that particular spot.[16]

The more closely we examine the overall structure of Gothic architecture, the more clearly we see the simplicity and directness of its grand design. The Gothic cathedral is a microcosm—every student of architecture knows that—but no one has yet, to my knowledge, noticed how faithfully late medieval architecture reflects each of the components of microcosmic theory that are outlined in the preceding chapter. The spatial and temporal plenitude which we have just begun to see as a broad governing principle here also operates both at intermediate levels of cathedral design and in the smallest details (as they must for the microcosmic model to have any general validity). Most scholarship to date has restricted itself to looking at these details, and even there the full range of microcosmic theory is only rarely applied.

Several scholars have analyzed Gothic buildings in terms of geometric proportion. Moessel's extensive historical study of the geometric bases of art maintains that the Middle Ages' passionate adherence to canons of geometrical mysticism was lost with the onset of Renaissance building:

> Ich glaube Grund zu haben zu der Annahme, daß mit dem Einsetzen der Renaissance die Handhabung der Proportion eine Wandlung erfuhr und vermute folgenden Zusammenhang. Die mittelalterliche Baukunst hatte die Geometrie leidenschaftlich gepflegt; sie war ihr zuletzt zum Selbstzweck, zum Spielwerk geworden—die Scholastik der Baumeister.[17]

Von Simson notes the inseparability of aesthetic and geometric design in medieval discussions of architecture theory.[18] The geometry of the circle always receives particular emphasis in such studies; Moessel shows it to govern not only the largest structures but many smaller features as well:

> Bauteile und Bauformen und Bildwerke kleineren Maßstabs, in denen die Kreisteilung bedeutsam Gestalt gewinnt, sind unter manchen anderen die Radfenster und Fensterrosen, Radleuchter, Taufbecken, zuletzt in außerordentlicher Vielfältigkeit das Maßwerk des späteren Mittalters.[19]

Moessel's studies work implicitly with the circle as a microcosmic structure, though he is not familiar enough with philosophical sources to make observations informed by microcosmic tradition itself; nonetheless, his work points in the right direction. Particularly useful is his identification of the medieval altar with the center of one or more circles providing a geometric core for the entire architectural design. This central point, he notes, coincides with the intersection of the two lines of the cross formation discussed above. (The traditional coincidence of circle and cross is widespread and has provided the subject for two book-length studies.)[20] The inscribed cross centers on the eucharistic body of Christ (and often on the body of a saint in a crypt below), and constitutes a source from which all circular and straight geometric structures radiate. Moessel describes the consecration of the altar, in which the bishop traces a cross over a round, central eucharistic paten, and again over the four corners of the altar table, as a representation of the church's overall cross-structure at its geometrical point of origin.[21] The "corporeal" origin of this central circle becomes especially evident in a Francesco di Giorgio drawing reproduced by von Simson: a human figure is inscribed within a cathedral plan, and on its chest is drawn a large circle whose center point coincides both with the center of the chest and the precise intersection of the structural "cross."[22] It is not surprising, then, that Moessel bases his circle-based analysis on the notion of an all-encompassing "Kernpunkt" residing inside man himself:

> Die Elemente, aus welchen die architektonische Gestaltung sich aufbaut, sind also dieselben Elemente, welche durch die Geometrie ihre Regelung erfahren. Wurden die Bauwerke auf geometrischer Grundlage entwickelt, also auf den Figurationen, welche sich aus den regelmäßigen Teilungen des Kreises ergeben oder ihnen entsprechen, so waren sie von einer Gesetzgebung erfaßt, eine Ordnung wurde ihnen zuteil, von einem Kernpunkt ausstrahlend und auf diesen Kernpunkt bezüglich; ein Regelmaß, das alle räumlichen Einzelheiten zu einer umfassenden räumlichen Einheit

> höherer Ordnung verbindet, aus der jene wiederum zu fließen scheinen (Kosmos). Diese Ordnung ist nichts anderes als die sichtbare Erscheinung einer im Inneren des Menschen selbst unwandelbar gegründeten Gesetzgebung.[23]

Elsewhere he calls this "Kernpunkt," part of a tradition originating with Plato, "ein Zentrum, das doch nicht gefaßt und mit Namen genannt werden kann. Es ist der Begriff der gestaltenden organisierenden Kraft."[24] As the necessary result of this centripetal arrangement, circular geometry predominates over rectangular geometry in Gothic architecture. Lesser makes this point concisely:

> After what has been said, we shall be permitted to distinguish between "rectangular" and "circular" geometry. We now venture to say that, during the Middle Ages, a church dedicated to Omnipotence had of necessity to be conceived and planned according to a "hierarchical" geometry where all parts and measures radiate from a central point which marks the apex and focus of the design: in other words, a circular or, if we may so put it, a centripetal geometry. Compared with this ideal, a merely rectangular or "proportional" geometry would appear secular and profane. Therefore we may expect that such rectangular relations are, in mediaeval church design, admitted in an ancillary role only.[25]

The importance of such "center-based" design in medieval architecture is acknowledged by many scholars. K. Freckmann calls it "eine religiöse Grundform."[26] Ohly sees it as the consequence of a typologically ordered world view.[27] And it is a basis of design with broad ramifications for many other art forms as well, since Gothic architecture itself provides a "kultischer Mittelpunkt" for all of the arts.[28] In architecture theory in general, "centeredness" is frequently linked with microcosmic structure.[29]

In the light of what has already been published about the geometry of circle and center in Gothic architecture, there is good reason to believe that cathedrals in the High Middle Ages conform closely to the mystical portrayal of the universe as an endless series of concentric circles whose center contains its circumference (as described in the previous chapter). The entire symbolic space of the cathedral is contained by the round eucharist at its center, which is in turn contained by a series of concentric layers, each of which figures as an allegorical equivalent of the body of Christ. The cathedrals taken as a whole were not round, but the arches that arrange themselves in concentric layers over the side chapels until they merge at the ceiling of the nave show the fundamental integrating principle of circular form. The altar, as we have seen, is where both architectural space and time reside in their fullness. The other circular formations within the cathedral—rose windows, labyrinths, chandeliers (*coronae*), etc.—constitute microcosms which themselves contain all space. The individual chapels, each with its own altar, are an especially striking recapitulation of the entire space of the cathedral (complete with its eucharistic center) at the structural circumference. The main altar's daily reenactment of the Incarnation that constitutes time's center resonates outwards towards the altars that occupy multiple points at the building's edge.

The preceding paragraphs have attempted an overview of microcosmic design in Gothic architecture as a whole; as such, my analysis may thus far appear oversimplified. It should, after all, be characteristic of any quest for microcosmic structure that the most essential evidence be found not in the whole, but in the parts. The remainder of my discussion concerns itself with architectural details. I begin here where all meaning begins, at the altar, and then move outwards towards rose windows, labyrinths, façades, etc., repeatedly highlighting the motif of cosmic concentric circles. At the chapter's end I will return to the altar, again following the flow of symbolism back to the middle which constitutes the building's beginning and end.

If the host is a microcosm, then the altar on which it lies must have microcosmic implications as well. Eliade writes: "Das Innere der Kirche ist das Welt-All. . . . Die Mitte des Kirchengebäudes ist die Erde."[30] Joseph Braun mentions the "die ganze Welt erfüllende[n] Altar," and cites medieval tradition associating its four corners with the four directions of the heavens.[31] And if the altar symbolizes the entire world, then it also represents the entire cathedral itself. Braun's plate 33 pictures an altar composed of columns and arches, a cathedral within a cathedral, and numerous medieval sources link the altar with the church.[32] The cathedral's center contains space in all of its plenitude; it encompasses and subsumes a number of traditionally holy sites in itself.

Exegetical tradition links it with paradise,[33] the tabernacle,[34] the manger,[35] the cross,[36] Golgotha,[37] and Christ's tomb,[38] all of which are associated allegorically with the macrocosmic structure of the cathedral as well.

The altar also encapsulates the plenitude of time. We have seen in Moessel how the church's consecration moves from the altar outwards; Eliade stresses "die enge Beziehung zwischen Kosmisierung und Konsakrierung," noting that the consecration reenacts microcosmically the creation of the world at the beginning of time.[39] Sauer discusses various altar ornaments representing the *plenitudo temporis*, such as a cloth hanging whose three colors symbolize a tripartite division of man's history (used at Easter, the calendar equivalent of time's center), and ivory carvings at the Cathedral of Salerno portraying scenes ranging from creation to Judgment.[40] The altar serves as a repository for history, a gathering place for memorable events, much as a living room's fireplace accumulates on its shelf photos and other mementos of a family's life together.[41]

The altar recapitulates the entire temporal and spatial sequence of the cathedral, because it, like the larger architectural frame, represents the body. Pseudo-Ambrosius writes: "Quid est enim altare nisi forma corporis Christi?"[42] The altar is Christ's body, and the stones with which it is constructed represent the many believers whose bodies together constitute the *corpus mysticum*.[43] But the altar is also the body turned inside-out. Scarry writes:

> The building of the altar externalizes and makes visible the shape of belief; the hidden interior of sentience is lifted out through work into the visible world. Itself the body turned inside-out, it in turn becomes the table on which the body will once more be turned inside-out.[44]

And again:

> It is now what is perceived to be in contact with this outward surface (God) that is most precious. That the altar's surface is the reversed lining of the body is made more imagistically immediate in all those places where blood is poured across the altar. . . . it is a turning of the body inside-out. . . .[45]

The Gothic Cathedral

Scarry connects the inside-outness of the altar with its paradoxical Old Covenant status as a locus where God resides and yet cannot be seen because of the many surrounding veils:

> Though there gradually comes before us in these endless tiers of tissue something that seems the magnificent and monumental tissue of the body of God, what at the same time comes before us is the veil, the materialization of the refusal to be materialized, the incarnation of absence.[46]

As a consequence, the altar is also associated with body parts that suggest an interior point of reversibility with relation to the whole body. The altar is the navel.[47] It is also, according to widespread patristic tradition, the cathedral's heart; Augustine writes: "Eius est altare cor nostrum."[48]

Among the other features of Gothic architecture evidencing microcosmic design, façades, in particular, have received attention for their synecdochal relation to the overall plan. Several scholars have pointed out our ability to trace a cross-section of the nave in the façade.[49] Sauer sees "die ganze Kirchensymbolik" epitomized by the façade, and attributes that relation of part to whole to the metaphorics of the body.[50] Of course, the corporeal sense of space here dictates not only a part/whole relation, but that of inside to outside; the façade is an exterior premonition of everything inside the building, just as the face reflects the emotions of the heart.[51] Though west portals receive the most attention in this regard, each of the four portals constitutes a projection from the central altar into one of the four directions of the world. Occasionally the altar screen figures as a mini-façade at the heart of the church.[52]

If the façade recapitulates the entire cathedral, then the rose window recapitulates both the façade, of which it is the "dominante formale Mitte,"[53] and by extension, the cathedral itself. The rose window is for the façade what the eucharist is for the entire building, a compact source of all meaning. This relation does not receive attention in scholarship, but can easily be substantiated. Eucharists since the ninth century were commonly molded in the shape of rose windows,[54] and Painton Cowen has assembled some evidence linking rose window design with the grail tradition.[55] Monstrances, used on special occasions (most commonly Corpus Christi Day) to display the eucharist, are often shaped like miniature façades in which the host replaces the rose window.[56]

Further, the rose window's dependence on various medieval representations of the cosmos has been convincingly demonstrated.[57] The tradition takes a variety of forms, but essential structural features can be identified. Christ's body, or Adam's, or that of an unidentified male figure, usually rests at the center of the depiction. This central body may also be replaced by a circle, or be circumscribed by one and/or contain one somewhere near its chest. The central figure is surrounded by circles forming a kind of wheel; the influence of the Wheel of Fortune tradition is always quite clear. These peripheral circles are sometimes attached to the central figure via "spokes" of some sort, and are in turn usually surrounded by a large, all-encompassing circle. These depictions, then, draw on a circle-based geometry patterned concentrically around a center point and capable of generating new centers/circles at the circumference; it is founded precisely upon the tradition we have seen in Mahnke's *Unendliche Sphäre und Allmittelpunkt*. As in Mahnke's description, these depictions find their center in the body.

The corporeal, microcosmic core of these *Weltbilder* emblemizes the spatial and temporal center of the universe. Often Christ is depicted on the cross, whose beams provide a spatial focus for an illustration of the universe's four elements and four directions, the four winds (normally illustrated at the four outer corners), or the four rivers of paradise. Occasionally the "spokes" join at the central figure's heart. Often the signs of the zodiac, the four seasons, or the twelve months of the year at the edges figure as macrocosmic extensions of the body's temporal centrality. Where the body is not depicted, the central circle constituting its equivalent often contains the words "Mundus Annus Homo," explicitly identifying the body as the source of space and time.[58]

One need only place reproductions of such drawings side by side with photographs of rose windows to see the striking similarity; often both *rosa* and *rota*, these window-wheels display a manifest dependence both on the content and concentric organization of the *Weltbilder*.[59] Rose windows commonly reproduce in miniature the shape of the whole both at the hub and at the ends of the "spokes."[60] Ellen Beer and others have traced the influence in detail, and their arguments require no repetition here. What research to date has not yet made clear is the extent to which traditional representations of the cosmos manifest themselves in less obvious details of Gothic architecture, and in its overall structure. Here microcosmic speculation and the corporeal, concentric understanding of time and space—until now not yet applied by scholars to the *Weltbilder* themselves—can further clarify certain architectural features.

The spokes of the rose windows' main "wheel" provide an important clue to the concentric organization of the entire cathedral. There are usually twelve of these spokes, and very frequently they are carved in the shape of columns, sometimes with two columns per spoke.[61] Not too much imagination is required to see a reference here to the double row of columns lining the nave (sometimes there are twelve, twelve being the number of the apostles, the "pillars" of the church[62]), though scholars largely ignore it.[63] Occasionally rose windows contain two different concentric layers of columns.[64] These columns typically "support" intervening "arches" which constitute the rounded outer edge of each "rose petal" between the columns. And as there are two layers of columns, there are also two layers of arches. In microcosmic terms, then, the *rota-rosa* window is a condensation of the entirety of a cathedral's space. Itself a displacement of the host at the building's utmost periphery, it provides a compact distillation of the structure of both façade and interior just as the façade in turn recapitulates the total architectural design.

By showing the essentially concentric relation of both interior and exterior layers of columns and arches to the eucharist on the altar, the rose window strongly reinforces the notion, proposed earlier, of Gothic architecture's fundamental dependence on the mysticism of circle and center. As the rose window is a miniature cathedral, so too the cathedral is a massive rose window. Each side altar recapitulates at the cathedral's edge both the building as a whole and the baldachin over the main altar, just as the *rota-rosa* is ringed with wheels identical to both the entire window and its hub. Both window and church picture a cosmos whose space and time begin and end with the body at the center.

Another microcosmic design, in many ways akin to the rose window, is the labyrinth; labyrinths are typically featured on cathedral floors, the best known perhaps being that of Chartres Cathedral. The labyrinth is an *imago mundi*; its convoluted path, if followed correctly, leads to salvation.⁶⁵ Christ was the first man to attain the center, and with his help, the secret route has been made available to all.⁶⁶ The "mühsam zugänglich[e] Kernraum" is thus the New Jerusalem, and the labyrinth as a whole may also be equated with that city.⁶⁷ Like the cathedral which contains it and itself emblemizes the holy city, the labyrinth displays at its center a microcosm of itself. Pilgrims following the labyrinth's winding path retrace Christ's *Leidensweg*; at the center they may also find Christ's body.⁶⁸ The labyrinth thus exemplifies, in miniature, the pilgrim's "journey" through the cathedral building itself.⁶⁹ Like the rose window and the macrocosmic structure of the cathedral, the labyrinth consists of successive concentric circles around an all-encompassing center; it enacts a *recapitulatio* of the cosmos, and is traditionally linked with representations of the zodiac.⁷⁰ Its geometric foundations become especially apparent in the famous Chartres design, whose chain of six circles at the exact center replicate both the *rosa* of round cathedral windows and the mystical proportions of the *Weltbilder* that those windows reflect. The Chartres example also repeats its core design with a chain of semicircles at its edge, emphasizing the equation of center and circumference.⁷¹ The labyrinth thus displays the form of a "knot" or "chain," a small-scale reproduction of the Great Chain of Being.⁷² And it helps us to see the analogous concentric and chained circles of the entire cathedral as a knot or chain as well.

The elaborate chandeliers which medieval sources call *coronae* exhibit a circular configuration recalling both labyrinth and rose window, and their original central location over the main altar gives them particular significance as microcosms.⁷³ Their overall shape is circular, but again, it is a circumference composed of semicircular segments. Like the rose windows and labyrinths, the *coronae* represent the New Jerusalem; the semi-circular segments have the shape of walls, connected at each point of intersection by a tiny tower.⁷⁴ To my knowledge, no one has yet suggested the influence of medieval cosmographic design on these chandeliers, but in light of the similar structures elsewhere in Gothic architecture the connection seems obvious enough. The number of semicircular walls in French *coronae* is commonly twelve,⁷⁵ identical with the number of petals in most *rota-rosa* windows and with the number of circles at the circumference of many *Weltbilder*. The crown image in Dante (*Par.* 22.119ff.) appears to be linked with the traditional cosmic representations of circle and wheel.[76] J. Baltrusaitis' thorough study of cosmographic circles in medieval iconography links traditional *Weltbilder* with the crown image throughout, though he does not discuss Gothic chandeliers.[77] His Figure 8 (70) provides an especially convincing link between *Weltbild* and crown via the intermediate image of the garland; here the traditional chains of cosmographic circles (which in turn arrange themselves concentrically around central figures) are held together with flower garlands.[78] Ian Bishop has already noted the symbolic equation of garland and crown in his work on *Pearl*, though he does not show awareness of the related iconographic tradition.[79]

One of the celebrated marvels of Gothic architecture is the fact that the proportional relation of the nave to the side aisles often may be derived from a cross-section of one of the piers; each pier, then, figures as a microcosm of the building. When we remember, in this connection, that the cathedral as a whole recapitulates the design of both cosmographic circle diagrams and *rota-rosa* windows, we can bring this detail into clearer focus. As we have seen, the piers that line the nave correspond with the columns forming the spokes of the *rota*. Both pier and column occur precisely at those points where the chain/crown of circles constituting the circumference of traditional *Weltbilder* overlap; the many columns that cluster into the pier normally branch out into separate, subordinate circular/arch structures as they progress towards the ceiling (where they again intersect at the bosses). Geometrical mysticism endows the overlap of circumferences with particular significance, because the point of intersection generates a new center; the center is everywhere and the circumference is, ultimately, nowhere. Iconographic use of the mandorla serves to underscore this geometric principle; the lozenge-shaped mandorla, the shape created by the intersection of two circles, commonly frames the figures of Christ and the saints—figures which represent the overlap of earthly and heavenly "spheres." Designers of *Weltbilder* occasionally highlight the importance of these points by drawing a cross at each intersection (I have even found such crosses drawn between the circular chapels of an ambulatory, in a cathedral plan evidencing particular awareness of cosmographic structure.).[80] Thus the body of Christ and the spatial centrality of the cross provide a source of meaning beginning at both center and edge. Of course, the association between the architectural column and the human body is a very old one,[81] as is the notion, in some cultures, that the world-body possesses a column of some sort at its center symbolically equivalent to the human spinal column.[82]

In view of the body-based geometric and theological significance of the column, it seems especially likely that the pier cross-section itself can be regarded as a representation of the cosmos akin to those providing the basis for rose windows, labyrinths, and *coronae*. The exact configurations of such cross-sections vary, of course, as do the *Weltbilder* themselves, but the basic design remains fairly consistent in both: a central circle surrounded symmetrically by subordinate circles. Particularly striking is how the cross-section of the *pilier cantonné*, the central column with four applied colonnettes used in the cathedrals at Chartres, Reims, and Amiens, resembles the common *Weltbild* configuration of a large central circle with four small circles attached.[83]

There is also some evidence for seeing traditional *Weltbild* structures in the geometry of the bosses that mark the east-west axis of the vault. The bosses occur at intersections of multiple ribs, and therefore carry the same potential geometric significance as the *pilier cantonné*. Their design can be quite elaborate, but is usually contained within a circle whose center provides the coordinate for symmetrical arrangement of subordinate parts. Often other circles occur both at the center and edge, and in an overlapping "chain" filling the space intermediate between center and edge in a design similar to the "petals" of rose windows.[84]

Having observed the *recapitulatio* of cosmos and cathedral at so many other points of geometric density, we are surely justified in seeking it at the "head" of the building itself. Though the apse might logically seem the most likely site for cosmographic representation, scholarship has to my knowledge ignored the possibility; however, a number of published observations, considered together, point in the right direction. The general symbolic equation of apse and head, of course, is nothing new to scholars;[85] it is reflected, for example, in the word "chevet" used in French to designate the apse.

Ferguson has traced the evolution of the apsidal formation out of the design of round churches, from which we can see the apse as a sort of archeological microcosm, a structural springboard for the remainder of the building.[86] There are historical grounds, then, for the apse's symbolic self-sufficiency. Moessel stresses the importance of the circle in apse design, and draws a parallel with rose windows, saying, "Hier wird die Geometrie selbst Gegenstand der Darstellung."[87] Sedlmayr notes its similarity to the *corona*, remarking that the apse, too, symbolizes the New Jerusalem.[88]

But the uniqueness of the apsidal termination within the overall cathedral plan has not yet received due attention. We may rightly compare it with the rose window and *corona*—and with the labyrinth, boss, and pier cross-section, for that matter—but these structures nonetheless comprise a group of architectural "details" (albeit very important ones) to which the apse does not fully belong. Nor is the apse merely another of the series of concentric layers (vessel, altar, baldachin, nave, etc.) clustering around the central altar. It is a space of more significance than a window or pier, yet of a different order from the other large spaces; clearly microcosmic in outline, it nonetheless possesses a structural independence denied to the building's other microcosms.

The relation of the entire Gothic cathedral to the apse graphically illustrates the paradoxical relation between the *corpus mysticum* and Christ, its head. Via participation in the mystical body, each believer shares "headship" with Christ, yet Christ's headship still predominates over that of each believer. Thus the apse constitutes a miniature church which fully integrates itself with the entire cathedral body at the same time that it resists the structural subordination to which the other microcosmic spaces must submit.

The mystical relation of head to body sheds light on the curious coexistence of two equally important altar sites in a large number of Gothic buildings: one at the transept crossing (often called the *Kreuzaltar*), and one at the center of the apse (*Choraltar*). Theological or aesthetic grounds for the coexistence of these two centers are, in the opinion of some scholars, not to be found. Sedlmayr writes:

> Die Existenz zweier Hauptaltäre auf der Hauptachse der Kirche ist weder aus dem künstlerischen, noch aus dem sinnbildlichen

Organismus des christlichen Kirchengebäudes zu begreifen . . . gerade innerhalb der Kathedrale, die überall die Tendenz zur Vereinheitlichung zeigt, wirkt es störend.[89]

But in fact the equal prominence of the two altars is fully consistent with the paradoxical unity of head and members in the mystical body; Christ's status in the church equals the joint status of those who follow him. Hence the geometric *Weltbild* configuration of the apse is separate from but equivalent to that of the entire building.

At issue, again, is the paradox of multiple centers, as discussed in the previous chapter. Every body part reproduces the whole in microcosm, yet some have more prominence than others; in the church building, not all altars have equal significance. Similarly, every point in the universe is a potential center, but some places—such as Jerusalem and Eden—are given more symbolic weight. Both the head and the heart are symbolic focal points of more or less equal importance: Christ is our head, yet we bear him in our hearts. Similarly, the altar, which medieval tradition understood to be the heart of the church, bears the host which constitutes the church's head. The development of main altars corresponding with the head and heart of the building, then, is fully consistent with medieval theology.

Scholarship on the apse provides a good example of what happens when the corporeal and microcosmic basis of cathedral design is not fully understood. It is not enough to compare the apse with the rose window or *corona*; the building's "head" is a *Weltbild*, and this cosmographic structure gives it a precisely definable relation to every other microcosmic super- and substructure drawing on the same tradition of cosmic representation. A separate strand of the *Weltbild* iconographic tradition itself, in fact, assigns prominence to the head as a second center and source of circular geometry, based on the analogy between the head's sphericity and the shape of the universe.[90]

Our examination of microcosmic structure throughout the cathedral has returned us, as it must, to the altar. Earlier in this chapter we noted in general how the altar creates a nodal gathering point for the spatial and temporal plenitude of cathedral symbolism via its traditional association with multiple corporeal centers (heart, navel, head) and its function as a point of reference for

The Gothic Cathedral

cathedral geometry. Having since analyzed how the altar projects itself into various architectural substructures, we are now prepared to see more clearly how the multilayered allegorical structure of the building radiates inward towards the altar itself. To this end, the remainder of this chapter concentrates primarily on the various liturgical vessels which constitute the altar's microcosmic components.

Bloomer and Moore write: "A chest or even an object upon a table may gain importance by recalling the columns and arches and even the roof of a house or a palace."[91] The façade-like shape of Gothic monstrances, in which the eucharistic host replaces the rose window, was noted above, as was the occasional microcosmic design of column and arch on the altar itself. Another eucharist-bearing vessel often designed like a miniature cathedral is the *ciborium*, an object whose name also designates the large canopied or vaulted structure that sometimes housed the entire altar, usually built with pillars or poles in such a way as to recall the tabernacle (again, a miniature church).[92] Chalices[93] and incense burners[94] also frequently mimic cathedral design, as do reliquaries.[95] The shape of the vessels intended for direct contact with the sacrament, then, provide a continual reminder that the entire building is a container for Christ's body.

Further, the multivalent symbolism of Christ's body itself endows each of its containers, at every level, with the capacity for multiple allegorical resonances; each layer of symbolic space signifies not only the church but also numerous images which exegetical tradition equates with the church. The altar table symbolizes both church and tabernacle, and its four legs remind many exegetes of the four levels of scriptural interpretation.[96] Just as the altar constitutes the heart of the church, so also the chalice,[97] paten,[98] incense burners,[99] and wine and water vessels[100] resting on it are linked with Christ's heart as well. Drawing on the archetypal conception of the Virgin as God's vessel, each container of the sacrament also emblemizes the body of Mary; taken together, the altar's liturgical equipment and decorations signify the various adornments used by the bride to please the bridegroom.[101] The *ciborium*, whose association with the tabernacle has already been noted, also bears resonances of the ark of the covenant, the urns used by the Israelites to hold manna, and Christ's tomb.[102] The chalice signifies both Christ's body and the tomb (both container and contained), while the paten used to cover the chalice is associated with both the stone that covered the tomb's entrance and the cross.[103] The altar table's linen covering reminds exegetes both of the church and of Christ's burial shroud.[104] Tradition links vessels for oil with Christ's body, and incense burners with both New Jerusalem and the image of the church as a ship.[105] As is the case with the successive architectural macrostructures that enclose it, the altar and its vessels reiterate many of the same allegorical associations at each level of proximity to the body in which all Christian symbolism finds it origin. Each container is the symbolic equivalent of the contained: Christ's body, the church which is his body's extension, and the plenitude of holy sites and objects understood as either literal or figural containers for that body find symbolic representation throughout the gradient of spatial enclosure.

Not only do the various altar vessels share the same microcosmic cathedral design and the same range of allegorical significance; many of them also evidence conscious imitation of traditional cosmographic representation, a fact that appears to have gone largely unnoticed in medieval scholarship. The rose window design often stamped onto the host has already been mentioned; when we examine the molds used to produce these hosts, the *Weltbild* structure becomes especially apparent.[106] It is not surprising, then, that the same cosmic design found its way onto the various liturgical containers. Thus monstrances, for example, often display the eucharist at the center of several concentric rings, with Christ's body occasionally featured, as in the *Weltbilder*, within the innermost circle (presumably under the host itself); sometimes a chain of jewels set just inside the outermost circle mimics the chain of circles featured by cosmic diagrams in the same place. The pattern of interlocking circles may also be reiterated at the base, or, when the monstrance is designed in the shape of a tree, in the tree's branches.[107] Occasionally featured just under the host is the shape of a waning moon, perhaps intended to hold the host in place; this detail recalls the inclusion of the waning moon near the center of some of the *Weltbilder* by Hildegard of Bingen and others.[108] One of the monstrances pictured in Braun displays the eucharist at the center of Christ's body, akin to the circles we have seen at the middle of the central figures in a number of cosmographic representations.[109]

The monstrances make abundantly clear the relation of cosmic structure to the eucharist at the core; other altar vessels display the same *Weltbild* design for the same reason, though they are designed to cover and enclose the host rather than display it. Medieval chalices frequently feature chains of interlocking circles around their base, occasionally at the periphery of interior concentric circles.[110] This base design can also be reflected on the sides of the chalice bowl, where the interlocking circles can take the form of columns and arches familiar in rose windows and eucharist molds.[111] The patens used to cover the chalice display cosmographic design even more clearly by virtue of their flat shape; in so doing, they reinforce the *Weltbild* imagery on the chalices with which they form a functional unit. Like eucharist molds, monstrances, and rose windows, they are ornamented with bands of chained circles layered within concentric circles, usually with Christ or a lamb pictured at the center.[112] Other liturgical equipment, including the *flabellum*, often displays analogous cosmic configurations, as occasionally does the altar itself.[113] Taken as a whole, this massive repetition of cosmic structure on liturgical vessels endows the altar with a density of microcosmic symbolism unparalleled by any other part of the cathedral.

Notes

1. For an overview of some such attempts see René Wellek and Austin Warren, "Literature and the Other Arts," *Theory of Literature*, 3rd ed. (New York: Harcourt, 1962) 125-35.
2. This claim has also been made, of course, sometimes in studies of architectural form in texts (see Jordan).
3. Sauer 36; cf. 301-02.
4. *Gothic Cathedrals and Sacred Geometry* (London: Tirantis, 1957) 148. See also Kantorowicz 71-72; Ernst Moessel, *Die Proportion in Antike und Mittelalter*, 2 vols. (München: Beck, 1926) 1: 113.
5. Guil. Durandus, *Rationale divinorum officiorum* 1.1, cited in Sauer 111. Cf. references to Villard d'Honnecourt and Vitruvius (the latter being quite influential in the ninth and fourteenth centuries) in Joseph Rykwert, *On Adam's House in Paradise: The Idea of the Primitive Hut in Architectural History* (New York: Museum of Modern Art, 1972) 94, 109ff. For early Italian Renaissance drawings showing the human body inscribed within a cathedral plan, see Wittkower, *Architectural Principles*.
6. Sauer 192-93.
7. See von Simson xxi; Adolf Katzenellenbogen, *The Sculptural Programs of Chartres Cathedral: Christ, Mary, Ecclesia* (Baltimore: Johns Hopkins, 1959) 55, 90, 127, etc.
8. Bloomer and Moore state their book's main thesis on 5: "Yet at its beginnings all architecture derived from this body-centered sense of space and place." Bachelard quotes Jules Michelet on 101: "La maison, c'est la personne même, sa forme et son effort le plus immédiat."
9. And yet one finds relatively few references to microcosmic theory in scholarship on the Gothic cathedral, and these are brief and superficial. It is striking, for example, that Sauer's widely-consulted book should begin by stressing the fundamental symbolism of the body of Christ, and then make no more than glancing allusions to microcosmic structure (e.g., 108). For the relation of architecture to the macrocosm at the most general level of discussion, see Bachelard 24, 61-63.
10. "Il n'y a qu'un Sauveur comme il n'y a qu'un Centre, mais de même que l'archétype engendre la répétition, le prototype polarise la multilocation: chaque autel est un haut-lieu." Idiart 358.
11. See Adamus Scotus, *De tripart. tabern. una cum pictura* 2.106 (*PL* 198.710-11); Friedrich Ohly, "Die Kathedrale als Zeitenraum," *Schriften zur mittelalterlichen Bedeutungsforschung* (Darmstadt: Wissenschaftliche, 1977) 173, 193; Cullmann 132-33, 136.
12. Sauer 223.
13. For the relation between architectural space and time, see Hermann Usener's discussion of the "templum/tempus" paradox in *Götternamen*, 2nd ed. (Bonn: Cohen, 1929) 191ff., and Eliade's continuation of the same idea in *Das Heilige und das Profane* 42ff. Cf. Ohly, "Die Kathedrale als Zeitenraum" 174-75; Sauer 383; Moessel 2: 174.

14. See Sauer, very generally on 3-4 and in connection with the use of Easter candles on 190; in Katzenellenbogen, as a principle of unity for the sculptural programs at Chartres, esp. 79, 90; Hans Sedlmayr, in analysis of *Bilderkapelle*, *Die Entstehung der Kathedrale* (1950; rpt. with afterword Graz: Akademische, 1976) 484-85.

15. Ohly 177. On the same page he links this conception with microcosmic theory: "Jene Welt ist in dieser Welt, und diese Welt ist kleiner als jene Welt, weil jene faßt, den diese zu fassen nicht imstand ist." Cf. 191-92.

16. Ohly 194n.

17. Moessel 1: 73; cf. 2: 5.

18. Von Simson 18-20. Also see Lesser; Gerda Soergel, *Untersuchungen über den theoretischen Architekturentwurf von 1450-1550 in Italien*, diss., U Köln, 1958 (München: n.p., 1958), especially chapter entitled "Proportionale Kreise" 69ff.

19. 2: 158. Cf. Katzenellenbogen 20 on the circle in the sculptural program of Chartres (in particular, the Liberal Arts sequence).

20. A. H. Allcroft, *The Circle and the Cross*, 2 vols. (London: Macmillan, 1927-30); Werner Müller, *Kreis und Kreuz: Untersuchungen zur sakralen Siedlung bei Italikern und Germanen*, Deutsches Ahnenerbe 2.10 (Berlin: Widukind, 1938).

21. Moessel 2: 154-55, 158. Wittkower writes: "as God is omnipresent, the Sacrament should be in the center upon which all the lines of the building converge" (*Architectural Principles* 12). Eliade discusses progress through religious buildings as a pilgrimage to the center of the world" (*Images et Symboles* 54). Cf. Sauer 155.

22. Pl. 7 (following 150).

23. Moessel 2: 175-76.

24. Moessel 1: 116.

25. Lesser 9.

26. "Maßverhältnisse der Rotunde von St. Michael in Fulda," *Fuldaer Geschichtsblätter* 33 (1957): 65, cited by Wolfgang Haubrichs, *Ordo als Form: Strukturstudien zur Zahlenkomposition bei Otfrid von Weissenburg und in karolingischer Literatur*, Hermaea, Germanistische Forschungen, N.F. 27 (Tübingen: Niemeyer, 1969) 87.

27. "Synagoge und Ecclesia," *Bedeutungsforschung* 325. Cf. Sauer 91-92; Katzenellenbogen 6.

28. Sedlmayr 100.

29. Christian Norberg-Schultz, *Genius Loci: Towards a Phenomenology of Architecture* (New York: Rizzoli, 1980) 18; Bloomer and Moore 50-51; Bachelard 35.

30. *Das Heilige und das Profane* 37.

31. *Der christliche Altar in seiner geschichtlichen Entwicklung*, 2 vols. (München: Koch, 1924) 2: 751, 852.

32. See Braun, *Altar* 751-52; Sauer 161; Sedlmayr 481.

33. See Eliade, *Das Heilige und das Profane* 37.

34. Sauer 175.

35. Katzenellenbogen 12-13; Braun, *Altar* 752.

36. Sauer 156-60, 164; Braun, *Altar* 752.

37. Graber 94.

38. Sauer 167; Katzenellenbogen 13; Braun, *Altar* 753.

39. *Das Heilige und das Profane* 18-20; *Eternel retour* 121-23.

40. Sauer 169-71. Similarly, Flavius Josephus writes that twelve pieces of bread on the altar table signify the twelve months of the year (*Ant. Jud.* 3.7.7, cited in Eliade, *Das Heilige und das Profane* 43).

41. Cf. Bloomer and Moore 49-51 and passim, where the phrase "body of memory" is used in this connection.

42. *De sacramentis* (*PL* 16.437; cf. 447). See Braun, *Altar* 751.
43. Sauer 159-60. Cf. Graber 111.
44. *Body in Pain* 204-05.
45. *Body in Pain* 189-90; cf. 237-38.
46. *Body in Pain* 211.
47. Bauer 148.
48. *De Civitate Dei* 10.3. Cf. Lactantius, *Divin. Instit.* 6.24 (*PL* 6.727). Secondary sources treating the equation of heart and altar in patristic tradition include the following: Bauer 149; Braun, *Altar* 753-54; Xenja von Ertzdorff, "Das Herz in der lateinisch-theologischen und frühen volkssprachigen religiösen Literatur," *Beiträge zur Geschichte der deutschen Sprache und Literatur* 84 (1962): 288; Ch. G. Kanters, *Le Coeur de Jésus dans la littérature chrétienne des douze premiers siècles* (Brussels: Beyaert, 1930) 89-90; Karl Richstätter, *Die Herz-Jesu-Verehrung des deutschen Mittelalters* (Regensburg: Kösel, 1924) 90; Dominique Sanchis, "Le symbolisme communautaire du temple chez saint Augustin," *Revue d'ascétique et de mystique* 37 (1961): 6.
49. Erwin Panofsky, *Gothic Architecture and Scholasticism* (Latrobe, PA: Archabbey, 1951) 44.
50. Sauer vii, 297, 324. In general, see chapter entitled "Die Bilderzyklen an Kirchenportalen und Kirchenfassaden, eine Zusammenfassung der ganzen Kirchensymbolik" 308-74.
51. Sauer 371-72; Bloomer and Moore 43-46.
52. Sedlmayr 289.
53. Sedlmayr 144.
54. E. Mersmann, "Die Bedeutung der Rundfenster im Mittelalter," diss., U Vienna, 1944, *Anmerkung* 67.
55. *Die Rosenfenster der gotischen Kathedralen* (Freiburg: Herder, 1979) 99-103. His reproduction of a medieval drawing of the Straßburg Cathedral's west façade shows a relation between portal and rose window relevant to the present discussion (38).
56. Sedlmayr 382, 479. See also Joseph Braun, *Das christliche Altargerät in seinem Sinn und seiner Entwicklung* (München: Hueber, 1932) pls. 62, 64, 66, 67.
57. See especially the work done by Ellen J. Beer: *Die Rose der Kathedrale von Lausanne und der Kosmologische Bilderkreis des Mittelalters* (Bern: Benteli, 1952); "Nouvelles réflections sur l'image du monde dans la cathédrale de Lausanne," *Revue de l'art* 10 (1970): 57-62. In this study, "representations of the cosmos" and similar designations provide a rough English rendering of the more concise German word *Weltbilder*. The terminology is, at best, misleading, suggesting Ptolemaic renderings of the earth surrounded by concentric heavenly spheres. The representations described here are not always so literal, often organizing more abstract categories within a concentric spatial and temporal framework.
58. Here "Annus" refers to the mythological God of time.
59. Not all Gothic rose windows evidence a clear "wheel" structure, but many did; in the latter, the spaces between the spokes figure as the "rose petals."
60. See Cowen 123, figs. 2-4.
61. See John Leyerle, "The Rose-Wheel Design and Dante's *Paradiso*," *University of Toronto Quarterly* 46 (1976/77) fig. 1 (282); Cowen, figs. 23-26, 46-52; Beer, *Kathedrale von Lausanne* fig. 55; Salomon fig. 72.
62. Sauer 297-98.
63. An exception is Leyerle; see "Rose-Wheel" 281.
64. E.g., Cowen figs. 46, 48, 49.
65. Gustav René Hocke, *Die Welt als Labyrinth* (Hamburg: Rowohlt, 1961).
66. Haubrichs 284.
67. Haubrichs 286.
68. Bauer 185. Sometimes the Minotaur appears at the center instead.

69. John James, *Chartres: The Masons Who Built a Legend* (London: Routledge, 1982) 87-88.
70. Haubrichs 287-88.
71. This outer ring of semicircles has often eluded scholarly notice. James' reproduction shows it clearly (87).
72. Hocke connects the labyrinth design with both the *vinculum universi* and the *Weltenverknotung (99-100)*, as in Dante's "forma universale di questo nodo" (*Par.* 33.91).
73. Sedlmayr notes that "die ganze Symbolik der Krone ist in gewissem Sinn bezogen auf die Symbolik des Altars" (127).
74. Sedlmayr details further correspondences with traditional features of the holy city on 126. For further iconographic evidence for the link between crown and building, cf. reproductions of Gallo-roman sculpted heads bearing hexagonal towers as crowns in Müller 101.
75. E.g., Sedlmayr 128.
76. See H. D. Austin, "Number and Geometrical Design in the Divine Comedy," *The Personalist* 16 (1935): 313.
77. "Cercles astrologiques et cosmographiques à la fin du moyen age," *Gazette des Beaux-Arts* 21 (1939): 75-76 and passim.
78. The exact nature of these three cosmic circles is reemphasized at the bottom of the same drawing, where a figure holds a staff at each end of which two sets of three garlands hang.
79. "The Significance of the *Garlande Gay* in the Allegory of *Pearl*," *Review of English Studies* ns 8 (1957): 12-21. He includes discussion of the same point in *Pearl in Its Setting*.
80. See Beer, *Kathedrale von Lausanne* fig. 38.
81. Columns have been carved in the shape of the human figure since the Greeks, hence the terminology to designate its parts: "capital," "pedestal." See Wittkower, *Architectural Principles* fig. 1c.
82. See Eliade, *Das Heilige und das Profane* 101.
83. For an analysis of the *pilier cantonné*, see Panofsky 49-52, 78-79; von Simson 196. The four-and-one circular cosmographic drawings can be seen in Harry Bober, "An Illustrated School-Book of Bede's 'De Natura Rerum,'" *Journal of the Walters Art Gallery* 19-20 (1956-57) figs. 2-3. It is also extremely common in the iconography of the five wounds of Christ, and will be discussed in my interpretation of the symbol of the heart in *Pearl* and *Sir Gawain*. This four-and-one design apparently grew out of a *Weltbild* tradition featuring personifications of the four winds at each corner of the page.
84. See James figs. 88-89 (151).
85. See Sicardus, *Mitrale, sive Summa de offic. eccles.* 1.4 (*PL* 213.21).
86. Cf. Petit 111-12.
87. Moessel 1: 72. Cf. fig. 44 (91).
88. Sedlmayr 142.
89. Sedlmayr 161-62.
90. See, e.g., Baltrusaitis fig. 18 (79) and circular designs around the heads of some of Opicinus' figures in Salomon, passim.
91. Bloomer and Moore 4.
92. See Braun, *Altar* pls. 152ff.; *Altargerät* pls. 54ff.; Sedlmayr 31.
93. Braun, *Altargerät* pls. 22-24, 29.
94. Braun, *Altargerät* pls. 130ff.; Sauer 205-06.
95. Sedlmayr 81-82.
96. Spitz 201-03.
97. Richstätter, *Herz-Jesu-Verehrung* 39-40; Kanters, *Coeur de Jésus* 177-78.
98. Sauer 199.
99. Sauer 207.
100. Sauer 204.

101. Holböck 2; Sauer 194.
102. Sauer 194-95.
103. Sauer 198-99; Graber 94.
104. See Graber 94; Sauer 199, 201-02.
105. Sauer 207-08.
106. See figures in Vloberg 227, 300.
107. Braun, *Altargerät* pls. 74-75.
108. Braun, *Altargerät* pls. 74-75, figs. 279, 281, 285; Singer, passim.
109. Pl. 74, fig. 282. This figure may reflect the symbolic equation of eucharist and heart that will be noted in connection with *Pearl*.
110. Braun, *Altargerät* pls. 22-24; see especially fig. 78.
111. Braun, *Altargerät* pls. 10, 12, 15.
112. Braun, *Altargerät* frontispiece and pls. 5, 19-20, 30, 42-45; *Altar* pl. 77; Vloberg 70. Cf. Sedlmayr 298.
113. Braun, *Altargerät* pls. 140-41. *Altar* pl. 75 shows the design on the base of a portable altar.

Chapter Three

BODY, SPACE, AND MICROCOSM IN MEDIEVAL LITERATURE

My first chapter offered a systematic presentation of microcosmic and corporeal spatiality in the Middle Ages, providing a framework for chapter two's analysis of spatial symbolism in Gothic architecture. While these two chapters were intended as original studies in their own right, the main focus of this study—an examination of textual spatiality in the Middle Ages—begins with the present chapter. My theoretical premise thus dictates the order of my argument: if the patristic understanding of the *minor mundus* constitutes a uniform principle of aesthetic organization, then the same body-centered temporal and spatial configurations will hold true not only for building design but also for many textual structures. Here I align myself with those who would push the study of spatial form to the forefront of literary research; as Mitchell has written, "Everything points to the conclusion, then, that spatial form is no casual metaphor but an essential feature of the interpretation and experience of literature."[1]

At the beginning of my exposition, I lamented the ironic neglect of the Middle Ages by those who study literary space. The intervening discussion should have made clear the uniform and pervasive influence of the corporeal matrix on theological and artistic form in general. But the implications of the body-based Christian *Weltanschauung* are particularly far-reaching in the realm of verbal art. If the creative Word's assumption of physical space constitutes the epistemological core of medieval culture, if verbal truth in the Middle Ages finds its highest fulfillment in a corporeal shape, then we must regard the form of medieval literature as an indispensable index to its meaning. That the medievals themselves regarded language in this way cannot be doubted. God, they believed, had authored two great books, the Bible and the created order of Nature.² The Incarnation endows the physical universe with a matrix of verbal coherence, puts it in an intelligible relation to the realm of speech. The Old Law's radical disjuncture of utterance and object is overcome; now signifier and signified interpenetrate and become interchangeable. Thus, by the fourteenth century, speculative grammar could maintain that language constituted a mirror (*speculum*) both of human conceptual structures and, macrocosmically, of the entire universe.

The equation of text and body finds its most explicit exposition in patristic exegesis; the Bible, especially, is often compared with the body of Christ. Thus commentators see the *apertio Scripturae* as analogous to the *fractio hostiae*.³ Origen sees in the head, feet, and entrails of the paschal lamb eaten by the Israelites in Exodus 12:6 the beginning, middle, and end of holy scripture, and his interpretation is elaborated by Jerome, Gregory, Hrabanus Maurus, and many others.⁴ Another early exegete, Eucherius of Lyon, bases his own threefold allegorical method on the metaphor of the "corpus . . . scripturae sacrae."⁵ The notion of scripture as a *liber involutus* provides a separate tradition based on the physical appearance of the Bible as a scroll; here the two sides of the scroll rolled together exemplify the inextricable union of Christ's two natures. Further, the relation of the New Testament written on the outer side to the Old Testament on the inner side manifests the relation of body to shadow.⁶ Based on the identity of Christ's blood and New Testament scripture, de Lubac finds the analogous equation of the New Testament and the eucharistic host to have been quite widespread.⁷ In general, the fundamental corporeality of scripture justifies interpretations presupposing the complementarity and organic unity of the whole despite the diversity of its components;⁸ the whole Christ, head and members, is the subject of all of scripture.⁹ And if the Bible is a body, it is also a microcosm of the rest of the world—a notion that provides the basis for patristic exegesis. Spitz concludes his massive study of exegetical tradition thus:

> Daß das Bibelwort ein beseelter Leib ist, der als Monade das Ganze der sichtbaren und gewußten Welt umfaßt, steht am Anfang der Tradition. Daß es eine logische Kraft besitzt, die Verläßlichkeit schafft, ist das Ergebnis christlicher Sprachheiligung durch die Inkarnation des Logos.¹⁰

This conception of the Bible as monad finds support in Frye, who stresses "one of the most striking features in the Bible: its capacity for self-recreation."[11]

Not surprisingly, then, the Bible imparts its own characteristic spatiality to the huge body of exegetical and literary texts of which it constitutes the center and monad. Löwith writes: "the history of salvation includes all the other stories, inasmuch as it is reflected in them."[12] The Bible is the great model of how a text manifests its content via its form; by studying the layers of patristic tradition around this core, we see the core's influence on its most proximate textual "enclosures." Selective digging among exegetical substructures thus yields an archeology of meaning.

Not only the Bible itself, but all other books are endowed with the symbolism of the body in the Middle Ages; Curtius emphasizes the medievals' "life relation" to books.[13] This symbolic equation came about partly via comparison between Christ's wounds and manuscript rubrication. Richard Rolle, for example, writes: "Þy body is lyke a boke written al with rede ynke; so is þy body al written with rede woundes."[14] The tradition begins as early as the fourth-century Spanish poet Prudentius, and later appears in Peter the Venerable's writings; it is consistent with widespread medieval literary portrayal of persons displaying letters or words on their bodies.[15] Not only the whole body, but also its various parts were equated with books; thus, in John of Hanville, both a girl's face (on which Nature has "rubricated" her lips) and calves are the symbolic equivalent of books and the pages of books.[16] Particular importance is given to the link between the human heart and books, based on 2 Cor. 3:3; under the new dispensation, God's Word is written "non in tabulis lapideis, sed in tabulis cordis carnalibus." This tradition is elaborated by Hildebert of Lavardin, among others, and may bear some relation to the analogy between rubrication and wounds, the heart constituting the central and theologically most significant wound.[17] The comparison between books and bodies extended itself to all manner of books, including legal volumes; Justinian called one of his laws a "piisima sive sacrosancta oblatio quam Deo dedicamus," and his idea was repeated by later lawgivers.[18]

Just as God speaks through the "writing" of the wounds on Christ's crucified body, so he also speaks through the bodies of all human beings brought into existence with the first creative Word. Scharl summarizes this aspect of the doctrine of *recapitulatio* thus: "Eine lange Rede war die Menschheit. Das Schöpferwort selbst hat sie begonnen."[19] God's revelation transmits itself not only through the written Word, but through the lived or corporeal Word. Following Christ necessitates participation in his wounds, becoming a part of the extended text that is the *corpus mysticum*.

The blurred distinction between body and text, then, makes possible a radical expansion of textual boundaries; just as Christ is the book "in quo totum continetur,"[20] so each book is a microcosm. The microcosmic relation of language to the created universe that speculative grammarians described has a flip side: the language of all of Nature appears written in the body of each human being. Alanus de Insulis elaborates this notion at some length in the context of man's relation to the four elements of the macrocosm, saying that *scripta natura* appears on each man's body.[21] Every human body is a Book of Nature, and every book is both body and microcosm.

This corporeal, microcosmic quality of textual space seems only to have been rediscovered recently. Lotman remarks: "The language of an artistic text in essence is a model of the universe."[22] Hall sees language as an extension into space akin to the more obvious technological means by which man mediates between himself and the universe; he claims that twenty percent of the English language's vocabulary are words describing a spatial relation.[23] Scarry compares literature with the many material artifacts representing a "turning of the body inside-out" in relation to the exterior world.[24] But these ideas have as yet found little application to medieval literature.

A corollary of the medieval association of text and body is the notion that texts may be constructed like buildings. The beginning of Geoffrey of Vinsauf's *Poetria Nova* makes the comparison very explicit:

> Si quis habet fundare domum, non currit ad actum
> Impetuosa manus; intrinseca linea cordis
> Praemetitur opus, seriemque sub ordine certo
> Interior praescribit homo, totamque figurat
> Ante manus cordis quam corporis; et status ejus
> Est prius archetypus quam sensilis . . .[25]

Vincent of Beauvais quotes these famous lines in his "De maturitate,"[26] and Chaucer translates them in *Troilus and Criseyde* (1.1065 ff.). The passage is especially striking for its emphasis on the derivation of meaning from man's *interior*, the *intrinseca linea cordis*. In light of the last chapter's investigation of the symbolism of the center and heart in Gothic architecture, it is tempting to see here a prescription for textual architectonics featuring a dense spatial center analogous to the altar. Though this possibility has received little attention by scholars discussing the passage, scholarship has established a long traditional connection between architecture and literary construction. Spitz has shown the ways that the several levels of medieval biblical exegesis paralleled layers of building structure, and Sedlmayr discusses how certain principles of Gothic architecture reflect themselves in Gothic script.[27] In this connection, Bachelard's conception of textual space is particularly apt:

> Il y a donc un sens à dire, sur le plan d'une philosophie de la littérature et de la poésie où nous nous plaçons, qu'on "écrit une chambre," qu'on "lit une chambre," qu'on "lit une maison." Ainsi, bien rapidement, dès les premiers mots, à la première ouverture poètique, le lecteur qui "lit une chambre" suspend sa lecture et commence à penser à quelque ancien séjour.[28]

Judson Allen's study of the late medieval *accessus* helps provide the theoretical underpinnings for these corporeal and architectural correspondences in literature, though his focus is neither body nor building *per se*. "Metaphors," he asserts, "are not so much the creative work of poets as they are reflections of the organization of reality."[29] He continues:

> The same atmosphere of involvement between words and things, and among all the things to which language can refer, is clearly revealed in the commentator's insistence that the character of the language and the character of the referent must correspond. Poetry is its sententious paraphrase; its metaphors join, in a fitting and rational way, the levels of being, depending on the similitudes which exist between them.[30]

Medieval metaphor does not consist in the violent yoking together of unlike images because the medieval cosmos was already poetic enough: "there was no need to claim for the poet greater powers than those of an honest reporter."[31]

Allen's work contains an implicit directive for students of literature: to interpret the controlling metaphorical framework of texts, we must first obtain a clear and detailed understanding of the structure and unity of the medieval cosmos. The present study takes as its thesis that all questions of unity in the Middle Ages, whether theological, architectural, or textual, begin and end with the body that is the universe's microcosm. De Lubac has shown that that mystery of the eucharist was always considered, first and foremost, as a *mysterium unitatis*.[32] Mersch observes that "the very [scriptural] texts that employ the images of a body strongly emphasize, and even place first, the idea of unity."[33] I propose that many of the thorniest interpretive problems in the scholarship on medieval literature have arisen, quite simply, out of ignorance of this basic principle. Since the advent of the New Criticism, scholars have repeatedly sought to unravel controlling themes and metaphorical structures that would facilitate coherent, unified readings of medieval texts, but most often they have allowed only for the possibility of an Aristotelian unity. The many different attempts to locate the thematic core of a given text often differ only in emphasis, not in their basic assumptions about textual coherence. This study suggests that the revival of classical notions of unity in the Renaissance coincided with a loss of the body-based aesthetics of the Middle Ages, a loss which medievalists must acknowledge before they will be able to read medieval texts in specifically medieval ways.

A point of departure for textual interpretation that takes full account of corporeal symbolism is the recognition of the special role that the synecdoche occupies in medieval figural expression. Of the four "master tropes,"[34] the synecdoche is the one most consistently linked with microcosmic speculation. Hayden White writes:

> this grasping together of the parts of a thing as aspects of a whole that is greater than the sum of the parts, this ascription of wholeness and organic unity to a congeries of elements in a system, is precisely the modality of relationships that is given in language by the trope of synecdoche. This trope is the equivalent in poetic usage of the relationship presumed to exist among things by those philosophers who speak about microcosm-macrocosm relationships.[35]

Synecdochic figuration is the necessary consequence both of a Ptolemaic universe of concentric spheres and of a trinitarian theology in which the Godhead resides fully in each of its three constituents. It is the textual counterpart of microcosmic cathedral design, making it possible for individual subsections, passages, and symbols within a text to bear a clearly definable relation to the whole.

Further, body-based literary structures may be expected to display a recognizable "center." Hans-Georg Gadamer writes: "Es ist die *Mitte der Sprache*, von der aus sich unsere gesamte Welterfahrung und im besonderen die hermeneutische Erfahrung entfaltet."[36] This center, like a cathedral's altar, is the point of greatest symbolic and thematic condensation, a point of convergence for the broadest concerns of the entire work and, simultaneously, the site where the themes of the text have their most intimate connection with extratextual structures. This point may or may not coincide with the text's "numerical" center (calculated by counting lines); often it will be represented by an especially crucial passage, but sometimes it cannot be identified with a specific portion of the text, instead recurring throughout the work as a floating symbol. It should in any case provide a nexus between the controlling themes of the text and the spaces (buildings, landscapes, etc.) depicted in it, and will usually bear an explicit connection with the human body and/or one of the body's multiple centers. Often we can find these textual centers simply by following the beaten paths of scholarly controversy. In this respect textual centers bear striking resemblance to Freud's notion of the "navel" of a dream, the moment where the symbolism of the entire dream merges compactly to make connection with the world exterior to the dream, making interpretation especially difficult.[37] The great exemplar for medieval texts is, of course, the Bible, in which the body of Christ constitutes both the temporal and spatial nexus and the central mystery.

The discussion entitled "Anagogic Phase: Symbol as Monad," concluding the second essay of Frye's *Anatomy of Criticism*, brings together a number of the key concepts here. Anagogic symbolism, he writes, points us "into the still center of the order of words," a "center of archetypes" where we may expect to find "a group of universal symbols"; at this level of symbolism, "nature becomes, not the container, but the thing contained," "an infinite and eternal living body."[38] He especially stresses the microcosmic implications of this way of reading texts:

> Thus the center of the literary universe is whatever poem we happen to be reading. One step further, and the poem appears as a microcosm of all literature, an individual manifestation of the total order of words. Anagogically, then, the symbol is a monad, all symbols being united in a single infinite and eternal verbal symbol which is, as *dianoia*, the Logos, and, as *mythos*, total creative act.[39]

The symbol as monad is linked with geometrical preoccupations we have already considered; Frye cites a letter by Rilke where the poet claims for himself a "perspective of reality like that of an angel, containing all time and space, who is blind and looking into himself," an "attempt to speak from the circumference instead of from the center of reality."[40] The poem is a self-contained universe of self-relexive meaning generated by a symbolic core:

> In other words, a poet's intention is centripetally directed. It is directed towards putting words together, not towards aligning words with meanings. . . . What the poet meant to say, then, is literally, the poem itself . . .[41]

In *The Great Code*, Frye applies this construct to the Bible itself, calling it a "centripetal body of words."[42]

Inevitably, then, textual centeredness generates a plenitude of literary space and time analogous to that in Gothic architecture. Following Augustine's observation that past, present, and future cohere in the reading of a psalm, Frank Kermode observes that books, like the Gothic cathedral, are world-models: "the book is a bibliocosm."[43] Erich Auerbach sees as a consequence of this new figural view of reality the breakdown of classical notions of textual space and time:

> This conception of history is magnificant in its homogeneity, but it was completely alien to the mentality of classical antiquity, it annihilated that mentality down to the very structure of its language, at least of its literary language, which—with all its ingenious and nicely shaded conjunctions, its wealth of devices for syntactic arrangement, its carefully elaborated system of tenses—became wholly superfluous as soon as earthly relations of place, time, and cause had ceased to matter, as soon as a vertical

connection, ascending from all that happens, converging in God, alone became significant.⁴⁴

This breakdown in classical linguistic structures accompanies medieval man's increasing sense of being lost "in the middle," of no longer having access to classical conceptions of narrative progress and causality. Jeffrey writes:

> Thus, the death which follows Eden is not only the loss of communion, the dissolution of the body and the estrangement of the soul, but, as for St. Augustine in the *Confessions*, the loss of a possibility of relationship to the whole story—time's full narrative. "Men perish," said the pre-Socratic philosopher Alcaemon of Crotona, "because they cannot join the beginning with the end." This old Greek statement might have been understood by medieval men as describing a literary problem, a problem of narrative. But in Christian thought down to the Middle Ages it is in fact the problem of joining which is seen to be the essential human problem, and its most immediate metaphors are often narrative, story, book metaphors.⁴⁵

Medieval texts attempt to reestablish a coherent relation between this new world order and the body of mankind at this center.

One of the consequences of microcosmic figural structure in medieval literature is textual *recapitulatio*. The head's ability to recapitulate the entire body within itself, we have seen, provides a basis for the plenitude of time and space—thus, for example, the six days of creation constitute a microcosm of all of history. It is therefore not surprising that biblical and literary texts, in which some medieval exegetes distinguished parts corresponding with head, feet, and entrails, were often found to contain the same structure. Classical rhetoric's longstanding recognition of the special status of introductory or concluding passages that summarized an entire chapter or book provided the basis for Irenaeus' conception of textual recapitulation, whereby an overview or summary passage stands in relation to an entire text as head to body. The notion found application to specific portions of scripture, as in the ability of the Decalogue's first two commandments to contain, by themselves, the whole of the law (Rom. 13:9).⁴⁶

Whatever its other contributions to medieval literary studies may be, the study of textual space provides compelling support for the application of patristic exegetical method to medieval literature. The Bible, we have seen, has the status of a monad at the center of all of medieval writing; medieval texts, in large measure, acquire their centripetal spatial and temporal configuration from it. Patristic studies, by clarifying these figural relations within the Bible itself, lay a foundation for understanding those relations in works modeled after that great exemplar. The Bible constitutes the heart of a huge body, the foundation of a massive literary edifice. C. G. Jung compares the human soul to a house whose respective stages reach far back into history, from a nineteenth-century second story to a Roman foundation, and even to the remains of life from the Ice Age.[47] Patristic research studies an analogous architectural structure: the successive encrustation of linguistic and traditional meaning onto a scriptural (and, to a degree, classical) core. Philology is linguistic archaeology. Patristic exegesis, at its best, reads medieval texts in medieval ways, based on principles of unity dictated by the Bible rather than neo-Aristotelian ones. It looks at texts as corporeal microcosms or *Weltbilder* imitative of the great microcosm at the center.

Crux-busting, that most hallowed rite of modern literary exegetes, assumes particular significance in this light; the solution of minute textual problems, we will see, can depend to a large extend on our ability to comprehend both the microcosmic relation of short passages to the entire text containing them, and the analogous relation of that entire text to the body of literature whose heart is the Bible. Philology, "just figuring out what the words mean," must as a consequence entail coming to terms with the broadest theoretical issues, just as, conversely, no theoretical approach can acquire any general validity without first proving its usefulness in untangling limited philological problems. The queerest, most recondite byways of exegetical tradition do not exist independently of the rest of medieval culture; neither can a textual crux be interpreted without extensive consideration of its macrocosmic textual and cultural frame. Every time we narrow our focus we must simultaneously broaden it.

Notes

1. W. J. T. Mitchell, "Spatial Form in Literature: Toward a General Theory," *Critical Inquiry* 6 (1980): 546.
2. Cf. Charles S. Singleton, *Commedia: Elements of Structure*, Dante Studies 1 (Cambridge: Harvard UP, 1954) 25ff.
3. See de Lubac, *Corpus mysticum* 80ff.
4. Origen, *In Joan.* 10.18 (GCS 4.188ff.); cf. Spitz 19-22.
5. Cited in Spitz 19.
6. Spitz 42-43.
7. De Lubac 217.
8. Jeffrey 12-13; Brown, *Love's Body* 194. Cf. the implicit link between Christ himself and the figure "Book" which personifies the Book of Scripture in *Piers Plowman*. R. E. Kaske, "The Speech of 'Book' in *Piers Plowman*," *Anglia* 77 (1959): esp. 132.
9. See Albertus Magnus, *Summa theol.* 1.1.3.
10. Spitz 247.
11. *The Great Code* 225.
12. Löwith 185.
13. Curtius 311ff.
14. *English Writings of Richard Rolle*, ed. Hope Emily Allen (Oxford: Clarendon, 1931); cited in Gray 84. Cf. in Chaucer's "ABC": "And with his precious blood he wrot the bille / Upon the crois, as general acquitaunce, / To every penitent in ful creaunce." All quotations from Chaucer taken from F. N. Robinson, ed., *The Works of Geoffrey Chaucer*, 2nd ed. (Boston: Houghton, 1957).
15. Curtius 311-12, 315-17, 319.
16. Cited in Curtius 316n.
17. See references to Hildebert in Curtius 318-19.
18. Kantorowicz 118-19.
19. Scharl 6-7.
20. See Curtius 332.
21. *De planctu Naturae* (*PL* 210.433).
22. Quoted by Ronald Vroon in preface to Lotman's *Structure of the Artistic Text*. Cf. Bronfen 20, 150.
23. Hall 3, 87.
24. *Body in Pain* 284.
25. Edmond Faral, ed., *Les Arts poétiques du XIIe et du XIIIe Siècle* (Paris: Champion, 1924) 198.
26. *Speculum Doctrinale* 4.93. Cf. Norman Davis, "Two Unprinted Dialogues in Late Middle English, and their Language," *Revue des Langues Vivantes* 35 (1969): 463; J. A. W. Bennett, *The Parlement of Foules* (Oxford: Clarendon, 1957) 4-5; Jordan 42-43, 76.
27. Spitz 205-18; Sedlmayr 701-03.

28. Bachelard 32; cf. 25, 51. Cf. Rudolf Arnheim's explanation of human cognitive organization: "When the human mind organizes a body of thought, it does so almost inevitably in terms of spatial imagery . . . any organization of thought assumes the form of an architectural structure . . . all human thought must be worked out in the medium of perceptual space." *The Dynamics of Architectural Form* (Berkeley, 1977) 272ff., quoted in Bronfen 169.

29. "Commentary as Criticism: Formal Cause, Discursive Form, and the Late Medieval Accessus," *Acta Conventus Neo-Latini Lovaniensis: Proceedings of the First International Congress of Neo-Latin Studies, Louvain 23-28 August 1971*, ed. J. Ijsewijn and E. Kessler (München: Fink, 1973) 38.

30. Allen 39.

31. Allen 39.

32. *Corpus mysticum* 111.

33. *Theology of the Mystical Body* 52.

34. See Kenneth Burke, "Four Master Tropes," *A Grammar of Motives* (New York: Braziller, 1955) 503-17.

35. *Tropics of Discourse: Essays in Cultural Criticism* (Baltimore: Johns Hopkins UP, 1978) 69; cf. 72-73.

36. *Wahrheit und Methode*, 3rd ed (Tübingen: Mohr, 1972) 433.

37. *The Interpretation of Dreams*, vols. 4 and 5 of *The Standard Edition of the Complete Psychological Works of Sigmund Freud*, ed. James Strachey, 24 vols. (London: Hogarth, 1900-01) 4: 111; 5: 525.

38. Frye, *Anatomy* 117-19. Cf. 125: "All poetry, then, proceeds as though all poetic images were contained within a single universal body."

39. Frye, *Anatomy* 121. On 125 he again refers to the Logos as a source of textual symbolism: "The study of literature takes us toward seeing poetry as the imitation of infinite social action and infinite human thought, the mind of a man who is all men, the universal creative word which is all words."

40. Frye, *Anatomy* 122.

41. Frye, *Anatomy* 86-87.

42. Frye, *The Great Code* 226.

43. *The Sense of an Ending: Studies in the Theory of Fiction* (New York: Oxford UP, 1967) 52. On 71 he adds: "When Augustine recited his psalm he found in it a figure for the integration of past, present, and future which defies successive time. He discovered what is now erroneously referred to as 'spatial form.' He was anticipating what we know of the relation between books and St. Thomas's third order of duration—for in the kind of time known by books a moment has endless perspectives of reality." Cf. 6, 53-54, 58. For further discussion of how textual time acquires spatial form see "Metaphorische Verräumlichung der Zeit," in Bronfen 294-309. Also relevant is Bachelard's treatment of microcosmic textual space: "Dans le commerce de la spatialité poétique qui va de l'intimité profonde à l'étendue indéfinie réunies dans une même expansion, on sent sourdre une grandeur" (183). Cf. 104, 185-86.

44. *Mimesis: The Representation of Reality in Western Literature*, trans. Willard R. Trask (Princeton: Princeton UP, 1968) 74; cf. 156-58 and passim.

45. Jeffrey 3-4.

46. Scharl 6-7.

47. Bachelard discusses Jung's idea on 18ff.

Chapter Four

PRELIMINARY TEXTUAL EXAMPLES

Before proceeding to my analysis of the *Pearl*-Poet, I must touch briefly on several other relevant texts. I do this not out of a compulsion for thoroughness, but because the uniform and ubiquitous character of textual spatiality in the Middle Ages requires something of a preliminary overview, and because some of the scholarship on those works impinges to some extent on my own. If microcosmic textuality is, in fact, as common as the preceding discussion implies, then we should expect to find at least tangential acknowledgment of it in research on the Middle Ages. No one, to my knowledge, has yet applied a broad acquaintance with microcosmic speculation, microcosmic cathedral structure, and patristic teachings on the body to the systematic interpretation of individual medieval texts. But several scholars' published observations clearly point in the right direction, though usually with little documentation beyond the internal evidence of the texts themselves. The work of the German school of numerologists (and of American scholars in the same tradition), in particular, has brought to light the symmetry of center and edge in several medieval texts, though their studies limit themselves primarily to formal literary construction; the controversy that has attended this school's work has resulted, in part, from its frequent failure to base its findings firmly on the appropriate aesthetic and theological sources.

The discussion that follows intends, first of all, to bring together the work of a number of scholars who, in some cases, have not realized what they have in common. The traditions outlined in the previous chapters offer a unifying framework for these disparate publications. To the numerologists, who *are* for the most part aware of the tradition in which they work, I offer a more solid cultural basis for their findings. The first studies discussed treat the influence of Latin symmetrical composition on medieval German and Old English literature; these will be followed by analysis of Middle English texts, including reference to selected works of Chaucer scholarship whose interests are not numerological, and of texts by Boethius and Dante. I conclude by noticing in Spenser a late stage in the evolution of these medieval forms. In each case, scholars' conclusions will be amplified or modified in the light of my own findings.

The most helpful numerological study in the present connection has been done by Wolfgang Haubrichs. He places Otfrid von Weißenburg's *Liber Evangeliorum* within a long tradition of Carolingian poetry, tracing, text by text, the evolution of a very uniform system of symmetrical number composition. These numerical structures, he claims, confer upon medieval texts an "Überschneiden von Bedeutungsebenen" imitative of the *Weltgebäude* built by Christ, "architectus noster."[1] Although parallels with the details of Gothic architecture or theories of the microcosm do not fall within the scope of his research, his painstaking observations concerning numerological centers in the texts studied lend considerable support to the fundamental theses already elaborated here.

Starting with the assumption that "jeder echten Zahlenbindung eine inhaltliche Bindung entspricht,"[2] Haubrichs details the correspondence of numerical centers within entire poems and their subdivisions with events depicted at those central points; in each case, the event bears particularly close connection to the central mysteries of the hypostatic union. Thus, for example, a description of the Incarnation constitutes the fifth of nine chapters in Audradus' *Liber de fonte vitae*;[3] the death and ascent to heaven of the hero is described in the middle chapter of the second half of Alcuin's *De vita Willibrordi episcopi*;[4] three lines summarizing the doctrine of the hypostatic union occur at the exact center of Otfrid's depiction of Christ's birth;[5] and so on. Further, these Incarnation-related events often correspond not only with the numerological middlepoint of an entire text or subsection, but with the center of a smaller core structure whose numerological disposition imitates, in miniature, the architectonics of the entire text or subsection. Thus, for example, the middle three books of Alcuin's commentary on the Book of John together contain the same number of chapters

Preliminary Textual Examples 65

(23) as the combined chapters of the two pairs of books which constitute the text's two "wings."[6] These texts, then, contain a numerological microcosm of their overall structure precisely at the point where all truth finds its compact origin in the body of Christ. Often, Haubrichs observes, the numerological relation of center to wings is chiastic, a relation accounted for by the inside out character we have noted in connection with altars and corporeal centers.[7] Not surprisingly, he finds a connection between one section of Otfrid's *Zentralbau* and the doctrine of Christ's birth from his Father's heart.[8]

Haubrichs also notices the influence of the doctrine of the *plenitudo temporis* at the numerological centers of the texts he discusses. Thus, for example, he writes concerning one such midpoint in the *Liber Evangeliorum*:

> Nun wird auch die sorgfältige Ausarbeitung des inneren Zeitgerüstes der Handlung deutbar: Otfrid interpretiert die "sehs daga" der Vorpassion als das Eingewiesenwerden der Zeit (". . . sih thiu zit nahta") in ihre Erfüllung, da die Welt 'geheilt' wird, die doch in sechs Tagen erschaffen war und sechs Weltalter dauern wird.[9]

The connection he notes between the middle and beginning of time brings to mind the doctrine of recapitulation, which manifests itself textually, we have seen, in introductory segments that stand in microcosmic relation to the sections they precede. Though Haubrichs does not invoke the doctrine of recapitulation as part of his explanation, he does show that the number of lines in the introductions to two of Otfrid's books bears a chiastic relation to the book's total number of lines, and that these books' preoccupation with aspects of the hypostatic union in Christ is responsible for that structure.[10]

Mary F. McCarthy sees in the *Nibelungenlied* a structure bearing some affinity with those traced by Haubrichs. She divides the story's total of 39 *âventiuren* into two symmetrical halves around the central twentieth *âventiure*, then subdivides each half into quarter sections arranged symmetrically around *âventiuren* 20 and 30. Each of these central *âventiuren* is pivotal for the plot development: The twentieth depicts the first presentation of the marriage proposal to Kriemhilt; the tenth and thirtieth describe Gunther and Prünhilt's first sexual consummation (with Sîfrit's help), and the first open conflict between Kriemhilt's men and the Burgundians, respectively. The text's architectonics thus reinforce numerically the interlace of the two main lines of the plot, the action linked with the Burgundian court and that connected with Kriemhilt.[11] Edward Fichtner elaborates on McCarthy's theories, observing, for example, that the use of the word *nôt* in Margrave Gêre's marriage proposal speech (the speech itself occurring at the very center of *âventiure* 20) anticipates the last word of the poem.[12]

Because theological issues do not come as explicitly to the fore here as in other texts, the governing matrix of body and microcosm in the *Nibelungenlied* has not received scholarly attention. The striking resemblance to analyses of Gothic architecture by Panofsky, Sedlmayr, and others, however, should be quickly evident; by extension, the microcosmic cathedral structure outlined in chapter two applies here as well. Numerically, each part recapitulates the center-based design of the whole work. Further, the spatiality depicted supports the numerical framework. Sexual penetration into the body's innermost center lies at the core of the plot, the central issue of both the tenth *âventiure*'s wedding night description and the twentieth *âventiure*'s proposal; the thirtieth *âventiure*'s conflict arises as a consequence of these two preceding events, taking place between groups of allies constituting extensions of their respective "heads."[13] In medieval literature the intimate sexual space shared by hero and heroine often provides a nexus for both the architectural and political "extensions" of their bodies and for the microcosmic layering of the texts themselves.

J. A. Huisman's excellent excursus on symmetrical number composition offers analyses showing structures resembling that of the *Nibelungenlied*. In the Old High German *Georgslied*, he finds that "Das Zentrum ist zweischichtig symmetrisch gebaut." The central five chapters divide themselves into two 32-stanza halves, and each of the three-chapter "wings" around this core also contains 32 stanzas.[14] Similarly, three poems produced by the school of Walther von der Vogelweide display identical numbers of lines at both center and edge.[15] Huisman also finds an analogous structure in the *Marienleich* written by Walther himself.[16]

In many of these numerological studies, scholars compare texts' "center and two wings" structure with that of the triptychs (German *Flügelaltäre*) found at the altars of medieval churches, most often in Gothic churches. The comparison is especially pointed in the light of the multifaceted microcosmic implications of the altar, as discussed in chapter two. Just as the cathedral constitutes a symbolic and structural extension of the altar, these texts manifest an overall numerological configuration which extends and reduplicates the triptych principle at the center. The fact that Christ's crucified body in the triptych's middle panel provides a point of figural unity for the depictions of the side panels makes the correspondence particularly apt.

Triptych symmetry is not confined to medieval German literature; scholars have begun to find similar patterns in English literature as well. Thomas Elwood Hart, for example, applies this scheme to *Beowulf*.[17] And there is good reason to believe that the same numerological pattern influenced Middle English literature; A. Kent and Constance Hieatt present strong evidence for its appearance in a fourteenth-century poem called "The Bird with Four Feathers." The poem's treatment of a bird's four feathers, symbolizing "four qualities misused and lost," is reflected in symmetrical line structure patterning displaying a center and four structural "feathers." Form and content here, as elsewhere, correspond closely:

> the numerical midpoint and the midpoint in terms of subject matter coincide: the introduction and the laments for the first two feathers occupy 120 lines; the laments for the last two feathers and the conclusion occupy the remaining 120 lines. This is unlikely to have happened by chance.[18]

The Hieatts notice that the significance of the number four is reflected in the use of quatrains throughout, just as the number three's crucial symbolism in the *Divine Comedy* imprints itself in that work's *terza rima* scheme.[19] Drawing a very general analogy with late Gothic art, they see here the paradoxical coexistence of *Nebeneinander* and *Nacheinander* that we have noticed before:

> In more fundamental and theoretical terms, certain reflections about the relation between the *Nebeneinander* and the *Nacheinander*—the simultaneous and the successive aspects—in late medieval art and poetry are probably appropriate. It is obvious that a temporally consecutive series of occurrences is often represented as a spatially adjacent series in medieval painting. The

> problem concerning the opposite possibility for the temporal medium of language relates to the extent to which a pattern that posits the imagination of an "architectural" or "painterly" simultaneity for its appreciation might be built up through the sequential utterances of a poem. Perhaps "The Bird With Four Feathers" gives the scholar historical evidence for supposing that late medieval poets went further in the development of this purely logical possibility than had formerly been supposed.[20]

The Hieatts' analysis can be amplified considerably in the context of the present study. Both the thematic and structural configurations of the poem feature the symmetrical body of the bird; structural subsections bear a microcosmic relation to the entire text. Even at levels of organization intermediate between quatrain and quadripartite whole, the poet shows his preoccupation with microcosmic layering:

> he may have drawn satisfaction from the points that, as one of his totals is 4^2 quatrains, so one of the subtotals within it is 4^2 lines; and that, as another of his totals is forty-four quatrains, so one of the subtotals within it is forty-four lines.[21]

Not concerned with corporeal or architectural microcosmic theory *per se*, the Hieatts fail to notice two extra layers of numerical correspondence between the bird's "body" at the center and the periphery of the "wings." The total lines in the *two* middle stanzas (28) equals that of both the three opening and closing stanzas; at the next structural level, the *four* middle stanzas' total lines (52) equals that of both the first and last five stanzas.[22] Thus both the poem's center and each of the poem's two composite wings respectively contain, as a microcosm of the entire poem, their own center and wings. In light of these observations, we can enlarge upon these scholars' comments on the relation of space to time in the poem. Not only do *Nebeneinander* und *Nacheinander* coincide; the poem's space also gathers in successive microcosmic layers around both center and edge. The shape of the text corresponds with the shape of Gothic architecture even more closely than was at first suspected: both meaning and structure derive ultimately from the "body" (Christ's and the bird's) and triptych at the center.[23]

The English Corpus Christi cycles are another group of texts displaying obvious cosmographic structure. The cycles' dramatization of salvation history was deemed the appropriate means to celebrate the power of the *Corpus Christi*; that is, the plenitude of time was located, as always, in the body of Christ. Jerome Taylor has built a good case for seeing the eucharistic body of Christ as a principle of organization in the cycles.[24] Again Christ's body furnishes a temporal vortex, a locus of historical *Verdichtung*. The Corpus Christi feast is the moment in the liturgical calendar where time turns inside out; the feast is, as Kolve notes, "fixed to a date outside regular liturgical 'anniversary' time."[25] The cycle plays enact the plenitude of time by presenting all historical events as present events.[26]

Kolve's description of time in the cycle dramas is consistent with observations we have made elsewhere:

> The events chosen for dramatization are those in which God intervenes in human history; significant time, it follows, becomes simply the point of intersection between these actions, the will of God expressed in time from outside time, by which a connection deeper than temporal causality is stated. . . . It is like a series of essays into history from the same center, like the casting of a fisherman standing in midstream and making strikes in several degrees of a circle. The sequence of these essays has meaning and moves steadily closer to a goal, but the times between them matter very little. The shape of the drama is a linear progression, a sequence of pageant wagons or self-contained episodes on a stationary stage, but the metaphysic of its structure is centrifugal.[27]

This "centrifugal" structure is, of course, cosmographically precise; these dramas are "cycles," and "cycle" implies "circle," a history in which the *Verdichtung* at the center enables beginning and end to conjoin. In a striking way, the structure of the cycles resembles that of *Pearl*: the series of pageant wagons whose stories join their beginning and end present stories within a Story, like a chain of circles constituting a larger circle.

A spatial plenitude akin to the plenitude of time also governs the structure of the cycles. Kolve writes: "Just as in this drama the time is out of joint, so too is the geography of the action dislocated. As *time* was made medieval, so does *place* of action turn out largely to be English."[28] Russell Peck comments on the same phenomenon:

This complex time-sense dominates much of medieval literature as well as art, especially dream vision literature and the drama, and accounts for much of what philologists at the beginning of the 20th century regarded as quaint anachronism. In the Towneley *Second Shepherd's Play*, for example, we begin in 14th-century northern England with English shepherds struggling against a miserable winter, then discover that we are participating in a second time scheme as well, namely the birth of Christ in our very midst. Ultimately, the players and audience share a glimpse of eternity as all sing with the angels. Time is reborn, perfected and made complete in our very presence. The play is designed to help the audience reclaim its own fullness of time.[29]

Several studies of Chaucer's works together constitute a separate strand of scholarship informing the present discussion. Because their focus is more thematic than numerological, they would not normally be considered in connection with studies of structural symmetry. But given the uniformity of medieval spatial perception demonstrated thus far, we are surely justified in looking for the same spatial configurations at the level of theme that we have found in more formal analyses.

John Leyerle's essay, "The Heart and the Chain," offers an especially provocative analysis of what he calls "poetic nuclei" in Chaucer's work.[30] He argues that the heart as the seat of love and the chain as a metaphor for universal order (as in Lovejoy's classic study) constitute the thematic core of certain tales.[31] Thus, in the *Knight's Tale*, references to "bonds" help us understand the literal confinement of the knights in prison as a function of "the metaphoric sense of order in the created world, the *faire cheyne of love*."[32] The *Miller's Tale* parodies this chain of love with its nucleus, "holes," while the *Parliament of Fowls* displays a more balanced understanding of love and order in its repetition of the nucleus word "place." The frequent occurrence of the word "hert," the "membre principal / Of the body" (ll. 495-96), makes it the nucleus of the *Book of the Duchess*, particularly as the object of "hert-huntyng," and in *Troilus*, where the lovers' "exchange of hearts" provides a metaphoric nexus.

Against the background of medieval microcosmic speculation and cosmographic representation, Leyerle's findings lead us to several additional observations. His definition of a poetic nucleus corresponds very closely with the notion of a symbolic core or monad; it is both "a kernel, or seed, the latent beginning of growth or development" and "the center around which other parts or things are grouped." It unifies the text via its "centripetal force."[33] Like Christ's body at the center of theology and history, and like the midpoint of a circle, it is both the source and quintessence of paradox, the origin of both literal and metaphoric meaning:

> Indeed, the nucleus itself is usually ambiguous in significance. Each nucleus has a contradiction within itself: the hunting of the *hert* is accomplished when its loss is finally recognized; the *prisoun* of order imposes a restrictive captivity; and the holes of license produce a love that famishes the craving. A nucleus does not, of course, explain everything in a poem where it is found, but it does reinforce from the core the ambiguities present in the whole. Each nucleus has a literal sense, but as the poem develops, each also tends to become invested with a metaphoric sense representing the main abstract ideas present.[34]

Like a cathedral's altar, the poetic nucleus is the focus for a coalescence of multiple meanings; Leyerle indicates, for example, that the metaphor of love as a bond coexists with the heart image in *Troilus*, lighting up another facet of the same theme.[35] Further, these central images evidence some self-reflexivity; an image is capable of "containing" itself, as when Gaunt finds Blaunch's heart within his own.[36] Considered in the light of the iconography of the cosmos, where chains of circles create concentric layers around a human figure's heart at the center, Leyerle's comparison of the interlocking stories in the *Canterbury Tales* to a "faire cheyne of love" is especially striking.[37] Chaucer's *Tales* assume the traditional geometric features of a medieval *Weltbild*, a microcosm of the Christian pilgrimage in time ordered within concentric narrative space. The *Knight's Tale* and *Miller's Tale*, at the work's beginning, present the images of chain, knot, and hole both as an introduction to the entire work's metaphorical frame and as a clarification of the microcosmic relation of tale to *Tales*.

Leyerle does not attempt to correlate thematic nuclei with formal symmetrical structure, and some such study seems to be the next logical step, in view of extant numerological findings. Both the *Book of the Duchess* and *Troilus*, for example, appear to be constructed around a formal center. Gaunt's first speech in the *Book of the Duchess* (ll. 598-709) not only occurs at the numerical center of the poem; it also describes the graphic consequences of his heart-hunting. It divides the poem into two halves, the first containing primarily narrative, the second consisting exclusively of a series of three further speeches by Gaunt in which he expresses an attitude towards his lady's death that is less self-pitying than in the first speech; the speech thus marks a significant emotional transition.[38] Further, Gaunt gives considerable attention to Fortune and her wheel in this speech, comparing the sudden "turn" in Fortune's Wheel that caused his lady's death to an unexpected checkmate in chess; significantly, he uses the words "checkmate" and "myd poynt" in ll. 659-60, very near the numerical center of the poem (ll. 667-68). Nearby, the inversion of up and down connected with the images of head and tail suggests an inverted body much like the inverted body we will also see at the centers of *Pearl, Patience,* and some *Weltbilder*:

> That ys broght up, she set al doun.
> I lykne hyr to the scorpioun,
> That ys a fals, flateryne beste;
> For with his hed he maketh feste,
> But al amydde hys flaterynge
> With hys tayle he wol stynge . . . (635-40)

In fact Gaunt suffers as a consequence the whole series of tragic inversions with whose enumeration his speech begins: laughter to tears, light to darkness, sleep to waking, etc. Leyerle has shown in another article how the metaphor of the "game" also rests at the poetic nucleus of this poem, noting in several texts how interlocking games provide a unified plot structure.[39] There is good reason to believe that this speech, and especially this pivotal game, constitutes a nexus for the text's several games. [40] As Fortune's Wheel itself constitutes a variant of medieval cosmographic representation, this long explanation of the ways of Fortune is yet another occurrence of microcosmic symbolism at a structural center.[41]

The convergence of the bond and the heart as poetic nuclei in *Troilus*, noted in passing by Leyerle, suggests the possibility of a sustained microcosmic structure in that work as well. Another study by Leyerle and articles by Stephen Barney and W. Wetherbee provide a starting place for such an analysis.[42] In his study of how the significance of both Fortune's *rota* and love's *rosa* interact in literary handling, Leyerle accounts for the "doubleness" of Criseyde's character by analogy with the Gothic rose window: "Criseyde's heart is the poetic nucleus of the poem, the seat of love and the seat of change."[43] Wetherbee reads the consummation scene at the center of the text (3.1310-1582) as an extended parody of what Dante experiences atop Mount Purgatory, an episode that Singleton labels "the pattern at the center" of the *Commedia*; Wetherbee calls the image of Troilus engraved in Criseyde's heart (1499) a "small hard image at the center . . . pointing up the significance of the *alba* sequence as a whole."[44] (Cf. Jordan's discussion, in the context of architectural structure, of the centrality of Book Three within the "progressive divisibility" of the entire work.)[45] Barney traces *Troilus*' theme of bondage in detail, noting how traditions of the "cosmic bond" by which God controls Nature, the bond of a lesser order holding man in Fortune's sway, and the "bond of Love" operate in the story. The bond of love holds Troilus' heart securely, while Fortune keeps him tied fast to her wheel, allowing him to suffer two complete revolutions before he dies.[46] Barney underscores the confining, often cramped quality of the succession of spaces Troilus inhabits: the sickbed chamber, temple, closet, and walls of Troy give him an inescapable sense of his own spatial limitations. In a poem that underscores his "locale in space and time," Troilus shows a paradoxical wish for both confinement and freedom, as when he shuts all the windows and doors in his chamber, then proceeds to batter both himself and the room's walls.[47] Only death brings escape from confinement into paradise, where "the circular and the linear, and the free and the bound, become one"; Barney cites the last stanza's reference to God who is "uncircumscript, and al maist circumscrive."[48]

The medieval iconography of the cosmos can help us unite these disparate scholarly observations into the overarching framework of microcosmic speculation. *Troilus* evidences detailed patterning according to the symmetric and concentric circle configurations of the universe. At the textual periphery (the last stanza) is God, the circle containing all others and itself contained by none, residing when circle and line converge. At the center rests Criseyde's heart, a nucleus whose symbolic density is evidenced by the ability of this body "part" to contain the image of a "whole" (Troilus); in the same way, we have seen,

Christians bear Christ in their hearts just as, paradoxically, he bears all of them in his. In this respect, the spatial center of *Troilus* resembles that of the *Book of the Duchess*, where Gaunt's heart contains the heart of Blaunch. Further, the *rota-rosa* symbolism linked with Criseyde's heart endows it with the complex spatial and temporal configurations of the *Weltbilder* upon which Gothic rose windows are modeled. Though the largest circle is drawn at the edge of the text, the plenitude of the cosmos is contained at its center; this central paradox extends itself to the double character of Criseyde as portrayed throughout the story. As in the *Book of the Duchess*, the Wheel of Fortune makes its most manifest appearance at the middle of the work. Again, the influence of medieval *Weltbilder* displaying a heart at the center is evident; in the *Pearl* chapters to come, I will also discuss *Weltbilder* in which a circle replaces the heart at the center of the breast, including several diagrams in which either this circle or the heart contains the image of an entire body. This clear relation of circle to heart is evidenced in Troilus' prayer that Love should use his bond to "cerclen hertes alle" (1767). We have already seen the equation of rose window and heart in a façade-shaped monstrance in which the rose window replaces the heart of a superimposed human figure,[49] and via the symbolic equivalence of rose windows with the "heart" of the cathedral, the altars and altar vessels bearing the same *Weltbild* design. And, just as both rose windows in monstrances and altar vessels contain the eucharist, both the rose window and the heart emblemize, *pars pro toto*, the body of Christ.

As elsewhere in architecture and literature, then, Christ's body at the center of *Troilus* provides a point of convergence for the work's dominant thematic and spatial configurations. But it does so not only via the symbolism of the heart. The body, we recall, has multiple centers, the most closely linked being heart and womb. If Criseyde's heart "bears" Troilus' image as our hearts bear that of Christ, then the womb itself may be expected to exercise its own centripetal force on the spaces depicted in the text. Barney's analysis, viewed in the light of womb-centered cosmographic iconology, bears out this notion. The successive layers of architectural "bonds" traced by him imitate, quite simply, the successive enclosures of cosmographic space, the Great Chain of Being. The innermost center of Troy's walls and the walls of Troilus' chamber is his bed, or more precisely, Criseyde's womb. The lovers' consummation constitutes not only the midpoint of the plot (the center of the story's central book); it is also the nexus of the work's depicted space. Like the miraculous conception by the Virgin at the hub of Christian history, Troilus and Criseyde's most intimate point of sexual encounter lies at the entire text's spatial and temporal core. Criseyde's womb is the "heart" of *Troilus*'s architectural space, just as her heart provides the fertile origin of the story's symbolism.

The work of Boethius and Dante deserves particular attention because both authors have long been thought to have influenced the *Pearl*-Poet. Elaine Scarry's analysis of the geometry of the *De consolatione*, in particular, can be used to show that that text bears strong resemblances to the microcosmic form in *Pearl* and elsewhere. The *De consolatione* shares with *Pearl* both a concern with the reconciliation of the linear to the spherical, and a concentricity of circular textual structure:

> book 3, verse 9, the physical center of the *Consolation*, is the center of a circle whose circumference is defined by the remainder of book 3, and book 3 is the center of a sphere whose circumference is defined by books 1, 2, 4, and 5.[50]

Like several other texts I have discussed, the *De consolatione* features a bipartite center serving as a microcosm for a textual whole that is also bipartite:

> Book 3 is divided into two parts of almost equal length: the two differ by about one hundred lines. Sections 1 through 9 recall all that has been said in books 1 and 2; sections 10 through 12 anticipate all that will be said in books 4 and 5. Sections 1 through 9, like books 1 and 2, deal with and ultimately dismiss the false forms of happiness, while sections 10 through 12, like books 4 and 5, deal with the true form of happiness. Implicit in this distinction between the false forms and the true form is the distinction between finite diversity and divine unity, a distinction reflected in the differing treatments of the false and the true forms.... This distinction between diversity in the first half of the *Consolation* and unity in the second half is, in turn, reflected in the numerical divisions of book 3: the first half is comprised of nine sections and the second half of three; the second is, then, the square root of the first.[51]

We will see a similarly bipartite center in *Pearl*, based like the *De consolatione*, in part, on the number five as a principle of numerical organization. Scarry observes that the well-rounded sphere constitutes a more important image in Boethius than the more famous wheel of fortune, and we will see that it is precisely this former image that most influences *Pearl*. In fact it is Boethius' circle within a circle, conflated with the wheel within a wheel from *Ezekial*, that constitutes the paradigm for most cosmographic iconography.

We can consider the geometry of the center in Dante's *Commedia* from two perspectives: that of the depicted space, and that of the text itself. The center of the depicted space is, of course, the frozen lake of Cocytus which Rudy Spraycar has linked with the *lago del cor* in *Inferno* 1;[52] this is the *cor terrae* at the center of a hell whose regions Robert Durling has found correspond with the various interior regions of the body. He writes:

> After Virgil carries Dante down Satan's side, turns laboriously around, and climbs up out of Hell . . . , they are in a position to see Satan from a truer perspective—as upside down. In terms of the overall pattern of Hell as a body of which Satan is the head, it can now be seen not only as upside down but also as inside out, or imploded: it is as if Satan had been flayed and his skin stretched up over his head to envelop all his children.[53]

Dante associates the center of the universe, then, with both the heart and an inverted, upside-down body.

Two studies by Charles Singleton have suggested the centeredness of the *Commedia*. The pageant of revelation that concludes the *Purgatorio*, Singleton argues, intrudes the plenitude of Christian history into the middle of the *Commedia*;[54] the center of the pageant features the consecrated host in the person of Beatrice. But the pageant's centeredness is better understood in terms of depicted space (the Earthly Paradise) than textual space. More to the point, Singleton finds at the numerical center of *Purgatorio* numerological correspondences with iconographic representations of the numbers of creation; such representations—featuring a central circle surrounded by six semicircles—form a strand of cosmographic iconography.[55]

A brief look at the structure of Spenser's *Faerie Queene* will bring this chapter to a close. We have already seen surprising homogeneity in the spatial form of texts in both the Early and High Middle Ages; the *Faerie Queene* provides evidence for the persistence of many of the same forms into the early Renaissance. Based on Renaissance Platonism's understanding of circle and center, Baybak, Delany, and Hieatt find that the work's first three books display a clear spatial midpoint. They suggest that the mount pictured in the middle of Book Three's Garden of Adonis occupies a relation to the rest of Book Three akin to drawings featuring a circumscribed body with its pudenda at the center:

> The mount in Spenser's garden represents, then, the centre of the little world of man as well as the fruitful and generative centre of the poem's external world. And Spenser reinforced this position of double centrality by a device that has apparently not been noticed before: Stanza 43 of Canto vi, whose first line is "Right in the middest of that Paradise," occupies, in the 1590 text, the exact mid-point of Book III as the 340th of 679 stanzas.[56]

Corresponding with the *mons Veneris*, the mount is, among other things, the locus for Venus and Adonis' sexual union.

Alastair Fowler has written a book-length study of numerological and astronomical symbolism in *The Faerie Queene*, based primarily on medieval sources Spenser may have known. Book Five arranges itself symmetrically, he argues, around the depiction of the Isis Church in an arithmetically central stanza concerning "the 'like race in equall justice' of sun and moon which . . . occupies a key position in the astronomical structure of the poem;[57] he draws a parallel with Christ's ascent of his chariot at the numerological center of *Paradise Lost*, another Renaissance text whose symmetrical structure may reflect medieval influence.[58] Book Five's twelve cantos, we might add, stand in microcosmic relation to the entire work's twelve books; the central depiction of a building as a microcosmic nexus at structural transitions is a device we will see elsewhere. Fowler finds medieval precedent for the work's overall duodecad arrangement, the basic number twelve giving it (like the *Shepheardes Calender*) a microcosmic relation to both the months of the year and the signs of the zodiac. Further, the *Faerie Queene*'s subdivision into four groups of three books, he claims, reflects

Augustine's rationale for the identical structure of his *Civitas Dei*: the apostolic commission to take the gospel into the four corners of the world.[59] "The formal proportions of the *Faerie Queene*," he summarizes, "are the proportions of the cosmos itself."[60]

Especially relevant to the present study is the apparent influence of the notion of textual *recapitulatio* in the *Fairie Queene*; though Fowler does not refer to this doctrine, his analysis constitutes rather striking evidence for its detailed application here. He sees the work's first book as both an overview and thematic core for the remainder of the *Fairie Queene*, a microcosm at the center of successive concentric circles:

> As the greater number includes the less, so each book of the poem contains the themes of all earlier books: the structural diagram would resemble a tree's growth rings, not a row of separate globes.[61]

The character Una, personifying both the sun and Queen Elizabeth, is the thematic nexus of Book One and a unifying focus for successive books. The sun, according to both Plato and Macrobius, stands in relation to the other astronomical bodies as the number one to all other numbers. It is a monad; as the source of light, its relation to the "body" of the universe is traditionally compared with God's. Queen Elizabeth, "the administrative head," is also linked with the cult name *Una*, a designation of her monadic relation to the body politic.[62] Spenser's work shows his knowledge of how history's recapitulation of its very first week is reenacted in the creation of each individual:

> To fashion a noble person or a nobler self, Spenser had to fashion a true microcosm; and to do that he had to imitate in his poem, *in parvo*, the whole macrocosm, with each sphere that forms the emerging soul. How could this be done, without numbers? Was not all creation effected *ut in pondere et mensura, ita in numero*? The numbers of astronomy were uniquely suited to convey Spenser's vision of a nature constantly renewed and eternized in the cyclic repetitions that bring it ever nearer to the fulfilment of the great week of creation.[63]

Although Fowler does not treat the "corporeality" of the *Faerie Queene* in any detail, his first appendix, seen in the light of the present study, shows

Spenser's awareness of the close connection between the human body and geometry. The famous arithmological stanza,[64] as Fowler and others have noted, draws on the long pictorial tradition of bodies circumscribed by various geometric shapes. Though the stanza is cryptic, it appears to reflect the body's capacity to reconcile the most diverse geometric configurations both with each other and with the arithmetical principles of the cosmos ("the circle set in heavens place"). Mention of both masculine and feminine "proportions" has led commentators to invoke the mystery of the hypostatic union as a guide to the stanza's meaning. Whatever else it may mean, this stanza provides compelling evidence that the painstaking numerology of the *Fairie Queene*'s concentric, recapitulatory form is, in a fundamental sense, body-based.

Notes

1. Haubrichs 91-92, 374.
2. Haubrichs 91, 116.
3. Haubrichs 115-17.
4. Haubrichs 106-08.
5. Haubrichs 181-82. For other Incarnation-related events or descriptions linked with numerological centers see 90-91, 183-84, 256, 326.
6. Haubrichs 109-10. For other examples, see 86, 111, 127, 225-27. Haubrichs' explanation for this relation points in the right direction: "Die psychische Ausgewogenheit ('aequalitas') und Harmonie des 'inneren Menschen' beruht auf einer ontologischen Übereinstimmung zwischen dem Aufbau des Äußeren und des Inneren; anders gesagt—auf einer allseitigen Harmonie der Zahlen" (169).
7. See, for example, Haubrichs 177-79.
8. Haubrichs 207-08; cf. 223. Von Ertzdorff has also stressed the importance of the theology of the heart in Otfrid's *Liber Evangeliorum* ("Herz" 262, 280).
9. Haubrichs 238. For other examples, see 126-27, 215, 234-35. He fails to remark on an especially striking occurrence in a poem by Alcuin on Charlemagne which he finds numerologically symmetrical in other respects (85-86). The phrases "temporibus cunctis, annis atque omnibus horis" and "saecula multa" occur at the center, lines six and seven, of this thirteen-line poem.
10. Haubrichs 186ff.; 230-32.
11. "Architectonic Symmetry as a Principle of Structure in the *Nibelungenlied*," *Germanic Review* 41 (1966): 157-69. She further subdivides each "quarter" into four-chapter "eights," again arranged in symmetrical pairs around chapters 5, 15, 25, and 35.
12. "Patterns of Arithmetical Proportion in the *Nibelungenlied*," *Essays in the Numerical Analysis of Medieval Literature*, ed. Caroline D. Eckhardt (Lewisburg, PA: Bucknell UP, 1979) 230n.
13. The idea of the ruled as an extension of the ruler's body is ubiquitous in the Middle Ages, as convincingly shown by Kantorowicz.
14. *Neue Wege zur dichterischen und musikalischen Technik Walthers von der Vogelweide, mit einem Exkurs über die symmetrische Zahlenkomposition im Mittelalter*, Studia Litteraria Rheno-Traiectina 1 (Utrecht: Kemink en Zoon, 1950) 85-86. His diagram, however, fails to make the relation completely clear; to see it, one must add together the ten- and twenty-two-stanza segments shown under each half of the central five chapters.
15. Figures on 112, 115, and 117.
16. Huisman 53-65.
17. "Tectonic Metholodogy and an Application to *Beowulf*," in Eckhardt anthology.
18. "'The Bird with Four Feathers': Numerical Analysis of a Fourteenth-Century Poem," *Papers on Language and Literature* 6 (1970): 24.
19. Hieatt and Hieatt 31.

20. Hieatt and Hieatt 38.
21. Hieatt and Hieatt 36.
22. My new numerical totals can be quickly confirmed by simply recombining the number of lines per stanza presented in Hieatt and Hieatt fig. 1 (29).
23. For further information about numerological and symmetrical composition in the Middle Ages, see: Michael Stanley Batts, "Numerical Structure in Medieval Literature, with a Bibliography," *Formal Aspects of Medieval German Poetry*, ed. S. N. Werbow (Austin: U of Texas P, 1969) 93-119; Ernst Robert Curtius, "Excursus 15: Numerical Composition," *European Literature and the Latin Middle Ages*, trans. Willard R. Trask, Bollingen Series 36 (1953; Princeton: Princeton UP, 1973) 501-09; Alastair Fowler, ed., *Silent Poetry: Essays in Numerological Analysis* (New York: Barnes, 1970); Johannes Rathofer, *Der Heliand: theologischer Sinn als tektonische Form* (Köln: Böhlau, 1962); Charles Alan Robson, "The Technique of Symmetrical Composition in Medieval Narrative Poetry," *Studies in Medieval French Presented to Alfred Ewert*, ed. E. A. Francis (Oxford: Oxford UP, 1961) 26-75; Edmund Reiss, "Number Symbolism and Medieval Literature," *Medievalia et Humanistica* ns 1 (1970): 161-74.
24. "The Dramatic Structure of the Middle English Corpus Christi, or Cycle, Plays," *Literature and Society*, ed. Bernice Slote (Lincoln: U of Nebraska, 1964) 175-86; rpt. in *Medieval English Drama: Essays Critical and Contextual*, ed. J. Taylor and A. H. Nelson (Chicago: U of Chicago, 1972) 148-56.
25. Kolve 49.
26. Kolve 104; cf. 101.
27. Kolve 118-19.
28. Kolve 110.
29. "Number as Cosmic Language," *By Things Seen*, ed. David L. Jeffrey (Ottawa: U of Ottawa P, 1979) 70.
30. "The Heart and the Chain," *The Learned and the Lewed: Studies in Chaucer and Medieval Literature*, ed. Larry D. Benson (Cambridge: Harvard UP, 1974) 113-45.
31. Arthur O. Lovejoy, *The Great Chain of Being: The Study of the History of an Idea* (Cambridge: Harvard UP, 1936).
32. Leyerle, "Heart" 118.
33. Leyerle, "Heart" 113-14.
34. Leyerle, "Heart" 124.
35. "Heart" 125.
36. Cited in Leyerle, "Heart" in a different connection (118).
37. "Heart" 121.
38. Cf. Leyerle, "Heart" 117.
39. "The Game and Play of the Hero," *The Concept of the Hero in the Middle Ages and Early Renaissance*, ed. Christopher Reagan (Albany: State U of New York P, 1975).
40. See Baltrusaitis for iconographic representations of wheels whose spokes converge at the center of the human breast.
41. In a later study, I will discuss Jean de Meun's handling of Fortune's Wheel at the numerical center of the *Roman de la Rose*.
42. John Leyerle, "The Rose-Wheel Design and Dante's *Paradiso*," *University of Toronto Quarterly* 46 (1977): 280-308; Stephen Barney, "Troilus Bound," *Speculum* 47 (1972): 445-58; Winthrop Wetherbee, "The Descent from Bliss: *Troilus* III.1310-1582," *Chaucer's Troilus: Essays in Criticism*, ed. Stephen Barney (London: Scolar, 1980) 297-317.
43. "Rose-Wheel" 304-05.
44. Wetherbee 306-07.
45. Jordan 87-88.

46. Barney 456-57.
47. *Troilus* 4.232-45, cited in Barney 457; cf. 447.
48. Barney 458.
49. Braun, *Altargerät* pl. 74, fig. 282.
50. E. Scarry, "The Well-Rounded Sphere: The Metaphysical Structure of *The Consolation of Philosophy*," in Caroline Eckhardt, ed., *Essays in the Numerical Analysis of Medieval Literature* (Lewisburg, PA: Bucknell UP, 1979) 96.
51. Scarry "Well-Rounded" 109-10.
52. "Dante's *Iago del cor*," *Dante Studies* 96 (1978): 1-19.
53. "'Io son venuto': Seneca, Plato, and the Microcosm," *Dante Studies* 93 (1975): 119.
54. "The Pattern at the Center," *Commedia: Elements of Structure* 45-60.
55. "The Poet's Number at the Center," Eckhardt anthology 85ff. The medieval design reproduced on 87 features the inscription "microcosmos hoc" and "minor mundus."
56. Michael Bayback, Paul Delany and A. Kent Hieatt, "Placement 'in the middest', in *The Faerie Queen*," *Silent Poetry* 143.
57. *Spenser and the Numbers of Time* (London: Routledge, 1964) 44-45.
58. See *Spenser* 247n, where Fowler gives the credit for this interpretation of Milton to Gunnar Qvarnström, *Dikten och den nya vetenskapan: Det astronautiska motivet*, Acta Reg. Soc. Humaniorum Litterarum Lundensis 60 (Lund, Gleerup, 1961).
59. *Spenser* 51-52. He cites Vincent Hopper, *Medieval Number Mysticism* (New York: Columbia UP, 1938) 86, 87, 99, 102 to substantiate the widespread influence of Augustine's idea, most notably in Aquinas.
60. *Spenser* 90.
61. *Spenser* 122.
62. *Spenser* 77-79.
63. *Spenser* 257.
64. Stanza 22 of book 2, canto 9.

Chapter Five

PEARL'S VINEYARD PARABLE AS A TEXTUAL CENTER

The preceding chapters have attempted to provide both a new framework for understanding medieval aesthetic form and a *modus operandi* for the remainder of this study. The present chapter brings us to the core of our inquiry, the work of the *Pearl*-Poet. If I appear to have delayed too much in getting down to the main business at hand, I can only plead that the theory proposed here—that many medieval texts are shaped like bodies—is a complex one and one that, stated bluntly and without adequate illustration, might otherwise have sounded rather fanciful.

Some justification for the length of my discussion of *Pearl* itself may also be in order at this point. *Pearl* evidences, more clearly than the poet's other works, systematic application of corporeal and architectural facets of microcosmic theory, and thus furnishes a basis for interpreting the entire opus of the *Pearl*-Poet. Multiple formal and thematic "centers" endow *Pearl* with a distinct pattern borrowed from iconographic and architectural renderings of the cosmos; the poem is at once a *Weltbild*, a rose-wheel window, and a Gothic cathedral. It is also, much like the poet's other poems, a body structured around the formal and thematic nucleus of the heart—a heart that is literal as well as metaphorical, so that it need not be placed in quotation marks. That the poem is the structural equivalent of all of these things (not only in the vague sense in which, for example, scholars commonly note literary resemblances to Gothic form, but in its details), and all of these things *at the same time*, is my thesis and my justification for such protracted exposition. A microcosm points, by definition, in every direction, and each of these directions requires explanation. After seeing how the pattern works in *Pearl*, much shorter discussions of the same pattern in *Sir Gawain* and *Patience* will suffice.

Consideration of the theology of the body in *Pearl* began with Robert Garrett, who attempted to interpret the poem as an extended treatment of the doctrine of the eucharist.[1] Although his general perception of the relevance of eucharistic doctrine to the poem was, I believe, on target, the frail logic of his analysis and his relatively scant documentation have rightly prevented his theory from attaining any general scholarly acceptance; instead, his work acted to discourage further research in a potentially fruitful direction for many years. Only a few studies since Garrett have tried to pick up where he left off. Most of these have focused on what they call the "sacramental" quality of the poem's symbolism, observing that the *Pearl*-Poet "transforms" one image into another in a manner according generally with the traditional understanding of the eucharist's transformational character.[2] One study, a chapter in Cary Nelson's *Incarnate Word*, considers the influence of the geometry of the circle on the poem's corporeal imagery.[3] These more recent findings have added a greater measure of credibility to Garrett's original idea, and provide a basis for further exploration along the same lines.

In fact, the extensive reference in lines 457-68 to the hierarchy of head and limbs in the *corpus mysticum*, and the prominent allusion to the sacrament at the poem's end (1209-10) make it impossible to ignore the theology of the body as one of the *Pearl*'s major themes. Where Garrett and, to a lesser extent, studies in his wake have erred is in their inability to see the poem's thematic and formal structure within the context of a more general theory of body-based aesthetics. In other words, to say that *Pearl* is a poem "about" the eucharist is only as accurate as saying that all of medieval theology and architecture is "about" the eucharist, or that French culture is "about" stars. What must be clarified is the difference between a ubiquitous cultural matrix and the idiosyncracies of its application to a particular work of art. It is only when, as in the preceding chapters, we begin to juxtapose the elements of a shared matrix that individual patterns of variation manifest themselves. Each member of the body participates microcosmically in its fullness, but all have different gifts and functions.

The whole question of what a work of art is "about" is especially vexing in the case of *Pearl* and, if anything, too many reasonable scholarly responses to the question are available in the poem's ample literature. In any poem with *Pearl*'s dense symbolic texture, it is far too easy to propose a controlling theme and support it with appropriate citations. In this respect, I must agree with A. C. Spearing:

> Much discussion of *Pearl* begins by asking "What does it mean?" or "What is it about?"—questions we should have no need to ask of *Purity* or *Patience*. . . . Questions of this sort may seem to imply that the poem is a kind of cryptogram, difficult to solve, but offering a single definite solution to the skilled cryptologist. I do not believe that this is so with *Pearl*, and I believe that critics and scholars have often obscured the poem by coming too quickly to such crucial questions. I therefore prefer to begin more obliquely by considering what *kind* of a poem it is.[4]

Like Spearing, I will begin by asking "What kind of a poem?" and dwelling on that question at considerable length before coming to the question "What does it mean?" The corporeal symmetry of the poem, together with the corollary relation of each of its parts to the macrocosmic whole, constitutes an essential architectonic frame for any thematic interpretation. Thus I will first consider how the poet handles traditions of literary and spatial centers, noting his reliance on the body and its center in the heart as an aesthetic matrix. The text's spatial and temporal focus in the pearl symbol itself should become clear against this background, preparing for analysis of *Pearl*'s architectural form and the poem's basis in cosmographic iconography. I will devote special attention to details in the poem calling for reinterpretation in the light of specific facets of body theology, and will propose that the poem be read according to a "poetics of the body" governing not only the unity of the text itself, but the relationship of both author and reader to the text.

As in so many medieval texts, the source of the meaning of *Pearl* lies at its structural center; my interpretation begins, therefore, with an analysis of the Vineyard parable at the approximate middle of the poem and moves outwards from that point. The conception of this parable as a concise summary of the main themes of the poem appears in several studies and accords well with the shape of the text.[5] *Pearl*'s stanzas and stanza groups interlock to create circles within circles, the overarching structure being the round chain of stanza groups comprising the poem as a whole; the Vineyard parable occupies the "central position in the concentric symmetry of a poem that literally moves in circles."[6] The fact that this parable nowhere explicitly mentions the pearl which is the poem's most important symbol is consistent with concentric structures we have seen elsewhere. The center always points away from itself for the fulfillment of its meaning; the eucharistic host at the middle of a cathedral acquires its significance largely from the structures that enclose it.

The lesson of the Vineyard parable recapitulates the form of the poem: the last shall be first and the first shall be last. The Vineyard workmen, standing to receive their wage, microcosmically reproduce the structure of the text:

> Set hem alle vpon a rawe
> And gyf vchon inlyche a peny.
> Bygyn at þe laste þat standeȝ lowe,
> Tyl to þe fyrst þat þou atteny. (545-48)[7]

Like the *Pearl* text, the workmen form a line (*rawe*), but the equivalence of first and last in both bring the ends together to create a circle.[8] The parable's core paradox encapsulates the most difficult lesson that the dreamer must learn; his daughter enjoys the highest rank in the heavenly hierarchy, even though her early death brought her earthly toil to a premature end. Thus the poem's theme is solidly based in geometry. And the microcosmic relation of center to text is strengthened via the image of the penny: each workman, no matter how long he labored, receives a penny as payment. The row of workmen with their pennies constitute, in geometric terms, a line of equal circles linked at beginning and end, a large circle comprised of smaller ones.

The microcosmic relation of parable to text also appears to be supported by a further detail. In line 635, the pearl maiden supports the justice of paying a late-coming workmen "at þe fyrst fyne" (which Hillmann renders "at the first furrow's end"), answering the objection "þat I my peny haf wrang tan here" (614). In other words, the penny may rightfully be paid both to one who has worked only one furrow and one who has worked all the furrows; the microcosmic relation of part to whole has its geometric basis in the equivalence of line to circle. Similarly, the circular link-word configuration of the linear text makes each stanza and each group of five stanzas the microcosmic equivalent of the entire poem. As in Langland's *Piers Plowman*, the *Pearl*-Poet equates writing and plowing. The furrowed field at the center of *Pearl*, like the men who work in it, recapitulates the shape of the entire poem.[9]

Exegetical writings associating the Vineyard parable with the *plenitudo temporis* reinforce its geometric centrality in *Pearl*; for the church Fathers, the workmen entering the field at different times of day (underscored in *Pearl* with the link word *date*) signify both the ages of one man's life span and, macrocosmically, the successive eras of world history. Thus Augustine, Gregory the Great, and Innocent III find in the parable a reference to the five ages of both individual men and mankind.[10] Their exegesis bases itself upon a larger tradition whereby all of salvation history, arranged in a bipartite scheme around the coming of Christ, is represented as a process of sowing and reaping; the prophets and patriarchs sow the seed under the Old Covenant whose harvest must await Christ's advent and, ultimately, the Day of Judgment.[11] The comparison is a familiar one in medieval writings on the liturgy as well, providing evidence both for the pattern of liturgical references applied by Gatta to *Pearl*, and for the poem's structural affinity to Gothic architecture.[12] The *Pearl*-Poet is not the first to use the Vineyard parable as a temporal nexus at the center of a poem; Haubrichs notes a very similar occurrence of the parable's resonances of the *plenitudo temporis* at a crucial transition in a symmetrical Latin poem by Gottschalk.[13] The general connection with Christ's designation as "alpha and omega" is, of course, evident throughout patristic handling of the plenitude of time.[14]

Elizabeth Petroff writes: "The ideal landscape is . . . a magical center, outside of time, yet the place of all generation."[15] *Pearl*'s Vineyard stands outside of the plot's time scheme—it is part of a speech, not an event—yet it embodies all time. The parable recounts the events of a single day, but resonates simultaneously with the larger time frames of both the human lifespan and the whole of salvation history. As such it stands in striking microcosmic relation to the text containing it, a poem narrating both a single day from the life of the dreamer and, in its figural movement from the garden of loss to the New Jerusalem, the history of mankind.[16] As Louise Mendillo points out, "The image of a well-run Vineyard suggests on a natural level how the universe and our lives are nurtured on a cosmic level."[17] It is in keeping with the Vineyard's microcosmic relation to time, as Nelson has noted, that one of the parable's stanzas concisely summarizes salvation history's three stages—prelapsarian bliss, the Fall and its consequences, and the Atonement that ushered in a new age:[18]

> 'Inoȝe is knawen þat mankyn grete
> Fyrste watȝ wroȝt to blysse parfyt;
> Oure forme fader hit con forfete
> Þurȝ an apple þat he vpon con byte.
> Al wer we dampned for þat mete
> To dyȝe in doel out of delyt
> And syþen wende to helle hete,
> Þerinne to won wythoute respyt.
> Bot þeron com a bote astyt.
> Ryche blod ran on rode so roghe,
> And wynne water þen at þat plyt:
> Þe grace of God wex gret innoghe.' (637-48)

The eucharistic resonances of the penny used in the Vineyard parable support our understanding of the Vineyard as a place where time exists in its plenitude, and provides evidence for the spatial centrality of that locus as well. The exegetical equation of the Vineyard penny with the consecrated host was first noted by Robert Ackerman, who finds evidence for the traditional association in vernacular treatises available in fourteenth-century England; exegetes interpret the penny as a reference to the daily bread asked for in the Lord's Prayer.[19] Scholars have generally accepted this symbolic link; Gatta sees it as one of the multiple sacramental transformations of the pearl image, while Borroff incorporates it into her interpretation of similar images of circularity in the poem.[20] The penny as consecrated host constitutes a symbolic condensation of the parable's teaching: each laborer, including those who have spent only two hours in the field, receives the penny that patristic commentary links with eternal life.[21] There is even evidence that medieval hosts were imprinted with the Greek letters alpha and omega, a fact that also helps associate the penny/host with the teaching that "the first shall be last."[22] Just as the penny "equalizes" the workmen's different periods of labor, so too the eucharist unites all periods of salvation history in the moment of communion. Cullmann writes:

> diese Mahlfeier [schaut] zugleich rückwärts auf das Todesmahl des historischen Jesus und die Ostermahlzeiten des Auferstandenen mit seinen Jüngern, und vorwärts auf das Ende, das ja im Bilde des messianischen Mahles schon im Judentum vorgestellt wird. So geschieht in jedem urchristlichen Gottesdienst das für unser Problem Bedeutsame, daß hier in Christus die ganze Heilslinie deutlich wird. Nicht als ob damit die Einmaligkeit ihrer zeitlichen Entwicklung aufgehoben wäre, wohl aber gewährt Christus der versammelten Mahlgemeinde den Überblick über den Zusammenhang des ganzen Heilsgeschehens und läßt sie teilhaben an seinen Früchten.[23]

The eucharist/penny image endows the Vineyard parable with the spatial plenitude that is the corollary of its all-encompassing temporal scheme. As the host on the altar is the ultimate source for each cathedral's structure and iconography, so too the Vineyard constitutes a fertile point of origin for the manifold circular dimensions of the poem. It is the locus of textual reduplication, the place where the poem, folding in on itself, regenerates itself. All of the poem's other circular and spherical images—pearls, roses, stones, maidens, and the multilayered configurations of the text—find their origin here, in the body of Christ that multiplies itself out of itself. Patristic sources use the association of Vineyard penny and host as a basis for understanding God's relation to the giant sphere of the cosmos; the eucharist provides the governing form of medieval cosmographic representation.[24] As the *denarius* bears the image of Caesar, so too the host bears the image (the letters alpha and omega) of the heavenly king. Receiving their coin, the Vineyard laborers are remade in its image, bearing the identical imprint of the God for whom there is no "more and lasse" (601).[25]

The plenitude of space inherent in the penny/host image radiates outwards into the spaces that contain it, just as successive layers of enclosure manifest symbolic equivalence with the eucharist at a cathedral's center. The penny is compared with "þe mede sumtyme of heueneȝ clere" (620), and the Vineyard itself is likened to "heuen lyȝte" (500). The basis for comparison is the pearl symbol, which likewise "Is lyke þe reme of heuenesse clere" (735), and is itself traditionally equated with the eucharist.[26] Thus the bright circle of heaven, the circumference of the cosmos, is compared not only with the geometric superstructure of the pearl-shaped text, but with the Vineyard space at its center and the individual pennies/hosts produced at that center—the pennies themselves distributed in a fashion that recalls the paradox of line and circle underlying the textual superstructure. The *Pearl* text faithfully and precisely reproduces the medieval *Weltbild*'s orderly gradation of concentric circles, displaying the fullness of time and space at its center.

The several concentric layers' equivalence with the circle of heaven and each other is the consequence, as in analogous architectural layering, of their shared allegorical relation to the body of Christ. The penny/host that the laborers receive signals their participation in the mystical body. Thus baptism, as the maiden explains, is the prerequisite for entry into the Vineyard: "In þe water of babtem þay dyssente: / Þen arne þay boroȝt into þe vyne" (627-28). The body of Vineyard laborers, in fact, simply continues the famous body metaphor that immediately precedes the parable (457-80). And even the Vineyard itself, the space containing the laborers, is associated in exegetical commentary with the church that is Christ's body. Finally, the body of the pearl-shaped text, itself an analogue and extension of the body of the maiden named Pearl, constitutes the outermost corporeal layer. Thus four equivalent layers of textual space emerge, linked via their common association with Christ's body: penny, laborers, Vineyard, text.[27]

Exegetical tradition also clarifies an additional dimension of "reversibility" in the body of believers at the poem's center. A homily attributed to Saint John Chrysostom sees in the time scheme of first and last an allusion to the paradoxical order of salvation for Jews and Gentiles; the Jews, like the laborers who began the earliest, are the first to be called but the last to receive their reward.[28] The mystical body displayed at the center of the poem, then, is upside-down. Rabanus Maurus' commentary on the parable makes this point very clearly: "Judaei de capite vertentur in cauda, et gentes de cauda mutabuntur in capite."[29] Thus *Pearl* evinces a principle of corporeal reversibility at its center akin to the inside out quality of the altar in Scarry's analysis, or the chiasmic numerical configurations that Haubrichs finds at the center of texts. In this respect, the spatial center of *Pearl* strongly resembles the way that the Divine Comedy's spatial core in hell figures as an inverted body of Christ, featuring a perspective on the upside-down body of Satan.[30] The description of the laborers condenses the entire span of salvation history; because that representation designates the center and plenitude of history, it is reversed and must be read backwards.[31] Further, the metaphor extends itself outwards to the relationship between the Pearl Maiden and dreamer; like "þyse þat wroȝt not houreȝ two" (555), the Pearl Maiden "lyfed not two ȝer in our þede" (483), while the dreamer has lived much longer on the earth. The oft noted over-literalness of his arguments, and his slowness to grasp the maiden's discourse on the operation of grace, makes him a type of Old Covenant belief, just as she is a type of New Covenant faith. The dreamer's vision shows him a daughter ranked high among the heavenly hosts; their relationship has been turned on its head.

The poet's pattern of link words and verbal echoes provides a formal frame for his thematic and spatial centering. Stanza group nine begins the Vineyard parable with the link word *date*, underscoring the relevance of the *plenitudo temporis*. The link word *more* in stanza group ten emphasizes both the laborers' and dreamer's confusion when confronted with the paradoxical quality of Christian time; those who worked longer should, by earthly standards, receive a greater reward, but God's grace allows the other laborers equal status. This paradoxical geometry of grace finds its climactic formal expression in the lines linking the poem's two center stanza groups (ten and eleven):[32]

> 'Now he þat stod þe long day stable,
> And þou to payment com hym byfore,
> Þenne þe lasse in werke to take more able,
> And euer þe lenger þe lasse, þe more.'
>
> 'Of more and lasse in Godeȝ ryche',
> Þat gentyl sayde, 'lys no joparde,
> For þer is vch mon payed inlyche,
> Wheþer lyttel oþer much he hys rewarde' (597-604)

Here the occurrence of *more* and *lasse* in both of the two lines constituting the structural heart of the poem enacts a formal climax which is consistent with the link word pattern used elsewhere (whereby the *more* link of stanza group ten must be repeated in group eleven's first line) and yet supplemental to the normal pattern. The addition of the extra link *lasse* gives the center two lines a special status. It also reinforces, at the poem's core, the peculiar geometry of Christian space and time. The closer to the center we find ourselves, the further away we really are: "euer þe lenger þe lasse, þe more" is an epigram for both the poem's theme and its construction. Stanza eleven's link word *innoghe*, then, reflects the thematic resolution of the two central lines; all points in Christian space and time are equal and sufficient. Oddly enough, the peculiar status of the links in lines 600-01 has heretofore received no attention in studies devoted to *Pearl*'s verbal *concatenatio*.[33]

The poet strengthens his work's formal symmetry with other verbal echoes as well. Ackerman notices that *hyne*, centrally located in lines 505 and 632, anticipates *homly hyne* (1211), while the word *pay*, linking the poem's very first and last lines, also recurs repeatedly at the center (584, 603, 632, 635).[34] Within our geometrical scheme, the strategic repetition of *pay* underscores the quantitative concerns of the poem. Not yet noted by scholars is the similar use of *day* at the poem's center (541, 554, 597) and end (1202, 1210), supporting the synecdochic relation of the day of labor in the Vineyard to the day which constitutes the time frame for the dreamer's experience.[35] Similar verbal patterning occurs elsewhere in the tradition of numerical composition in which the *Pearl*-Poet seems to have placed himself. In the *Nibelungenlied*, the key word *nôt* in Margrave Gêre's structurally central marriage offer anticipates, like *pay* in *Pearl*, the very last word of the poem.[36]

In the case of the word *hyne*, in particular, scholars' ignorance of the poem's basis in the structures of the body has led to mistranslation and misinterpretation. Two studies, one of which takes the word as its main focus, mistranslate *hyne* with the singular "servant" or "worker," despite the plural renderings in glosses by Gordon and Hillmann.[37] Nearby plural references in the text themselves amply justify a plural rendering: *werkmen* (507), *þer* (508); *þay*, (repeated, 626-633); *vus* (1210, 1211). And the allusions to the mystical body implicit in the references demand it; Kean correctly sees in the phrase an allusion to the *domesticos fidei* of Galatians 6:10.[38] The word echo deliberately links the mystical body represented laboring in the Vineyard with *vus*, the body of believers who read the poem; looking in from the edge of the text, we readers notice our shared association with the group at the center. Failure to see the connection has given rise to a false distinction between the two occurrences of *hyne*, as in the following interpretation:

> There is . . . a significant difference between the "hyne" who perform their part in the parable and the "hyne" of this concluding prayer. The former were casual laborers, working for hire: the latter are "*homly* hyne," inmates of the Lord's household. . . .[39]

Against the background of the *Pearl*'s formal geometry of circle and center, we are in a better position to interpret the poem's difficult fiftieth stanza:

> Then more I meled and sayde apert:
> 'Me þynk þy tale vnresounable.
> Godde3 ry3t is redy and euermore rert,
> Oþer Holy Wryt is bot a fable.
> In Sauter is sayd a verce ouerte
> Þat speke3 a poynt determynable:
> "Þou quyte3 vchon as hys desserte,
> Þou hy3e kyng ay pretermynable."
> Now he þat stod þe long day stable,
> And þou to payment com hym byfore,
> Þenne þe lasse in werke to take more able,
> And euer þe lenger þe lasse, þe more.' (589-600)

The passage's main crux is *pretermynable*, a word that occurs nowhere else in Middle English, rhyming here with "a poynt determynable."[40] As this stanza immediately precedes the poem's formal center and is ringed by other verbal echoes sustaining *Pearl*'s spherical structure, the strikingly similar use of cognates of *determynable* in traditional explanations of the mystical geometry of the circle may be relevant. Bonaventure uses the word *interminabilitas* in a definition of eternity based on circular geometry:

> Ad illud quod obiicitur, quod aeternitas est interminabilitas; dicendum, quod non accipit totam rationem aeternitatis, quia non tantum dicit interminabilitatem, sed etiam simultatem; et sicut per modum interminabilitatis dicit circumferentiam quandam intelligibilem, carentem principio et fine; sic per modum simultatis simplicitatem et indivisionem dicit ad modum centri; et haec duo circa divinum esse simul ponuntur, quia simul est simplex et infinitum, et ideo circularitas in aeternitate intelligitur. . . .[41]

Poulet has demonstrated the dependence of this passage in Bonaventure on the *Liber XXIV Philosophorum*, whose importance for the geometry of concentric circles we have noted, and on Boethius' famous definition of eternity in the *De consolatione* (which contains the word *interminabilis*): "Aeternitas est interminabilis vitae tota simul et perfecta possessio."[42] Several scholars have seen the influence of the *De consolatione* in *Pearl*; the *Roman de la Rose*, also considered by some scholars to have influenced the *Pearl*-Poet, uses the corresponding Old French cognate *terminable* in an allusion to the same geometrical tradition:

> Car el sot des qu'el le portait
> Dont au porter se confortait,
> Qu'il iert l'espere merveillable
> Qui ne peut estre terminable,
> Qui par touz les son centre lance,
> Ne leu n'a la circonference . . .[43]

Another word in the *Pearl* passage that appears to allude to mystical geometry is *poynt*, occurring next to the key word *determynable*: "Þat speke3 a poynt determynable." Medieval explanations of the *punctus* at the center of time are closely linked in tradition with the *interminabilitas* of eternity. Poulet notes, in connection with the Boethian definition of eternity cited above, the similar concern of a *De consolatione* passage discussing the point at the center of a circle: "Igitur (fatum) uti est ad intellectum ratiocinatio; ad id quod est, id quod gignitur, ad aeternitatem tempus, ad puncti medium circulus."[44] It is an image we have already seen in Dante's allusion to the plenitude of time and space: "il punto / a cui tutti li tempi son presenti" and "là 've s'appunta ogni ubi e ogni quando."[45] (The *Commedia*, of course, has also often been taken as an influence on *Pearl*.) The image appears again in the opening line of the first of Dante's *rime petrose*, a poem in which Robert Durling finds systematic application of microcosmic conceptions of space and time: "Io son venuto al punto de la rota."[46] The *punctus* at the center reappears throughout medieval writings on the nature of Christian time.[47]

The Middle English *poynt* is most familiar to *Pearl*-Poet scholars from its more prominent appearance in *Patience*. There *poynt* is both the first and last word of the text and, as we will see in a later chapter, is linked via traditional exegesis with the whale image constituting the heart of the poem.[48] Anderson's gloss notes that *poynt* acquires a meaning in *Patience* that is unusual for this Middle English word; quite possibly its use in *Pearl*, so close to the word coinage *preterminable*, is idiosyncratic as well. Together with the other two words drawn from geometrical mysticism, it appears to bear a specific relation to the *spot* on which *Pearl*'s action begins and ends, just as the point of the hook at the center of *Patience* bears a geometrical relation to the word with which the text begins and ends.

The traditions alluded to with the words *poynt determynable* and *pretermynable* provide a subtle but important geometric basis for the *Pearl* passage in question, helping to integrate this concise structurally central statement of the poem's main themes with the overall geometry of the text. In the *Pearl* passage, the dreamer expresses in quantitative terms his continuing bewilderment at the distribution of heavenly rewards. He cites the last line of Ps. 61:12-13 as a proof text for the principle of unequal payment for unequal labor, claiming to have found in these verses a *poynt determinable*.[49] The Middle English phrase he uses implies both that the doctrine in question is *festgelegt* and inarguable, and that the distribution of rewards dictated by the verses is capable of precise and finite quantitive "determination": the amount of the wage should correspond, *quid pro quo*, with the length of time spent on the job. This principle he opposes to the economy of the Vineyard in which, as it seems to him, the wage increases in indirect proportion to the amount of labor: "Þenne þe lasse in werke to take more able, / And euer þe lenger þe lasse, þe more." But his paraphrase of the Psalms text itself belies his interpretation. God, the *hyȝe kyng*, is *pretermynable*, a word that Hillmann glosses "'Before the terminable (that which can be limited)'; hence, without limits of any kind, not contingent: therefore, 'Eternal, Infinite'"; in this connection she cites Étienne Gilson, who writes, "The perfection of being (God) not only calls for all realizations, it also excludes all limits, generating thereby a positive infinity which refuses all determination."[50] Thus the dreamer's own paraphrase betrays his misunderstanding of the geometrical principles of the *punctus* and *interminabilitas* of time to which he alludes, just as his Old Covenant legalism prevents him from interpreting his scripture text in accordance with the operation of grace. It is precisely within the paradoxical spatiality of the *poynt* that is simultaneously fixed in one place and dispersed into all places, at once center and circumference, that the operation of grace unfolds. And it is this *poynt*, the "point central . . . à partir duquel le monde se développe,"[51] that both *Pearl* and *Patience* texts take as their structural and thematic locus of origin.[52]

Notes

1. "The *Pearl*: An Interpretation," *U of Washington Publications in English* 4 (1918): 1-45. Also published separately: Seattle, WA: U of Washington, 1918.

2. Joyce Rogers Emert, "*Pearl* and the Incarnate Word: A Study in the Sacramental Nature of Symbolism," diss., U of New Mexico, 1969; John Gatta, Jr. "Transformation Symbolism and the Liturgy of the Mass in *Pearl*," *Modern Philology* 71 (1974): 243-56; Elisabeth Petroff, "Landscape in *Pearl*: The Transformation of Nature," *Chaucer Review* 16 (1981): 181-93.

3. "*Pearl*: The Circle as Figural Space," *The Incarnate Word* (Urbana: U of Illinois P, 1973) 25-49.

4. *The Gawain Poet: A Critical Study* (Cambridge: Cambridge UP, 1970) 96.

5. See Carleton Brown, "The Author of *The Pearl*, Considered in the Light of His Theological Opinions," *PMLA* 19 (1904): 115-45, published separately, Baltimore: MLA, 1904; René Welleck, "*The Pearl*: An Interpretation of the Middle English Poem," *Prague Studies in English* 4 (1933): 1-33, rpt. in Blanch 3-36; D. W. Robertson, Jr., "The 'Heresy' of *The Pearl*," *Modern Language Notes* 65 (1950): 152-55, rpt. in Conley 291-99.

6. Dennis William Moran, "Style and Theology in the Middle English *Pearl*: Patterns of Change and Reconciliation," diss., U of Notre Dame, 1976, 137.

7. All citations from E. V. Gordon edition (Oxford: Oxford UP, 1953).

8. Marie Borroff points out that the image of workmen in a *rawe* is the poet's addition to the account in Matthew, adding: "The line of laborers is to be read 'back' in time, from later to earlier, and 'backward' in space, as if, in terms of Western culture, a line of print were to be read from right to left instead of from left to right." "*Pearl*'s 'Maynful Mone': Crux, Simile, and Structure," *Acts of Interpretation: The Text and its Contexts, 700-1600: Essays on Medieval and Renaissance Literature in Honor of E. Talbot Donaldson*, ed. Mary J. Carruthers and Elizabeth D. Kirk (Norman, OK: Pilgrim, 1982) 163ff.

9. Cf. Jordan 17-18 for the relation of "middle" to "first" and "last" in Plato's definition of geometric proportion.

10. Augustine, *Sermo* 81 (*PL* 38.530-33); Gregory the Great, *Hom. in ev.* 1.19 (*PL* 76.1154ff.); Innocent III, *Sermo in Dom. Septuag.* (*PL* 217.351-52). Cf. Honorius of Autun (*PL* 172.858). The practice of dividing a body of people into sections corresponding with time divisions is at least as old as ancient Greece and Rome; see Brown, *Love's Body* 20. S. Lorenz's summary of how Nicolas of Cusa understood the plenitude of time within the framework of mystical geometry bears tangential relevance to the *rawe* of workmen: "Die Zeit ist daher die aneinander gereihte Gegenwart." "Das Unendliche bei Nicolaus von Kues," *Philologisches Jahrbuch* 40 (1927): 63.

11. See Augustine, *Sermo* 101 (*PL* 38.605-13); Hugh of St. Cher, *Opera omnia in universam Vetus et Novum Testamentum* (Venice, 1703) 6: fol. 191v.

12. See Ohly, "Die Kathedrale als Zeitenraum" 254-59.

13. Haubrichs 137-39.

14. See, e.g., Scharl 73-74.

15. "Psychological Landscape in Fourteenth Century Poetry and Painting," diss., U of California (Berkeley), 1972, 47-48.

16. An important temporal referent is the phrase "Oute of oryent" (3) which Borroff interprets as, among other things, an allusion to the rising of the sun at the poem's beginning.

17. "Word Play in *Pearl*: Figures of Sound and Figures of Sense," diss., U of California (Berkeley), 1976, 174.

18. Nelson 29-31.

19. "The Pearl Maiden and the Penny," *Romance Philology* 17 (1964): 614-23. Reprinted in Conley 149-62.

20. See especially Gatta 253-56; Borroff 165.

21. See Ann Douglas Wood, "The *Pearl*-Dreamer and the *Hyne* in the Vineyard Parable," *Philological Quarterly* 52 (1973): 9-19.

22. See Sauer 196-97.

23. Cullmann 64. Van der Leeuw writes: "Der Ritus des Abendmahlssakraments ist ja wesentlich nichts als die Aktivierung des Christusmythus . . . eine Versetzung des Urgeschehens aus der Vorzeit in das Heute" (25). Cf. Graber: "Wie Taufe und Firmung, so weist auch die Eucharistie hinüber über das Grab in die Ewigkeit" (112). Also see Eliade, *Das Heilige und das Profane* 43.

24. Sauer 196-97.

25. In addition to the passage in Sauer just cited, see the discussion of how both man and the heavens are "coined" in God's image in Bernard F. Huppé, "Petrus id est Christus: Word Play in *Piers Plowman*, the B text," *Journal of English Literary History* 17 (1950): 172-73. A long passage from Alanus de Insulis' *De planctu naturae* (PL 210.453-54) uses the metaphor of coining to explain how God, as architect, fashions the material world in his image. The process begins in the *praeconceptionis thalamus* and moves outward (I will discuss the wedding chamber as a corporeal and textual center in chapter seven).

26. Friedrich Ohly, "Die Geburt der Perle aus dem Blitz," *Schriften zur mittelalterlichen Bedeutungsforschung* (Darmstadt: Wissenschaftliche, 1977) 294.

27. Actually, yet another layer exists, intermediate between the penny and the group of workmen: the body of each individual laborer. That it was conceived by the poet as a separate layer will become clearer in the course of our later examination of how the individual maidens' pearl ornaments (at the center of their breasts) parallel each workman's penny.

28. This homily is the thirty-fourth in the collection entitled *Opus Imperfectum in Matthaeum* (*PG* 56.822), cited in Borroff 163n. Cf. James P. Oakden, "The Liturgical Influence in *Pearl*," *Chaucer und seine Zeit: Symposion für Walter F. Schirmer*, ed. Arno Esch (Tübingen: Niemeyer, 1968) 346-47.

29. *Comm. in Matth.* (*PL* 76.1157), cited in Wood 10.

30. See Durling 117-19; Charles Singleton, "Campi semantici dei canti XII dell'*Inferno* e XIII del *Purgatorio*," *Miscellanea di studi danteschi* (Genova: Bozzi, 1966) 11-22.

31. Cf. again Brown, *Love's Body* 134-35, on the reversibility of head and tail in corporeal metaphors for the state.

32. The symmetrical stanza group arrangement and link word patterning described here point to lines 600-01 as the poem's formal center, even though its precise numerical center is line 606.

33. Such studies include Macrae-Gibson and Mendillo, cited above, and Edward Wilson, "Word Play and the Interpretation of *Pearl*," *Medium aevum* 40 (1971): 116-34. Note that the link word *more* also occurs in stanza group three, and *lasse* in group fifteen.

34. Ackerman 161. For more information on the pun on *pay*, see Wilson 124; Mendillo 45.

35. Further, the phrase "vche a daye" (1210) describes the viewing of the consecrated host, and points back to the eucharistic implications of the Vineyard parable.

36. See Fichtner 230n. Although there is certainly no reason to believe that the *Pearl*-Poet knew the *Nibelungenlied*, evidence from "The Bird with Four Feathers" discussed above indicates that Middle English poets had some access to the same tradition of symmetrical composition.

37. Wood 9-19; Louise Dunlap, "Vegetation Puns in *Pearl*," *Mediaevalia* 3 (1977): 180-81.

38. Kean, *The Pearl* 232.

39. Bishop, *Pearl in its Setting: A Critical Study of the Structure and Meaning of the Middle English Poem* (Oxford: Blackwell, 1968) 79.

40. I have adopted Gordon's reading of the manuscript's *ptermynable*, but a good argument can also be made for the rendering *pertermynable*. However we may interpret this difficult prefix, the resemblance to *determynable* supports the idea of a deliberate contrast between the two words.

41. *Quaestiones disputatae, De mysterio Trinitatis*, q. 5, a. 1, 7-8 (Quaracchi, ed., *Opera omnia* 5.91).

42. *De consolatione* lib. V, prosa 6.

43. Ernest Langlois, ed., Société des anciens Textes francais, 5 vols. (Paris: Firmin-Didot, 1914-24) 4: 254ff. Cf. K. Sneyders de Vogel, "'Le cercle dout le centre est partout et la circonférence nulle part' et le *Roman de la Rose*," *Neophilologus* 16 (1931) 248.

44. *De consolatione* lib. 4, prosa 5. Poulet xxv; cf. ix.

45. *Paradiso* 17.18, 29.12; cf. Poulet xii-xiii.

46. Durling 52ff.

47. See Cullmann 27, 33; Tillich 173-74; Quispel 115-16, 122; Eliade, *Das Heilige und das Profane* 13, 17-18.

48. John B. Friedman discusses the exegetical link between the "point" image and the hook used to fish for the whale in "Figural Typology in the Middle English *Patience*," *The Alliterative Tradition in the Fourteenth Century*, ed. Bernard Levy and Paul Szarmach (Kent, OH: Kent State UP, 1981) 107. Line 68 of *Patience* shows the close thematic relation of the words *place*, *poynt*, and *hert*. All citations of the poem are from the J. J. Anderson edition (Manchester UP, 1969).

49. The designation "verce ouerte" contributes to the poem's elaborate scheme of enclosures and containers, begun in line two's phrase "To clanly clos."

50. *The Spirit of Mediaeval Philosophy*, trans. A. H. C. Downes (New York: Scribner's, 1936) 55; Mary Vincent Hillmann, *The Pearl* (Notre Dame: U of Notre Dame P, 1961) 93n.

51. Poulet xx.

52. An allusion to the tradition of mystical geometry via the word *pretermynable* does not necessarily preclude R. E. Kaske's translation, "speaking or declaring enduringly," which he bases on exegetical understanding of "Semel locutus est Deus" in the Psalm verse. His rendering, preferring the manuscript spelling *pertermynable*, also appears to play on God's ability to speak *semel*, i.e., only once and yet enduringly, throughout all time. The Word, spoken at the beginning of time and enduring eternally, provides a recapitulatory structure for Christian time. In any case, the evidence presented here provides ample grounds for disagreeing with A. C. Spearing's assertion that the poet's own explicit interpretation of the parable precludes the necessity of exegetical knowledge on the part of the audience. *The Gawain Poet: A Critical Study* (Cambridge: Cambridge UP, 1970) 102-03.

Chapter Six

"TO CLANLY CLOS"
PEARL'S CONCENTRIC SETTINGS

The corporeal basis for the poem's geometry is, of course, the body of the Pearl Maiden. Herself a pearl, she is also a container for the pearl at the center of her body: "Lo, euen inmyddez my breste hit stode" (740, cf. 222).[1] Once again, our interpretation must begin with this center and move outwards. Scholarly ignorance of the relation of enclosure to the enclosed in medieval cosmography and architecture has given rise to numerous attempts to find a symbolic distinction between the maiden herself and the pearl on her breast. Sister Mary Madaleva argues that the pearl on the maiden's breast, rather than the maiden, is the lost pearl which the dreamer seeks:

> the Maiden is not his pearl, and the pearl is not a child. . . . the Maiden bids the poet "get for thee *thy* spotless pearl." This, again, establishes her identity as distinct from the pearl he is seeking.[2]

Paul Piehler writes:

> The dialogue culminates in the maiden's explanation of the significance of the pearl upon her breast; it is at once the pearl of great price for which the jeweller gave all his goods, and the gift of the Lamb in "token of pes." Here it is clear that the maiden does not stand allegorically for the kingdom: the pearl is her chief decoration but, although maiden and jewel are both pearls, they are kept separate.[3]

In fact, the pearl worn by the maiden constitutes a symbolic and structural core for successive layers of equivalent enclosure akin to the spatial nexus of the

Vineyard. Just as the Vineyard field and workers create a concise recapitulation of the overarching geometry of both poem and cosmos, so too the maiden equates the pearl she wears with "þe reme of heuenesse clere" (735); the outermost circumference of the universe projects itself into the innermost space of the poem. This arrangement reflects the dispersion of spatial centeredness effected by the Incarnation, whereby the body of each believer is both a temple for the Holy Spirit and a new center for the universe. The *poynt* at the poem's structural center is reiterated in the middle of the human body:

> Le point divin est le centre même de l'âme, c'est Dieu intérieurement possédé dans un moment humain. . . . Dieu est un point, parce qu'il est centre, non seulement de l'univers, mais de l'âme.[4]

Thus the Pearl Maiden's pearl is shared by the entire host of maidens that the dreamer sees in his vision of the New Jerusalem. Like the symbolic analogue in the penny distributed to each Vineyard worker, the multiplicity of pennies and maidens effects a radical decentralization of textual space and time. The pearl, like the eucharist and the "navel" of a dream, is the locus where the poem's themes weave so tightly as to defy interpretation; akin to the mystery of the Incarnation at the center of history, the pearl lies outside the scope of human reason:

> A manneȝ dom moȝt dryȝly demme,
> Er mynde moȝt malte in hit mesure.
> I hope no tong moȝt endure
> No sauerly saghe say of þat syþt. (223-26)

Traditional cosmological associations with the pearl symbol support its status in this text; a common funerary image, it represents a midpoint between the finite and the infinite, signifying both Christ and the human soul.[5]

Just as the text itself is a macrocosm of the geometry of the Vineyard, so also it reduplicates the geometry of the pearl. Both the Pearl Maiden and the words she speaks are pearls: "A juel to me þen watz þys geste, / And iueleȝ wern hyr gentyl saweȝ" (277-78).[6] Itself a circular extension of the Pearl Maiden's body and chief ornament, the text also reflects the diversity of centers by which the

Pearl Maiden's body is extended into the larger community of Christ's body represented by the host of maidens. Groups of five stanzas, each a structural circle containing five circles, parallel the maidens' understanding of their own numerical relation to each other: "vchon enle we wolde were fyf" (849), and again, "vchon fayn of oþereȝ hafyng, / And wolde her corounez wern worþe þo fyue."[7] The twelve-line stanzas and 1,212 total lines of the text reflect the number of maidens—144,000, the product of twelve and twelve thousand. The maidens thus sing together in a chorus whose geometry imitates the text's *corona* structure; medieval choruses often arranged themselves in a garland shape around the altar, and both Durandus and Isidore of Seville find an etymological link between *chorus* and *corona*.[8] Pearls are the chief *adubbement* of both the maidens' bodies and the body of the text.

The Pearl Maiden's young age not only plays a part in the poem's concern with the theology of time; it also highlights the special status of children and childlikeness within the doctrine of the mystical body. In chapter one we saw in the image of the child the same inside out structure as that present at the body's center. Human bodies (and, by analogy, aesthetic forms) reproduce themselves from within; the wounding of Christ turned his body inside out, just as the birth of the church from his side (and the birth of any child) constitutes an exteriorization of his body's interior. Scharl demonstrates the relation of becoming childlike (*renovare*) to *recapitulatio*; conversion is a recapitulation of Christian space and time, a symbolic return to the body's center that appropriates the Incarnation at the center of history for each believer.[9] Baptism requires reimmersion in the water that flowed from Christ's wound/womb: the *novus homo*'s ontogony recapitulates Christian history's phylogeny. Children are microcosms within their parents, and the dreamer's quest is a search for his own center. Bishop writes: "the mourner's child is thus a 'type' or 'figure' of what he must himself become 'spiritually' in order to enter the Heavenly City.[10] And the dreamer's pearl is both literal daughter and literary offspring. His search for his daughter leads him, in the end, to refashion himself in the image of his bodily and aesthetic interior—to become, with his readers, "precious perleȝ" (1212).[11]

Since publication of Bishop's Pearl *in Its Setting*, scholars have generally acknowledged the poem's sustained concern with the multiplicity of literal and figural "settings" enclosing the pearl. The poet's intent "to clanly clos" (2) the pearl is taken, accordingly, as a *modus operandi* for a whole complex of images of containment, including the *coroune, garlande gay, byʒe, cofer, forser,* and *kyste,* the three landscapes depicted, and the enclosing structure of the text itself, many of which are circular or spherical like the pearl they contain.[12] Bishop's study, however, concerns itself primarily with background materials as an interpretive setting for the poem; scholars have not yet given sufficient attention to the specific images of enclosure used by the poet himself, or to the relationships that these images bear to each other.[13] Nor has enough work been done to establish the influence of medieval architectural and cosmographic theory on the poem's configurations of successive enclosure. Nelson's study, however, points firmly in the right direction by positing a corporeal matrix for the text's multifaceted circularity.

My analysis of *Pearl*'s extended metaphor of enclosure bases itself on the relationship of the body to its containers dictated by the theology of the vessel; the concentric spaces of the text, I believe, manifest the same allegorical equivalence to each other as the altar vessels discussed in chapter two. Just as the Virgin's womb contained that which, paradoxically, contained both her and the whole of the universe, so the pearl is at once smaller and greater than all of its enclosures. The manner in which the Pearl Maiden's body extends its own characteristics into its containers is implied, for example, in the dreamer's statement: "As ʒe ar maskeleʒ vnder mone, / Your woneʒ schulde be wythouten mote" (923-24).[14] The Incarnation effects a mysterious union of inhabitor and habitation; Christ is both the church and the body within the church:

> Sic quippe corpus Unigeniti domus Dei dicitur, sicut etiam templum vocatur; ita vero, ut unus idemque Dei atque hominis filius ipse sit qui inhabitat, ipse qui inhabitatur.[15]

Thus, as Dominique Sanchis explains,

> L'église en effet est ainsi nommé uniquement parce qu'elle contient l'Ecclesia: l'assemblé des appelés . . . on appelle couramment le contenant du nom du contenu, qu'il signifie et symbolise.[16]

Emma Jung's description of traditional characteristics of the vessel in her study of the grail legend, in particular, recalls the central symbol of *Pearl*—its unity, circular shape, and allegorical relation to both "þe reme of heuenesse clere" and the innermost space of the body:

> Das Gefäß ist immer eines, es muß rund sein in Anlehnung an die Himmelssphäre, damit die Gestirnseinflüsse am Werk teilnehmen können. Es wird auch oft eine Matrix oder Uterus genannt....[17]

The Pearl Maiden, herself a vessel containing the pearl on her breast, is in turn contained by a succession of other enclosures sharing her spotless perfection.[18]

The theology of the vessel interacts, in *Pearl*, with the metaphor of the shell, the inevitable corollary of the pearl image. Because the text makes no explicit mention of the pearl's origin within the oyster, the image has received no scholarly notice; it is nonetheless implicit in the layers of enclosure around the pearl in the structure of both the text and the "containers" depicted in the poem. Ohly's careful study of patristic exegesis applied to the pearl symbol shows the close interdependence between traditions depicting the Virgin as a vessel and the oyster's shell:

> Die Auslegung sagt: Das Meer ist die Welt und die Muschel Maria, die, im Tempel stehend, das Brot des Himmels, Christus, in sich aufnahm, das in sie einging wie der Blitz, der, aufgenommen im Inneren der Jungfrau, den heiligen Leib erleuchtete, den der Inkarnierte annahm. So ist aus ihr Gottes Wort geboren ohne männliche Verbindung wie die reine und höchst kostbare Perle.[19]

He even finds some evidence of a tradition seeing the mollusk bearing the pearl as a book metaphor.[20] Haubrichs, whose study of symmetrical composition can be applied to the *Pearl* text's structure in so many other ways, sees the shell metaphor as one important basis for the concentric layering of numerical structures around a text's moment of *plenitudo temporis*; he terms this compositional process "Schalenbildung."[21] Bachelard's discussion of literary space devotes considerable attention to traditions of the shell both as an image of the resurrected body and as an indication of the intimate relation of body to architecture. Like the pearl's various round settings, the shell's shape is dictated by the shape of the mollusk within, and is itself part of the mollusk's body.[22]

One of the settings depicted in close proximity to the Pearl Maiden's body is the *coroune*:

> A py3t coroune 3et wer þat gyrle
> Of mariorys and non oþer ston,
> Hi3e pynakled of cler quyt perle,
> Wyth flurted flowre3 perfet vpon.
> To hed hade ho non oþer werle.... (205-09)

Bishop's well-known article has established a link between the *coroune* and *garlande gay* (1186) via traditional associations of both with the *corona* chandelier hanging over the main altar of many Gothic cathedrals; he notes that exegetical understanding of the *corona* as a representation of the New Jerusalem clarifies the relation of both images to *Pearl*'s concluding description of the heavenly city.[23] In the light of chapter two's discussion of cathedral *coronae* and microcosmic theory, it is clear that the poet intended the crown as an image of the cosmos, an image that is all the more striking in view of traditional *Weltbilder* (also mentioned in that chapter) depicting the cosmos as a giant garland. Evidence from a number of different sources can be adduced to amplify Bishop's interpretation in the context of architectural and iconographic representation. A passage from *Cleanness* explicitly links the New Jerusalem with the "gay" *corona* over the altar:

> Þe jueles out of Jerusalem wyth gemmes ful bry3t,
> Bi þe syde of þe sale were semely arayed;
> Þe aþel auter of brasse watz hade into place;
> Þe gay coroun of golde gered on lofte ... (1441-44)

Sedlmayr's observation that the *corona* over the altar depicts the descent of the heavenly city (as described in chapter twenty-one of the Apocalypse) corresponds with the dreamer's vision of the city that "watz lyzt fro þe heuen adoun."[24] Pseudo-Chrysostom likens the "circle" of workers in the Vineyard parable to a *corona*, showing that the crown image bears a close relation to the numerical center of the poem just as the chandelier hangs at the center of a cathedral.[25] The circular *corona* worn by the Pearl Maiden underscores her head's microcosmic relation to her entire body; as we saw in chapter one, the sphericity of the head recapitulates both the entire body, conceived mystically as a sphere, and the cosmos.[26] The maiden's *corona* reiterates the shape of both her body and the pearl at the center of her breast, just as the *corona* of the New Jerusalem at the poem's end projects itself into the circle of Vineyard laborers at the numerical center. Similarly, as shown in chapter two, the design of the Gothic apse at the cathedral's "head" echoes the *corona* hanging over the building's "heart"; Sedlmayr sees the design of the apse as a "Kranz" (garland) as well.[27]

Kantorowicz' extensive study of the juridical status of the crown, based primarily on legal writings from late medieval England, further illuminates the *coroune* in *Pearl*.[28] He finds that the crown, like the halo,[29] signified the plenitude of time of the New Jerusalem; the crown invested each mortal king with symbolic immortality, endowing him with the authority of an unending line of predecessors and successors.[30] The crown also invoked the plenitude of space inherent in the notion of the king's two bodies; the king ruled, simultaneously, his physical body and the extended political body constituted by his subjects.[31] Kantorowicz writes:

> There can be no doubt that in the later Middle Ages the idea was current that in the Crown the whole body politic was present—from king to lords and commons and down to the least liegeman. . . . In this respect indeed the Crown and the "mystical body of the realm" were comparable entities. . . . For the Crown would have been incomplete without both the king as the head and the magnates as the limbs.[32]

The Pearl Maiden uses the analogous image of the *byȝe* ("ring") to express the relation of head to limbs in her famous speech on the mystical body:

> 'Of courtaysye, as saytȝ Saynt Poule,
> Al arn we membreȝ of Jesu Kryst:
> As heued and arme and legg and naule
> Temen to hys body ful trwe and tryste,
> Ryȝt so is vch a Krysten sawle
> A longande lym to þe Mayster of myste.
> Þenne loke what hate oþer any gawle
> Is tached oþer tyȝed by lymmeȝ bytwyste.
> Þy heued hatȝ nauþer greme ne gryste,

> On arme oþer fynger þa3 þou ber by3e.
> So fare we alle wyth luf and lyste
> To kyng and quene by cortaysye.' (457-68)

The ring demonstrates the participation of each member of the mystical body in the privileges of the head; the speech occurs as part of the maiden's response to the dreamer's repeated objections to her right to wear a crown. As in medieval political theory (whose reliance on religious conceptions of the mystical body Kantorowicz amply demonstrates[33]), the crown image in *Pearl* contributes considerably to the sense of temporal and spatial plenitude generated by the poem's other microcosmic structures. Invoking the plenitude of both the heavenly city and the structure of the poem itself, each pearl maiden's crown, like the pearls they wear, signals their common claim to eternal life. The doubleness of the crown symbol in *Pearl*, like the twofold nature of the king's body, allows it to signify both an ornament worn by the maidens and the larger corporate structure of the New Jerusalem and the text.[34]

Further, the image of the phoenix reinforces our sense of the doubleness of the crown. Questioning the Pearl Maiden's right to wear a crown that belongs to the Virgin, the dreamer says:

> 'We leuen on Marye þat grace of grewe,
> Þat ber a barne of vyrgyn flour;
> Þe croune fro hyr quo mo3t remwe
> Bot ho hir passed in sum fauour?
> Now, for synglerty o hyr dousour,
> We calle hyr Fenyx of Arraby,
> Þat freles fle3e of hyr fasor,
> Lyk to þe Quen of cortaysye.'
> (425-32)

Kantorowicz notes that medieval juridical writings invoke the phoenix to explain the double nature of rulership; the sources he cites repeatedly stress its "singleness" (with L. *singulare, singularissima*; cf "synglerty" here).[35] In *Pearl* the image of the phoenix helps explain the doubleness of queenship that allows the Virgin to share it with the pearl maidens.

The ring itself is a second in the series of settings for the pearl; like the crown with which it is traditionally linked, the ring's circular form conforms with the shape of the enclosed.³⁶ Kantorowicz discusses the widespread medieval practice of placing a ring on a new king's hand at coronation. Based on the doctrine of Christ's mystical marriage with the church (and the analogous use of the ring in ordination ceremonies for bishops), a king's ring symbolizes his marriage to the extension of his own body constituted by his realm, or body politic. The ring thus signifies the paradoxical relationship between the king's two bodies: "the realm is in the king, and the king in the realm; the subjects are incorporated in the king, and the king in the subjects."³⁷ A ring on the hand expresses the participation of each "limb" of the *corpus mysticum* or body politic in the fullness of the crowned head. This corporeal relation of part to whole found its precise justification in mystical geometry; thus, for example, S. Lorenz finds numerous passages in Nicolas of Cusa's geometrical writings that explain this special relation of hand to head: "In jedem Teile spiegelt sich das Ganze, der ganze Mensch spiegelt sich in der Hand, vollkommener im Haupte. Hierauf beruht die Vollkommenheit der Welt und jedes Einzelglieds in ihr."³⁸ The Pearl Maiden's most explicit metaphorical handling of the *corpus mysticum* draws on this traditional connection between hand and head, in the context of the marriage relation of "kyng & quene":

> Þy heued hatȝ nauþer greme ne gryste
> On arme oþer fynger þaȝ þou ber byȝe.
> So fare we alle wyth luf and lyste
> To kyng and quene by cortaysye. (465-68)

The special status of crown and ring within corporeal symbolism prepares us to examine the broader significance of the Pearl Maiden's clothing and adornment. That the poet attaches particular significance to this "container" is evident from the length of the description accompanying the maiden's first appearance in the poem. Lines 157-229 depict, in addition to the *coroune*, her *bleaunt*, *beau biys*, *cortel*, *poyned*, and *hemme* in minute detail, in each case emphasizing the *adubbement* with pearls, and climaxing with the central pearl on her breast; the link word "pyȝt" underscores the importance of the description. The special relation of clothing to the one clothed is emphasized in the implicit comparison of the whiteness of her face ("her fyre frount, / Hyr vysayge whyt as playn yuore," 177-78; "Her lere leke al hyr vmbegon. . . . Her ble more bla3t þen whalle3 bon," 210-12) with the glistening whiteness of her adornment ("Al blysnande whyt wat3 hir beau biys," 197; "Wyth whyte perle and non oþer gemme, / And bornyste quyte wat3 hyr uesture," 219-20). A later reference to Christ's garment recalls the maiden's adornment ("As praysed perle3 his wede3 wasse," 1112); Christ has clothed her in his image:

> 'O maskele3 perle in perle3 pure,
> Þat bere3,' quod I, 'þe perle of prys,
> Quo formed þe þy fayre fygure?
> Þat wro3t þy wede, he wat3 ful wys.' (745-48)[39]

The metaphor of clothing and adornment not only defines the relation of the maiden's body to her garments; it also helps us to see other "containers" in the poem as successive layers of clothing. Thus the link word *adubbement* in the second stanza group's passage of landscape imagery prepares for the presentation of the maiden's *adubbement* immediately following;[40] in particular, the dreamer compares the *rych rokke3* to textiles woven by men:[41]

> Where rych rokke3 wer to dyscreuen.
> Þe ly3t of hem my3t no mon leuen,
> Þe glemande glory þat of hem glent;
> For wern neuer webbe3 þat wy3e3 weuen
> Of half so dere adubbemente. (68-72)

Elsewhere the poet invokes the clothing metaphor again to describe the maiden's enclosure in the soil of her grave: "To þenke hir color so clad in clot. / O moul, þou marre3 a myry iuele" (22-23).

The shining whiteness that characterizes both the flesh and its clothing is a standard feature of the glorified appearance of believers after the resurrection. This tradition found its basis in Christ's Transfiguration, a type of the general resurrection to come. C. S. Lewis writes of the Transfiguration: "One rather curious detail is that this shining or whiteness affected His clothes as much as His body."[42] The doctrine finds its way, for example, into *St. Erkenwald*, where the miraculous preservation of both body and clothing causes the bishop to exclaim:

> Þi body may be enbawmyd, hit bashis me noght
> Þat hit thar ryve ne rote ne no ronke wormes;
> Bot þi coloure ne þi clothe, I know in no wise
> How hit my3t lye by monnes lore and last so longe. (261-64)[43]

Hence, in the language of St. Paul, believers must *induere* Christ in order to participate in the resurrection.[44] To obtain membership in the *corpus mysticum* we must "don" Christ's body, just as he accepted the mantle of mortal flesh during his earthly ministry. Origen uses the metaphor of vesture explicitly in this connection:

> Sicut "in novissimis diebus" verbum Dei ex Maria carne vestitum processit in hunc mundum . . . ita et cum per prophetas et legislatorem verbum Dei profertur ad homines, non absque competentibus profertur indumentis.[45]

Augustine draws on the same metaphor when he equates the church with an "amictus" or "stola."[46] Thus the Pearl Maiden's layers of *adubbement*, extending from her garb outwards into the landscape and the pearl-studded shape of the text itself, reflects the unity of body and clothing implicit in the metaphor of the Word made flesh.

The ways in which exegetes applied the theology of the Incarnation to allegorical interpretation of priestly vestments further clarifies the relation of the maiden to her clothing. John Burrow draws on this tradition to show how Gawain's armor in *Sir Gawain* reveals, via the "homo exterior" the "interioris hominis proprietates";[47] the prominence of an "endele3 rounde" (738) ornament both on the maiden's breast and on Gawain's chest and shield suggests a similar relation of garment to body in both poems.[48] Outer vesture indicates interior character on the basis of the incarnational structure of successive enclosure, whereby container and contained manifest symbolic equivalence. Thus, to cite another Middle English parallel, the armor worn by *Piers Plowman*'s "Christ-Knight" allegorizes both *humana natura* and *consummatus deus*; Raymond St.-Jacques finds the basis for this allegory in exegetical interpretations of priestly robes provided by Rupert of Deutz, Honorius Augustodunensis, Durandus, and others.[49] Holböck derives this symbolic doubleness of priestly vesture—its ability to point in two directions at once—from the *Doppelcharakter* of the consecrated host itself:

> Die Wahrheit, daß die hl. Messe das Opfer Christi und der Kirche zugleich ist, brachte man der mittelalterlichen Symbolik entsprechend häufig auch dadurch zum Ausdruck, daß man im Opferaltar bald die Kirche, bald wieder Christus versinnbildlicht sah. Oft betonte man auch, daß der Priester am Altar sowohl im Namen Christi als auch im Namen der Kirche opfert: Man sagte, der Priester am Altar sei Minister Christi capitis, er handle in persona Christi capitis. In schöner Weise brachte man diesen Doppelcharakter des zelebrierenden Priesters auch dadurch zum Ausdruck, daß man das Messgewand, mit dem der Priester am Altar bekleidet sein muß, gleichzeitig auf Christus und auf die Kirche deutete: "Casula est vestimentum Christi, quod est Ecclesia."[50]

Just as the eucharist represents the heavenly king's two bodies (the mortal body and its mystical extension in the church), so both priest and garment each partake of an equivalent double-layered symbolism. Each layer of symbolism points towards that which it encloses and, simultaneously, that by which it is enclosed. The Pearl Maiden and her clothing symbolize, individually, both Christ and the church; as a consequence, each also symbolizes the other. And her clothing resembles priestly garb in other respects as well: Sedlmayr cites the common practice, described in Suger of Denis, of decorating bishops' chasubles with "kreisrunde Ornamente."[51] Also relevant here is Conger's discussion of an old tradition in which priestly vestments represent a microcosm of creation.[52]

Within the manifest architectural resonances of the poem, the traditional allegorical equation of clothing and church building clarifies the relation of the maiden's garb to the heavenly city in which she dwells and the "building" of the text itself. Frye notes the connection between the white stone (*calculus candidus*, Apoc. 2:17) and the white raiment (*vestimenta alba*, Apoc. 3:5) of the New Jerusalem; each believer is a living stone in the architecture of the church, just as each, in an analogous metaphor, is a part of the warp and woof of the church conceived as a seamless garment.[53] Chartres Cathedral, dedicated to the tunic of the Virgin, both centers on and extends the structure of the tunic in much the same way that Otfrid, according to Haubrichs' study, extends the structure of the *tunica Christi* at a textual center.[54] The Pearl Maiden's appearance recalls the regally ornamented and crowned personifications of the church in late medieval iconography; one of the ornaments featured in such representations, a model of a church resting on the figure's arm, suggests the same equivalence of ornament/garb to body as found in *Pearl*.[55] Since at least the nineteenth century, studies of body-based architecture and literary space have shown a similar interest in the relation of clothing to architecture.[56] In medieval churches, the equivalence of raiment and building becomes especially evident in allegorical interpretations of liturgical cloths covering the altar. These sacred cloths symbolized both the shroud covering Christ's body at burial and the clothing worn by the church to please her bridegroom;[57] spatially, they comprised an intimate layer in the series of enclosures culminating in the "garment" of the outer church walls. The Pearl Maiden's clothing, worn by a girl who was both recently buried and recently made a bride of Christ, evidences the same relation to the heavenly city and textual suprastructure which constitute her outermost containers.[58]

The allegorical association between the pearl-shaped text and the maiden's pearl-studded clothing also finds its basis in longstanding exegetical tradition. Origen interprets Christ's clothing as "sermones et litterae evangeliorum quibus Jesus est indutus."[59] The luminous white robes of Christ at the Transfiguration, in particular, recall for Ambrose the way in which scripture's allegorical meaning is only apparent to those who view it with the eyes of faith:

> uestimenta uerbi sermones sunt scripturarum et quaedam intellectus indumenta diuini, quia sicut ipse Petro . . . in altera specie apparuit et uestitus eius albus refulsit, ita et oculis tuae mentis iam diuinarum lectionum sensus albescit.[60]

Thus the poet's description of the maiden's *adubbement*, with all of its resonances of the Transfiguration, describes the shape of the text as well. Medieval exegesis also links the seamless robe which soldiers cast lots for at the Crucifixion with the indivisibility of scripture,[61] and parallels the weaving of Joseph's coat with the process of biblical inspiration: "texuerunt digiti Dei omnem Scripturam; ... Fecit ergo Pater Filio suo tunicam polymitam varie pulchram, et pulchre variam."[62] Dante applies this same clothing metaphor to poetic fiction:

great embarrassment would come to one who, having written things in the dress of an image or coloring of words, and then, having been asked, would not be able to strip his words of such dress in order to give them their true meaning.⁶³

In *Pearl*, the interwoven patterning of the text is just one of several layers of "dress" that must be stripped away to uncover the nuclear meaning of the pearl symbol itself.⁶⁴

The next image of enclosure to be considered is the coffer or chest represented by the words *cofer*, *forser*, and *kyste* in the following speech by the maiden:

> That juel þenne in gemmeȝ gente
> Vered vp her vyse wyth yȝen graye,
> Set on hyr coroun of perle orient,
> And soberly after þenne con ho say:
> 'Sir, ȝe haf your tale mysetente,
> To say your perle is al awaye,
> Þat is in cofer so comly clente
> As in þis gardyn gracios gaye,
> Hereinne to lenge for euer and play,
> Þer mys nee mornyng com neuer nere.
> Her were a forser for þe, in faye,
> If þou were a gentyl jueler.
>
> 'But, jueler gente, if þou schal lose
> Þy ioy for a gemme þat þe watȝ lef,
> Me þynk þe put in a mad porpose,
> And busyeȝ þe aboute a raysoun bref;
> For þat þou lesteȝ watȝ bot a rose
> Þat flowred and fayled as kynde hyt gef.
> Now þurȝ kynde of þe kyste þat hyt con close
> To a perle of prys hit is put in pref.
> And þou hatȝ called þy wyrde a þef,
> Þat oȝt of noȝt hatȝ mad þe cler;
> Þou blameȝ þe bote of þy meschef,
> Þou art no kynde jueler.' (253-76)

Here the maiden rebukes the dreamer for the foolishness of considering his pearl lost and *al awaye*, when by virtue of her coffer she lives eternally, "Hereinne to lenge for euer and play." What he lost was only a *rose* which, "Þurȝ kynde of

Concentric Settings 115

þe kyste þat hyt con close," has acquired temporal permanence. Again we can turn to Kantorowicz for a better understanding of the coffer image within the theology of the body; the peculiar status of effigy-bearing coffins for late medieval French and English kings draws on an application of the doctrine of the king's two bodies relevant to the chest that is the pearl's coffin.[65] The coffin effigy, which played a crucial role in funeral ceremonies, represented the king's atemporal body, the body constituted by both the sum total of his subjects and of his ancestors and heirs on the throne; his transient, mortal body was contained within the intransient one. Thus, paradoxically, the body which was invisible during the king's life became, at death, visible, and vice versa:

> Wherever the circumstances were not to the contrary, the effigies were henceforth used at the burials of royalty: enclosed in the coffin of lead, which itself was encased in a casket of wood, there rested the corpse of the king, his mortal and normally visible—though now invisible—body natural; whereas his normally invisible body politic was on this occasion visibly displayed by the effigy in its pompous regalia: a *persona ficta*—the effigy—impersonating a *persona ficta*—the *Dignitas*.[66]

The paradox of the visible and invisible bodies is consistent with the speech immediately following this one (289-312), where the maiden rebukes the dreamer for only believing that she exists because he can see her. The contrast, in her speech about the various coffers, between the transience of the dreamer's lost *rose* and the permanence she has acquired by virtue of her new container, may be illuminated by Kantorowicz' concluding remarks on the tradition of coffin effigies:

> Our rapid digression on funerary ceremonial, effigies, and sepulchral monuments, though not directly related to the rites observed for English kings, has nevertheless yielded at least one new aspect of the problem of the "two Bodies"—the human background. Never perhaps, except in those "late Gothic" centuries, was the Western mind so keenly conscious of the discrepancy between the transience of the flesh and the immortal splendor of a Dignity which that flesh was supposed to represent.[67]

Like the medieval king's coffin, the pearl's coffin constitutes both an extension of her own body and a dramatization of the distinction between the visible and invisible, mortal and immortal bodies that all Christians share with their heavenly king. An integral part of the extensive series of enclosures depicted in the poem, the pearl's coffin is linked explicitly with the landscapes constituting the next highest level of containment both in this speech ("in cofer so comly clente / As in þis gardyn gracios gaye") and in the opening description of the *huyle* wherein the pearl is *spenned* (53).

Bachelard's long discussion of the coffer as a category of literary space, based on psychoanalytic notions of enclosure whose relevance we have seen elsewhere, also broadens our understanding of the coffer in *Pearl*.[68] As repositories for memory (memorable objects), coffers, like medieval funeral coffins, constitute a locus for the plenitude of time:

> Dans le coffre sont les choses inoubliables, inoubliables pour nous, mais inoubliables pour ceux auxquels nous donneront nos trésors. Le passé, le présent, un avenir sont là condensés. Et ainsi, le coffre est la mémoire de l'immémorial.[69]

Also like the royal coffins which emblemize the infinite expansiveness of the king's body through the bodies of past and future subjects, Bachelard finds an all-encompassing spatiality within the most intimate confines of the coffer:

> Et achevant la valorisation du contenu par la valorisation du contenant, Jean-Pierre Richard a cette dense formule: "Nous n'arrivons jamais au fond du coffret." Comment mieux dire l'infinité de la dimension intime? On ouvre le meuble et l'on découvre une demeure. Une maison est cachée dans un coffret.[70]

Because of the dense symbolic importance of its contents, Bachelard claims, we may say that a coffer contains the entire house that contains it; likewise, the consecrated host within a church's innermost enclosure encompasses the entire symbolism of the building itself. Reading our way through the layers of landscape, clothing, and coffer in *Pearl*, we find ourselves confronted with the outermost structure of the text itself in the contents of its most intimate space.[71]

Concentric Settings

The landscapes themselves, whose association with the other pearl enclosures I have already noted, call for more detailed examination at this point. Scholars generally agree in identifying three separate landscapes in the poem: the *erber grene* with which the poem opens and to which it returns at its conclusion, the pearl-studded land traversed by the jeweller throughout his dream, and the unattainable region across the stream where the jeweller sees both the Pearl Maiden and the New Jerusalem. Studies of these three loci normally explore either the transformation of landscape imagery and its relation to the central figure of the Pearl Maiden or, less frequently, parallels between landscape environments and the dreamer's own psychic transformation.[72] The shared assumption of such studies is the peculiar relation of landscape enclosure to enclosed figure, although it is rarely stated in those precise terms. The corporeal matrix presupposed by the present study provides a basis of unity both for more extensive treatment of the three landscapes' relation to each other and the figures contained by them, and for more thorough handling of the landscapes' relation to the pearl's other layers of enclosure. The natural world is, in Freudian terms, an inverted extension of the body.[73] Much like the knight of medieval romance, whose "prickynge" over the land leads to conquest both of the heroine's body and the kingdom which constitutes that body's extension, *Pearl*'s dreamer must come to terms with the maiden's pearly landscape setting as a prerequisite to "finding" the lost pearl itself. His progress through this most exterior layer of enclosure is, again, a movement in the direction of corporeal interiority, the search for a center. Thus some scholars have found that each *Pearl* landscape draws on and elaborates the imagery of the preceding ones; the further the dreamer goes, the more definitively he finds himself in the same place.[74] Each landscape points towards the plenitude of the Vineyard at the middle of the poem; the dreamer ends his journey in the same landscape where it began, re-enacting in his own experience the same relation of "first" and "last" outlined in the central parable.

A number of scholars have remarked on the seminal quality of the *erber grene*'s compact cluster of images. Petroff finds a similarity in this respect between *Pearl*'s opening landscape and the *selva oscura* at the beginning of Dante's *Commedia*:

> We know how much of the poem is compressed into the first stanza group. . . . The *selva oscura* and the *erber grene* exist not only as introductory landscapes in which one orients oneself to the topography of the poem; they are also containers for the seeds of the future landscapes in the poem.[75]

She describes this traditional relationship among landscapes in geometrical terms:

> the interrelationship of successive landscapes in each poem is not only linear, but circular and reciprocal. The first landscape contains the seeds of all the others. . . . In both poems we find that the opening landscape is not fully understandable until we see its final transformation in the last landscape of the poem.[76]

Bishop makes a similar observation, noting the analogous structure dictated by the various *Artes praedicandi*, in which

> the *thema*, enunciated at the beginning of the discourse, was the single root out of which the whole composition was to grow like a tree, branching out into digressions, distinctions, and correspondences.[77]

Kean and Piehler draw similar conclusions about the opening garden.[78] Other scholars see in the *erber grene* a figure for the church.[79]

In the light of the mystical geometry of center and edge, we should recognize in the *erber grene* a microcosmic structure already familiar to us from the opening book of the *Fairie Queen*, a structural *recapitulatio*. The symbolism of the entire *Pearl* poem is given compact expression in the garden at the text's periphery just as it will emerge again in the central Vineyard; both landscapes evoke the full spatiality of the church. In this respect *Pearl*'s opening imitates the microcosmic status of the portal façades of the Gothic cathedral; the dense symbolism of the portal, like the *erber grene*, adumbrates and encompasses the entire theological structure of both the central altar and the building as a whole.[80] The lesson which the dreamer must learn about the relationship among the poem's different landscapes is consistent with the Pearl Maiden's teaching about post-Incarnation spatiality. Like the Vineyard which constitutes the geometrical center of textual layers surrounding it, the *erber grene* provides an imagistic middlepoint for successive landscapes.

Concentric Settings   119

Just as the entire poem centers on the *corpus mysticum* of the Vineyard, so also the *erber grene* which recapitulates the space of the poem centers on the body of the Pearl Maiden in the *huyle* which is her grave. Petroff calls this mound "the visual center of the garden."[81] The phrase "clad in clot" shows the grave mound to be an important layer of enclosure in its own right, linked with other enclosures via the clothing metaphor.[82] The *huyle* bears a clear figural relationship to the *hil* (976, 979) on which the New Jerusalem appears in the poem's concluding vision. The poet's paraphrase of Ps. 23:3 in line 678, "Lorde, quo schal klymbe þy hy3 hylle, / Oþer rest wythinne þy holy place?" provides a scriptural basis for the two hills: exegetes link the *mons* of the scriptural verse with the church, paradise, and Mt. Sinai or Zion.[83] Thus medieval tradition identifying Mt. Zion as the center of the universe is incorporated into the structure of spatial plenitude in *Pearl*.[84] After rashly attempting to reach the *hil* on which the heavenly city is pictured in his final vision, the dreamer is forced to return to the *huyle* on which he began (1205). The geometry of grace requires each believer to discover the spiritual center within himself, and the decentralization of Christian space makes every point of the universe a potential midpoint; the dreamer must learn how to find his center in the initial *spot*. Both the *huyle* where the pearl is buried and the mountain bearing the pearl's eternal home are the mountain of which Augustine writes: "Ipse est mons qui ex parvo lapide venit, et totum orbem crescendo implevit. In illo aedificatur Ecclesia quae abscondi non potest."[85] Both hills take their origin from the *parvus lapis* contained within them.[86]

That the *erber grene* description centers firmly on the body of the maiden is underscored by its unmistakable reference to the resurrection:

> Þat spot of spyse3 mot nede3 sprede,
> Þer such ryche3 to rot is runne;
> Blome3 blayke and blwe and rede
> Þer schyne3 ful schyr agayn þe sunne.
> Flor and fryte may not be fede
> Þer hit doun drof in molde3 dunne;
> For vch gresse mot grow of grayne3 dede;
> No whete were elle3 to wone3 wonne.
> Of goud vche goude is ay bygonne;
> So semly a sede mo3t fayly not,

> Þat spryngande spyceȝ vp ne sponne
> Of þat precios perle wythouten spotte. (25-36)

The pearl is a *sede* whose death and rebirth is consistent with the poem's larger pattern of harvest and plant imagery. The flowers that "schyneȝ ful schyr agayn þe sunne" recall the luminosity of the glorified body at resurrection. Commentators find a scriptural basis for this resurrection imagery in John 12:24 and 1 Cor. 15:34-38.[87] Petroff observes that the plants mentioned "all suggest mortality" and "are noted for cleansing, healing, masking the odor of decay"; she, with others, finds allusion in this opening description to the Feast of the Assumption of the Blessed Virgin (August 15), the celebration of Mary's bodily ascension into heaven.[88]

Within the geometrical plenitude of the poem, the link word *spot*, designating the central location of the maiden's body, underscores the microcosmic relation of the *erber grene* to the entire textual structure, which itself contains a *poynt* at the middle. The pearl that is *wythouten spot* is, via deliberate punning, both "without flaw" and "incapable of spatial limitation."[89] The dreamer errs in mourning his pearl's confinement to a single location; her body extends itself in space through a multiplicity of enclosures. To understand the geometry of grace, he himself must leave that *spot* ("Fro spot my spyryt þer sprang in space," 61), yet at the poem's other "edge" he returns to it. Just as the first landscape displays in kernel form the total imagery of the other two, so also the pearl buried in the initial *spot* contains the space of the entire pearl-shaped text that follows. Like the point at the core of the universe's many concentric circles, the *erber grene*'s *spot* signifies both the boundless circumference and infinite constriction of incarnational space, qualities that it shares with the *poynt* at the poem's center. The moon, by comparison, is *spotty* (1070); its physical imperfection precludes participation in the spatial plenitude of the pearl.[90]

The poem's second landscape (the first dream landscape) extends and elaborates the imagery of the *erber grene*, continuing to evidence that first landscape's special relation of figure to ground. The pearly gravel under the dreamer's feet and the striking luminosity of the vegetation surrounding him prepare for the first appearance of the Pearl Maiden herself. Piehler observes here that every feature of the *erber grene* has been "raised to a state of visionary transformation."[91] Itself an extension of the initial geometry of the *spot*, the first dream landscape is "ever-extending rather than enclosed," a quality that Petroff contrasts with the *hortus conclusus* with which the poem begins: "The openness and expansiveness and all-inclusiveness of the place suggest the need (and possibility) for a similar spiritual expansion within the narrator."[92] This new landscape's imagistic expansiveness parallels the Pearl Maiden's stern teaching at this point: she urges the dreamer beyond an over-literal interpretation of both scripture and landscape to a broader allegorical understanding of what he sees and hears.[93]

The dreamer's vision culminates in his description of the New Jerusalem, the final landscape of the poem; Petroff calls it "the perfection of all the earlier landscapes, and the standard by which they should be judged."[94] Like the *erber grene* at the beginning and the Vineyard of the central parable, this last landscape, again, evokes the plenitude of the poem's time and space via its relation to the body. Frye writes: "The real apocalypse comes, not with the vision of a city or kingdom, which would still be external, but with the identification of the city and kingdom with one's own body."[95] This vision of the heavenly city is granted in response to the dreamer's statement: "As ȝe ar maskeleȝ vnder mone, / Your woneȝ schulde be wythouten mote" (923-24).[96] The city must be spotless as a consequence of the unblemished purity of the bodies which inhabit it; the dreamer's vision of that city is a final lesson about the nature of the pearl itself, the concluding stage of a learning process that has brought him to terms with a long series of settings for that gem. The New Jerusalem is the triumphal setting for the glorified, resurrected body—"þe borȝ þat we to pres / Fro þat oure flesch be layd to rote" (957-58)—and is itself the body of Christ, the temple of the New Covenant.

Thus the boundary between inside and outside, inhabitant and habitation, is blurred. The parallels between the first description of the Pearl Maiden and the dreamer's vision of the heavenly city are striking. The dreamer's first glimpse of both provokes a similar state of dazed awe: "I stod as hende as hawk in halle" (184); "I stod as stylle as dased quayle" (1085). The maiden who "Ryseȝ up" (191) anticipates the moon that "con rys" (1093) in the final landscape. The "fygure" (170, 1086) of both maiden and city is depicted as "ryally" arrayed

(191, 193, 986), with emphasis on their shining white color and the effect of both on the dreamer's heart.[97] Just as the New Jerusalem is a dwelling constructed of multiple inner dwellings ("woneȝ wythinne," 1027), it is likewise a body comprised of the multiple, microcosmic bodies in the procession of maidens within it. Its dimensions, a series of squares within squares (and cubes within cubes), parallel the dimensions of its inhabitants: each maiden, herself wearing a sphere on her breast, is a sphere within the larger sphere of the mystical body.[98] The number of maidens (144,000, lines 869-70), like the dimensions of the city, is a product of twelves. Brown describes the peculiar corporeality of the Apocalypse thus:

> All flesh shall see it together. Apocalypse is the dissolution of the group as numerical series, as in representative democracy, and its replacement by the group as fusion, as communion. As in totemism, we participate in each other as we participate in the object.[99]

The final vision fuses enclosure and enclosed, eradicating the boundaries between body and building.[100]

Traditional personifications of the New Jerusalem as the bride of Christ, as in Hildegard's hymn, "O Jerusalem," support this interpretation of *Pearl*'s heavenly city as an extension of the Pearl Maiden's body. Details from Hildegard's text parallel the maiden's description: she portrays the city as a *vas* bearing a crown, regally adorned with precious stones (*vivis lapidibus*), and containing no spot of imperfection (*nullam maculam*). Like the Pearl Maiden, the New Jerusalem is linked with childhood (*O beata pueritia*), and associated with both the images of the mountain (*sicut nec mons valli celatur*) and field (*flos campi*).[101]

In chapter one I discussed the medieval understanding of the New Jerusalem (and of the earthly paradise) as the heart or navel of the universe.[102] Like the relation of center to circle in medieval geometry, the heavenly city is a corporeal and universal midpoint which, paradoxically, is capable of containing all space. Just as the pun on *wythouten spot* signifies both the unblemished purity and geometric expansiveness of the maiden's body, *wythouten mote* designates both the city's immaculateness and its spatial boundlessness.[103] The New Jerusalem need contain no church, because Christ's body itself has taken over this function:

> Kyrk þerinne watȝ non ȝete,
> Chapel ne temple þat euer watȝ set;
> Þe Almyȝty watȝ her mynster mete . . . (1061-63)

Frye writes: "there is no temple in the New Jerusalem, as the body of Christ has replaced it."[104] Similarly, the heavenly city requires no other light source besides the body of Christ of which it constitutes an architectural extension; the "lombe" is its only lamp:

> Of sunne ne mone had þay no nede;
> Þe self God watȝ her lombe-lyȝt,
> Þe Lombe her lantyrne, wythouten drede;
> Þurȝ hym blysned þe borȝ al bryȝt. (1045-48)

Relevant here is the pseudo-Aristotelian doctrine of the *lux primaria* or *infinita* which illuminates the entire orb of the universe from a geometric center outside of space and time.[105] Paré has shown how this notion of a universal light source manifests itself in Albertus Magnus' teachings on the microcosm, and Frye writes of the "transparent and luminous" quality of the Apocalypse vision, characterized by "its annihilating of space and time as we know them, . . . the disappearance of shadows . . . in a world where everything shines by its own light."[106] The "lombe-lyȝt" thus shines not only on the New Jerusalem; it is also the center and source of light for the entire poem. Johnson writes:

> The other "lights" the dreamer encounters in the visionary landscape are similar, both in appearance and in effect, because each reflects the "lombe-lyȝt," also the source of heaven's light. Thus, the various things he sees that cast light are alike because each borrows its light from God.[107]

The dreamer's quest is a search for a center. His rash attempt to cross the stream at the poem's end dramatizes his inability to distinguish the heavenly Jerusalem from its earthly counterpart, the consequence of confusing the Old Law with the New Law (919-48). His final return to the initial *spot* teaches him an all-important lesson about the decentralized spatiality of grace. There is no church in the New Jerusalem; rather, each believer's body becomes a new geographic center when it transforms itself into a temple for the indwelling Spirit. Salvation is offered to the living within the confines of their own bodies, in any earthly *spot* they may happen to occupy. The heavenly city is only accessible to the righteous dead: "Þy corse in clot mot calder keue" (320). The poem's concluding eucharistic reference underscores the dreamer's new sense of the centrality of his own body; by partaking of Christ's flesh, he encloses the New Jerusalem within the most intimate space of his corporeal shell.[108]

The spatial and temporal compactness of this concluding landscape, like that of the *erber grene* and the Vineyard, reaches outwards to encompass the structure of the entire poem; the poet represents the whole text at its end, as at both its beginning and center. Most obvious, of course, is the numerological similarity of city and text: just as the heavenly city is built on twelve foundations (993), with twelve gates (1035) and twelve square furlongs in each of its subsections (1030), so too the poem organizes itself into twelve-line stanzas.[109] *Pearl*'s structure thus draws on a longstanding tradition of microcosmic numerical composition; Haubrichs finds, for example, that Otfrid bases the numerology of his *Liber Evangeliorum* on the architectural prescriptions of the same scriptural source.[110] Both Otfrid and the *Pearl*-Poet, like many medieval builders, imitate in the structure of their works one of scripture's most famous architectural exemplars.[111]

Notes

1. Cf. the similar designation of a center in 835: "Inmydeȝ þe trone, þere saynteȝ sete."
2. *Pearl: A Study in Spiritual Dryness* (New York: Appleton, 1925; New York: Phaeton, 1968) 172-73.
3. *The Visionary Landscape: A Study in Medieval Allegory* (London: Arnold, 1976) 151.
4. Poulet xiii, discussing the "punto solo" in Dante, *Par.* 33.94. Cf. Origen's notion that the Passion repeats itself at the "breast" of the circles of cyclical time (Puech, 71-72).
5. Ohly, "Geburt" 293; Eliade, *Images et Symboles* 178-98.
6. These lines derive particular significance from their occurrence in the very first stanza group where the Pearl Maiden speaks, and from the surrounding lines' general preoccupation with the nature of speech. Henry Rupp finds in "geste" a pun on the meanings "guest" and "story, tale"—further evidence for the allegorical equivalence of the maiden's body and the *Pearl* text. "Word-Play in *Pearl*, 277-78," *Modern Language Notes* 70 (1955): 558-59.
7. These are the poem's only two explicit references to the number five.
8. Sauer 132.
9. Scharl 11-12, 22-26.
10. *Pearl in Its Setting* 61; cf. his discussion of how the Pearl Maiden's description draws on the traditional livery, etc., of the newly baptized (113-21).
11. Scarry describes faith as the moment "when the object created is in fact described as though it instead created you. It ceases to be the 'offspring' of the human being and becomes the thing from which the human being himself sprung forth" (*Body in Pain* 205). Cf. Curtius 132-33 on the tradition of the book as child of the author. I will add no further commentary on the old allegory vs. elegy debate here. The studies of figural typology by Auerbach and Salter cited earlier have made abundantly clear, I believe, how the pearl can signify both a literal daughter and any number of allegorical meanings.
12. The key phrase "to clanly close" itself effects a kind of syntactic enclosure, bracketing the adverb between the two components of an infinitive. Hillmann's gloss suggests that the phrase "in vche araye" (5) may also refer to a variety of potential settings for the pearl. Cf. line 909: "Now, hynde, þat sympelnesse coneȝ enclose."
13. An exception is Bishop's excellent study of the *corona* and *garlande gay*. "The Significance of the *Garlande Gay* in the Allegory of *Pearl*," *Review of English Studies* ns 8 (1957): 12-21.
14. Cf. lines 947-48: "And as hys flok is wythouten flake, / So is hys mote wythouten moote."
15. Gregory the Great, *Moralia in Job* (*PL* 76.693).
16. "Symbolisme communautaire" 17.
17. *Die Graalslegende in psychologischer Sicht*, Studien aus dem C. G. Jung-Institut Zürich 12 (Zürich: Rascher, 1960) 149; cf. 147-48, 150, 184-85.
18. McLuhan argues that modern technological culture has returned to a medieval conception of the relation between "inner" and "outer" (254).

19. "Geburt der Perle" 304.
20. Ohly, "Geburt der Perle" 310.
21. Haubrichs 87-88 and passim.
22. See "La coquille," *Poétique de l'espace* 105-29, esp. 114-18. Cf. Brown, *Love's Body* 44-45, where sleep is described as a retreat into the cosmic shell; the dreamer's sleep in *Pearl* creates an inner shell structure within the frame of action occurring in the *erber grene* at the poem's beginning and end.
23. "The Significance of the '*Garlande Gay*' in the Allegory of *Pearl*," cited above.
24. Sedlmayr 139.
25. In the thirty-fourth homily of *Opus Imperfectum in Matth.* (*PG* 56.822): "Sicut enim in corona, cum sit rotunda, nihil invenies quod videatur esse initium aut finis: sic inter sanctos, quantum ad tempus in illo saeculo, nemo novissimus dicitur, nemo primus." Cited in Borroff 164-65n.
26. The recapitulatory relation of head to body may underly the similarity between these statements about the group of pearl maidens: "Bot vchon enle we wolde were fyf" (849) and "Bot vchon fayn of oþerez hafyng, / And wolde her corounez wern worþe þo fyue" (450-51).
27. Sedlmayr 89.
28. "The Crown as Fiction," *The King's Two Bodies* 336-83.
29. For "corona" as the familiar designation for round halos, see also Gerhart B. Ladner, "The So-called Square Nimbus," *Mediaeval Studies* 3 (1941): 20.
30. "All that seems even more true with regard to Jerusalem, although transcendental Jerusalem means timeless Eternity rather than continuity within Time. The original city of Christ, Jerusalem's material body, had been destroyed by Titus; Aelia Capitolina, Hadrian's new foundation on the ruins of David's city, was void of metaphysis. Yet, 'Jerusalem haloed' might descend to earth at any moment, if for no longer than the festal hour in which a new shrine was consecrated, and then bestow the lustre of Eternity on any insignificant town or even on the village church. Hence, the 'halo' always indicated, in some way or another, a change of the nature of Time. It signified that the haloed individual, person or place, participated also in a category of 'Time' which was different from the one determining the natural life on earth as the mediaeval mind understood it. The halo, it is true, did not remove its bearer into the *aeternitas Dei* which is without continuity because in it all times, past and future, are present. Yet, the halo removed its bearer too: removed him, scholastically speaking, from *tempus* to *aevum*, from Time to Sempiternity, at any rate, to some continuum of time without end: the haloed person, or rather the person *qua* halo, his *ordo*, 'never died'" (Kantorowicz 83-84; cf. 337-38).
31. "There was a visible, material, exterior gold circle or diadem with which the Prince was vested and adorned at his coronation; and there was an invisible and immaterial Crown—encompassing all the royal rights and privileges indispensable for the government of the body politic—which was perpetual and descended either from God directly or by the dynastic right of inheritance" (Kantorowicz 337; cf. 340-42).
32. Kantorowicz 363-64. Cf. 362-63: "Hence, the preservation of the *status coronae* amounted to preserving the *status regni*. The Crown, therefore, was not something apart from the body politic and its individually changing constituents. This was pointed out explicitly two generations later, in 1337, when the Bishop of Exeter, John of Grandisson, declared that 'the substance of the nature of the Crown is found chiefly in the person of the king as head and of the peers as members.' The composite character and corporate aspect of the Crown could not have been expressed more poignantly than by linking it to the old image of head and limbs describing the corpus politicum or mysticum of the realm." Also cf. 336.
33. The *corona* was, for example, equated with the *ecclesia* in some respects (Kantorowicz 378).

34. Kantorowicz places the tradition of the "crowning" of the newly baptized within the broader double symbolism of the crown discussed here (490-95); Bishop has already studied the influence of baptismal crowns on *Pearl* in Pearl *in Its Setting* 113-18.

35. Kantorowicz 387-92.

36. The poet nowhere explicitly links the *by3e* with the pearl, but a ring is an obvious setting for precious stones, and its circular shape integrates it into the cluster of other round settings in the poem.

37. Kantorowicz 223; cf. 212, 221-22.

38. "Das Unendliche bei Nicolaus von Kues," *Philosophisches Jahrbuch* 40 (1927): 61-62. Lorenz shows how this relation holds, in Nicolas of Cusa, as part of the broader microcosmic structure of the universe, specifically including the relation of sun and moon to the rest of creation. The microcosmic symbolism of sun and moon also plays an important part in the spatiality of *Pearl*.

39. Cf. ll. 765-68:

> He gef me my3t and als bewté;
> In hys blod he wesch my wede on dese,
> And coronde clene in vergynté,
> And py3t me in perle3 maskelle3.

40. The word *dubbed* describes her clothing in l. 202.

41. Other details in this stanza group prepare for the shining, white appearance of the maiden as well: "crystal klyffe3 so cler of kynde" (74), "Holtewode3 bry3t" (75), "As bornyst syluer þe lef" (77), "glem of glode3" (79), "schymeryng schene ful schrylle þay schynde" (80), including an explicit comparison of gravel to "precious perle3 of oryente" (82).

42. *Miracles: A Preliminary Study* (1947; London: Collins, 1974) 156.

43. *St. Erkenwald: A Middle English Poem*, ed. Henry L. Savage (1926; Hamden, CT: Archon, 1972).

44. See Rom. 13:14, 2 Cor. 5:2, Eph. 4:22-24, Col. 3:12.

45. *In Lev.*, hom. 1.1 (GCS 6.280), cited in Spitz 17.

46. "Stola porro ejus quam lavat in vino, id est, mundat a peccatis in sanguine suo, cujus sanguinis sacramentum baptizati sciunt, unde et adjungit, *Et in sanguine uvae amictum suum*, quid est nisi Ecclesia?" *De civ. Dei* 16.41 (*PL* 41.520). Cf. Brown, *Love's Body* 74.

47. *A Reading of Sir Gawain and the Green Knight* (London: Routledge, 1956) 38-39.

48. Of the pentangle in *Sir Gawain*, the poet writes: "And ayquere hit is endelez; and Englych hit callen / Oueral, as I here, þe endelez knot" (629-30). All *Sir Gawain* citations are from Norman Davis' revision of the Tolkein and Gordon edition (Oxford: Clarendon, 1967). The parallels between the monadic symbols of pearl and pentangle and the respective poems' corporeal, geometric and thematic structures are, in fact, quite extensive; I have reserved detailed consideration of this parallel for chapter eight.

49. "Langland's Christ-Knight and the Liturgy," *Revue de l'Université d'Ottawa* 37 (1967): 154-57.

50. Holböck 226-27. He quotes Rupert of Deutz (PL 170, 22B).

51. Sedlmayr 39.

52. Conger 18.

53. *The Great Code* 157-58.

54. Haubrichs 240-43.

55. See Sauer 247-49.

56. Otto Semperer, the great nineteenth-century German theorist, stresses the etymological link between *Gewand* and *Wand*, as discussed by Dolf Sternberger, *Panorama oder Ansichten vom 19. Jahrhundert*, 2nd ed., Suhrkamp Taschenbücher 179 (Frankfurt: Suhrkamp, 1974) 159-61. André Lefèrre writes in *Les merveilles de l'architecture* (1880), "The individual dwells as he is

clothed"; quoted in Joseph Rykwert, *On Adam's House in Paradise: The Idea of the Primitive Hut in Architectural History* (New York: Museum of Modern Art, 1972) 19. More recently, Bachelard writes of the "maison-vêtement" (101).

57. See Sauer 167-74; Holböck 2; and, in general, Braun, "Die Altarbekleidung," *Altar* 9-132. The cloth construction of the tabernacle, of course, provides one traditional basis for the equivalence of church and garment; see Scarry *Body in Pain* 211-12.

58. We have already noticed the similar symbolism of the altar cloth (G. *Korporale*). Honorius Augustodunensis explains that, when folded, the altar cloth has neither beginning nor end; thus it shares the qualities of the body it encloses. *Gemma animae* ch. 1.

59. *In Matth.* 12.38 (GCS 10.154); Spitz discusses this citation, along with some of those listed below, under the heading "Kleid," 40ff. Spitz finds a continuity between this clothing metaphor and exegetical understanding of the veils and curtains around the altar in the temple, providing a link with the architectural dimension of the clothing metaphor that we have just noticed.

60. *In Luc.* 7.13 (*Corpus christianorum: series latina* 14.219).

61. See Alanus de Insulis, *Distinctiones* (PL 210.1000).

62. Rupert of Deutz, *In Gen.* 8.20 (PL 167.507).

63. *La Vita nuova* 25, trans. Mark Musa (1957; Bloomington: Indiana UP, 1962) 55. For further discussion of the metaphor of the book as garment, see Curtius 316.

64. My interpretation of the role of the clothing metaphor in *Pearl* does not necessarily contradict Bishop's theory; he finds parallels in traditional baptismal garb for the maiden's robe and crown (Pearl *in Its Setting* 113-21). By choosing to disregard the "other ornamental details" (114) of her raiment, however, he underplays the crucial symbolic centrality of the pearl on her breast, and blurs the connection between the many pearls on her clothing and the pearly landscape and textual structure that constitute outer layers of clothing. It is surely an oversimplification to claim that "the basis of the maiden's apparel consists of nothing other than the ceremonial dress of the newly baptized" (114).

65. O. D. Macrae-Gibson observes that *kyste* and *cofer* may signify "coffin" in addition to their other meanings. "*Pearl*: The Link-Words and the Thematic Structure." *Neophilologus* 52 (1968); rpt. in Conley 203-19, see esp. 207. Cf. Herbert Pilch: "Figuratively, the coffin ennobles the rose and makes it a precious pearl." "The Middle English *Pearl*: Its Relation to the *Roman de la Rose*," trans. Heide Hyprath, in Conley 170. Trans. of "Das mittelenglische *Perlengedicht*: Sein Verhältnis zum *Rosenroman*," *Neuphilologische Mitteilungen* 65 (1964): 427-46.

66. Kantorowicz 137; his discussion of funeral effigies begins on 419.

67. Kantorowicz 436.

68. "Le tiroir. Les coffres et les armoires," *Poétique de l'espace* 79-91.

69. Bachelard 88.

70. Bachelard 89. Cf. on 88:

Nous étuderions dans un chapitre ultérieur la dialectique du dedans et du dehors. Mais au moment où le coffre s'ouvre, plus de dialectique. . . . Le dehors ne signifie plus rien. Et même, suprême paradoxe, les dimensions du volume n'ont plus de sens parce qu'une dimension vient de s'ouvrir: la dimension d'intimité.

Pour quelqu'un qui valorise bien, pour quelqu'un qui se met dans la perspective des valeurs d'intimité, cette dimension peut être infinie.

71. Bachelard writes: "Dans un chapitre antérieur, nous déclarions qu'il y a un sens à dire qu'on lit une maison, qu'on lit une chambre. On pourrait dire de même que des écrivains nous donnent à lire leur coffret" (86).

72. Discussions of the dreamer's relation to *Pearl* landscapes include John Finlayson, "*Pearl*: Landscape and Vision," *Studies in Philology* 71 (1974): 314-43; Madaleva 106-09; Petroff, "Landscape in *Pearl*," 182, 187; Spearing, *The Gawain Poet* 140-41. Other treatments of the

poem's landscapes can be found in Gatta, Kean, W. Johnson, and Petroff, as well as Paul Piehler, "*Pearl*," *The Visionary Landscape: A Study in Medieval Allegory* (London: Arnold, 1971) 144-62. See also Louise Dunlap, "Vegetation Puns in *Pearl*," *Mediaevalia* 3 (1977): 173-88.

73. See Brown, *Love's Body* 36-37, 50.

74. See Kean 204-05 for verbal parallels in descriptions of the three landscapes. The presence of light and the color white in all three landscapes receives attention by Louis Blenkner, "The Pattern of Traditional Images in *Pearl*," *Studies in Philology* 68 (1971): 31, and Petroff, "Landscape in *Pearl*" 185. Cf. the intricate pattern of parallels between corresponding cantos in the three major landscapes of the *Divina Commedia*; Petroff notes in "Psychological Landscapes" 295 that the relation between landscapes and human figures' psychic states in *Pearl* resembles that in Dante's work.

75. "Psychological Landscape" 306. She also remarks on the possible influence of the Garden of Deduit in the *Roman de la Rose* (297); I will discuss the seminal quality of the imagery in the latter garden in a later study. Cf. Singleton, *Commedia: Elements of Structure* 7.

76. "Psychological Landscape" 368-69.

77. Pearl *in Its Setting* 35.

78. Kean 53; Piehler 145-49.

79. Wood 14; Hamilton 47.

80. In addition to chapter two's analysis of portal façades, see especially Bloomer and Moore 47-48, and Sauer 310-12.

81. "Psychological Landscape" 315.

82. The phrase "clad in clot" has figured prominently in the old allegory vs. elegy controversy, but by now scholars have generally recognized in it a reference to human burial, particularly in the light of the attendant imagery of resurrection. For an extended discussion of similar expressions elsewhere in Middle English literature, see Wilson 124-25.

83. See Hamilton 48-50; Johnson 200-02. Similarly, the *colle* Dante encounters at the beginning of the *Inferno* (1.13) prefigures Mount Purgatory; Carol Kaske has shown traditional resonances of Mt. Sinai in Mount Purgatory. "Mount Sinai and Dante's Mount Purgatory," *Dante Studies* 89 (1971): 1-18.

84. In addition to the discussion in chapter one, see especially Sanchis 11ff.; Sedlmayr 99-100; Eliade, *Das Heilige und das Profane* 23-24.

85. *In dedicat. Eccles.* 3, *Sermo* 338 (*PL* 38.1478). Augustine's statement draws on the theology of the cornerstone, whose importance to the poem will be explored in a later study.

86. No one has yet suggested the influence of the Celtic "green mound" on the *huyle* in *Pearl*'s *erber grene*; in the light of its prominent appearance as the Green Castle in *Sir Gawain*, some such influence is at least a possibility. The green mound acted as a geographic point of contact with the Celtic otherworld, the kingdom of the fairies, and thus a locus of transition analogous to the various geographic centers in Christian mythology. As such, it is an appropriate place for the jeweller's entry into a supernatural dream world. Cf. Eliade, *Das Heilige und das Profane* 22-23.

87. See Bishop, Pearl *in Its Setting* 19; Petroff, "Landscape in *Pearl*" 185; Hamilton 46; Wilson 13-14.

88. "Landscape in *Pearl*" 181, 184.

89. For further analysis of this pun, see Johnson, *The Voice of the Gawain Poet* 169-70, 194; Macrae-Gibson 204-05; John C. McGalliard, "Links, Language, and Style in *The Pearl*," *Studies in Language, Literature, and Culture of the Middle Ages and Later: Studies in Honor of Rudolph Willard*, ed. E. Bagby Atwood and Archibald A. Hill (Austin: U of Texas P, 1969) 282-83.

90. In addition to chapter one's explanation of the geometry of concentric spheres around a central point, see especially Mahnke 148; Lorenz 69, 73; Peck 66ff. Bachelard makes a relevant

literary application on 63; Crane writes of "spots of Time" in *Sir Gawain* in "Four Levels of Time in *Sir Gawain and the Green Knight*," *Annuale Medievale* 10 (1969): 65-80.

91. Piehler 147.
92. "Landscape in *Pearl*" 187.
93. See Petroff "Landscape in *Pearl*" 188-90.
94. "Landscape in *Pearl*" 190.
95. *Fearful Symmetry: A Study of William Blake* (Princeton: Princeton UP, 1947) 431.
96. Cf. l. 904.
97. See multiple references in stanza groups 3 and 18.
98. The "new song" which the maidens sing (879-82) plays a role in microcosmic tradition; Clement of Alexandria argues that this new song brings harmony both to the macrocosm and to the little universe which is every human being. See Conger 30.
99. *Love's Body* 255.
100. Cf. Bloomer and Moore 105.
101. See the edition of this hymn by Pudentiana Barth et al., *Lieder* (Salzburg: Müller, 1969). The hymn concludes with a reference to servants (*famulantes*) in that *habitatio* that is similar to the *homly hyne* reference at the end of *Pearl*.
102. In this connection, see especially: Bruno Nardi, "Il Mito dell' Eden," *Saggi di filosofia dantesca*, Biblioteca pedagogica antica e moderna italiana e straniere 57 (Milano: Società anonima Dante Alighieri, 1930) 359; Eliade, *Das Heilige und das Profane* 24, 27.
103. Cf. Macrae-Gibson 215-16; Johnson 45; W. A. Davenport, *The Art of the Gawain-Poet* (London: Athalone, 1978) 46-47.
104. *The Great Code* 157. Cf. Sanchis 9.
105. See Mahnke 202.
106. Paré 114; Frye, *The Great Code* 167-68.
107. Johnson 202-03.
108. For discussion of the Christian pilgrimage towards a "center" and the decentralized geometry of Christian space, see Idiart 279-82. Cf. Lorenz 73-74.
109. Also the trees depicted in the same vision bear "twelue fryte$_3$ of lyf" twelve times a year (1078-79).
110. See "Die Maße der Gottesstadt als harmonisches Leitbild der Gesamtstruktur des 'Liber evangeliorum,'" 348ff; cf. 248.
111. Rykwert examines this practice in connection with the medieval notion of the body as a microcosm (118-23). The New Jerusalem description also parallels the structure of the *Pearl* text via the arrangement of its pearly gates; I will discuss this point in the context of the poem's broader preoccupation with doors and gates in a later study's treatment of the poem's "architecture."

Chapter Seven

THE SPATIALITY OF THE HEART IN *PEARL*

I have discussed how body-based conceptions of centrality have informed the poet's depiction of the Pearl Maiden, the structure of the text itself, and the three landscapes featured in the poem. The next step of my argument brings us back to the center of all of these enclosures again, to the pearl at the center of the Pearl Maiden's breast. I propose that the placement of this pearl, corresponding with the location of the human heart, works together with numerous other textual references to the heart to endow the poem with a distinctively heart-centered spatiality. My first chapter has already offered a brief outline of the heart's role as one of the multiple centers of both body and universe; as men find their midpoint in their heart, so too hell constitutes the *cor terrae*. Here I intend to expand on that initial discussion, drawing on a broad range of sources to demonstrate how closely all notions of corporeal centeredness rely on that most indispensable of organs. The present chapter will entail lengthy and detailed exposition because the issue at hand is crucial to my interpretation of *Sir Gawain* and *Patience*, and because I intend it also as a general introduction to how the theology of the heart can govern medieval aesthetic structure. If a poetics of the Incarnation may endow texts with corporeal spatiality, then we are justified in looking for textual hearts.

I believe that microcosmic spatiality governs many medieval texts, and that often the spatiality of the heart plays a key role in these structures. But tracing out such structures depends largely on comparisons with similar structures. *Pearl* does not contain an elaborate set of explicit references to the spatiality of the heart, though it contains some; in the light of the previous chapters' analysis, however, I believe we can recognize important heart-based spatial patterns. The discussions of other *Pearl*-Poet texts which follow should then reinforce our sense of such patterns.

A commonplace in the history of man's self-perception is the observation that man's center has migrated, since the Renaissance, from the heart to the head. A vast and growing volume of recent scholarship on the theology of the heart (a concomitant, perhaps, of increasing interest in the mystical body) has now established beyond any doubt the popularity attained by the Cult of the Sacred Heart in Western Europe by the eleventh century. This cult, enthusiastically propagated by such major writers as Hugh of St. Victor and by the Franciscans, grew to exert a major influence on popular devotion in England, France, Italy, Germany, and Spain by the end of the thirteenth century.[1] Not confined to devotional literature, the cult soon made a lasting impact on courtly poetry as well.[2] With time, devotion to the fleshly heart of Christ transformed itself into a reverence for the growing number of theological virtues (above all, love) associated with the Sacred Heart. By the High Middle Ages, the heart as symbol had acquired a devotional status equal to or exceeding Christ's physical heart itself; the heart came to be regarded as a *summa*, an emblematic condensation of the best that Christianity had to offer.[3]

References to the heart in *Pearl* are linked most explicitly with the tradition of the heart as a fountain: through the wound in Christ's side, his heart poured forth the water and blood of baptism, simultaneously creating the four rivers of paradise. This liquid effusion constituted the birth of the church, the figural coordinate of Eve's birth from Adam's side; the heart, as we have seen, shares the generative function of the womb.[4] The poet's description of this central event mentions the heart explicitly:

> Bot a wounde ful wyde and weete con wyse
> Anende hys hert, þurȝ hyde torente.
> Of his quyte syde his blod outsprent. (1135-37)

The *welle* issuing from that wound, he stresses, is baptism (649-53). Further, the dreamer describes his own heart as a *welle* in a moment of remorse early in the poem: "My herte watȝ al wyth mysse remorde, / As wallande water gotȝ out of welle" (364-5). Elsewhere, the heart is usually alluded to at moments of especially strong emotion, as in the dreamer's reaction to the first dream landscape (128, 135). The dreamer's first glimpse of the maiden "stonge myn hert ful stray atount" (179); his vision of the New Jerusalem is one "No fleschly hert ne my3t endeure" (1082). The word *hert* occurs eleven times in the text,[5] a fact that is not particularly striking for such a commonplace word, but one that merits consideration in light of existing scholarship about the heart's crucial symbolic status in *Patience*.[6]

The fountain flowing from the hearts of both the dreamer and Christ is especially noteworthy in view of Hugo Rahner's study of this image. The scripture text on which he focuses (John 7:37-38) is surely the basis for *Pearl*'s image of the breast as a fountain: "in novissimo autem die magno festivitatis stabat Iesus et clamabat dicens, 'si quis sitit, veniat ad me et bibat; qui credit in me, sicut dixit scriptura, flumina de ventre eius fluent aquae vivae.'" Rahner traces two separate exegetical traditions applied to this scripture text: the oldest tradition, first formulated by Origen, locates the fountain's source in the *venter* of Christ; a later interpretation finds the source in the breast of individual believers themselves. (Rahner also provides patristic evidence associating the *venter* in this passage with the heart, a point that I will substantiate more fully below.)[7] Rahner concludes that the older interpretation was unknown to the Middle Ages, only to be revived by German Pietists in the seventeenth and eighteenth centuries.[8] But the *Pearl*-Poet shows knowledge of both traditions.

The corporeal centrality of the heart, we have noted, links it with the pearl at the center of the maidens' breasts. Like the pearl, the hearts of Christ and Mary are traditionally characterized by their spotlessness.[9] Kanters and Richstätter, basing their observations on exegetical materials, compare Christ's heart specifically to the precious pearl of the New Testament.[10] The *Pearl*-Poet applies the word *wele* to the lost pearl (14), associating it with the *welle* of Christ's heart via the serious punning that is his trademark. The poem's pearl symbol also recalls the heart of Christ via the intermediate image of the rose: "For þat þou leste3 wat3 bot a rose" (269); "And þou so ryche a reken rose" (906). A number of medieval sources call Christ's heart a rose, and occasionally the central wound is depicted iconographically in the form of several adjoining rose petals.[11] Heart and rose coincide in heart-centered cosmographic representation, whereby Christ's central organ recapitulates microcosmically the shape of the universe. As the pearl on the maiden's breast is the source of the poem's overall shape, Christ's rose/heart dictates the configurations of the rose-window shaped universe. The relation of the pearl symbol to the thematic and numerological structure of the text is thus strikingly similar to the way that Criseyde's heart constitutes a poetic nucleus for the *rota-rosa* configurations of *Troilus*.

The symbolic congruence of heart and pearl images in the poem is also supported by their common association with the eucharist. Christ's heart is the fount of the sacraments, the origin of both the host and the consecrated wine. Medieval iconography often pictures the devout holding a chalice under Christ's bleeding heart; one fifteenth-century engraving even shows what appears to be a host emerging from the pierced heart.[12] Artists also sometimes superimposed the Sacred Heart on representations of the host.[13] The mystical identification of the eucharist with Christ's heart began in the thirteenth century, coinciding with the introduction of Corpus Christi Day solemnities. Albertus Magnus produced the first extensive doctrinal formulation of this symbolic connection, and his ideas were elaborated by Meister Eckhart, Gregory, and others.[14] Albertus compares the host within Christ's heart to the manna contained in the ark of the covenant.[15] Petrus Cellensis writes: "Eucharistia siquidem locum tenet in corpore Ecclesiae, quem humanum cor in homine."[16]

The symbolic link between eucharist and heart adds another resonance to the poet's concluding reference to the "bred and wyn / Þe preste vus scheweʒ vch a daye" in order that we may become "precious perleʒ." Ambrose writes that Christ's birth in our hearts occurs as the result of our reception of the eucharist: "omnis itaque anima quae recipit panem illum descendentem de caelo domus panis est . . . incipit ergo concipere anima et formari in ea Christus quae recipit adventum eius."[17] Bearing Christ in our hearts, he writes, each of us becomes a new mother of Christ.[18] The pearl worn over the heart of each pearl maiden provides an especially striking representation of the rebirth of Christ within the heart of each believer: the "gay juelle" within is Christ (1124), and each maiden herself becomes a pearl as a consequence of her heart's sacred burden.[19] Each maiden is a mother of Christ by virtue of the pearl on her chest. This special status prompts the dreamer to ask whether his own Pearl Maiden has been granted an equivalent place with Mary in the heavenly hierarchy, to which she responds that all the maidens are queens in that realm (421-56). Thus the theology of Christ's birth from our hearts supports the geometry of the poem: the pennies/eucharists received by the Vineyard workmen, as we have seen, are the geometric equivalent of the maidens' breast pearls; the latter are a consequence of the former. And Christ's birth from believers' hearts, like the reception of the eucharist, occurs "vch a day." Albertus Magnus writes: "Christus parit Ecclesia *quotidie* per fidem in cordibus auditorum,"[20] and many other Fathers use the word *quotidie* similarly to describe this continually re-enacted mystery.[21]

The image of the heart underscores the poem's concern with the plenitude of space. Just as the maiden's breast pearl (analogous with the Vineyard space at the poem's center) encompasses the entire space of *Pearl* within itself, the heart on which that pearl lies acts as a nexus for the many sacred spaces in Christian tradition. Coinciding with the point of intersection between the cross's two beams, Christ's heart is a universal center, gathering north, south, east, and west into itself. Like the altar at a cathedral's crossing-point, Christ's heart evokes, simultaneously, many different loci: the ark of the covenant,[22] the tabernacle,[23] the Holy of Holies and Solomon's Temple,[24] the Garden of Eden (and other gardens),[25] and the New Jerusalem (or heaven in general).[26] The heart image in *Pearl* thus bears a specific relation to the other settings depicted. L. Johnson and Wilson mention the equivalence of garden and heart in the treatment of *Pearl*'s landscapes.[27] Dorothee Finkelstein finds a shared structural equivalence between the New Jerusalem and the breast pearl via exegetical interpretation of Aaron's breastplate;[28] this latter relation is strengthened by passages stressing purity of heart as a prerequisite for entering the heavenly city (135-38; 677-83). Several patristic sources identify the human heart with a cultivated field in which God's Word must be sown; some refer specifically to the New Testament Vineyard which forms the heart of the *Pearl* text.[29]

Thus the heart symbolizes the *plenitudo*, the gathering together of all space and of the entire New Law of grace. Brun von Schoenbeck, a contemporary of St. Mechthild von Magdeburg, writes:

> In Corde ipsius sinceritatis et legis plenitudo,
> In seynem herczin wohnt der Reinheit Gut,
> Und des Gesetzes Fülle in ihm ruht.[30]

In the sixth century, Venantius Fortunatus composed a hymn to Mary, praising her heart's ability to encompass earth, sun, moon, and the entirety of the universe within itself; it begins with these verses:

> Quem terra, pontus, aethera
> Colunt, adorant, praedicant,
> Trinam regentem machinam
> Claustrum Mariae baiulat.
>
> Cui luna, sol et omnia
> Deserviunt per tempora,
> Perfusa coeli gratia
> Gestant puellae viscera.
>
> Mirantur ergo saecula,
> Quod angelus fert semina,
> Quod aure virgo concipit
> Et corde credens parturit.
>
> Beata mater munere
> Cuius supernus artifex
> Mundum pugillo continens
> Ventris sub arca clausus est.[31]

Like the body's other center in the womb, the spatial plenitude of the heart exemplifies the paradoxical spatiality of grace—the radical juxtaposition of "more and lasse." As a consequence of extensive twentieth-century researches into the patristic understanding of the Sacred Heart, the encyclical "Haurietis aquas" in 1956 especially stresses the *plenitudo* of the heart: "Omnia complectentis plenitudinis Dei clarissima imago est ipsum Cor Christi Jesu."[32]

The *plenitudo* emblemized by the heart is temporal as well as spatial. Peck observes how the heart coincides with the center point of concentric layers of time in medieval theology:

> Augustine, Anselm, the Victorines, and the Franciscans all suggest that one's sense of immortality, so obscured by the Fall, is

> recovered by a journey inward, Eternity being discovered in the
> heart where the soul resides. With recovery of that center, one's
> triple time-sense is complete and his sense of Being focused within
> the concentricities of personal time, historical time, and eternity.
> The cycle of reference grows full.[33]

Individual Christians share in the mothership of Mary. The original birth of the Logos reenacts itself continually, throughout time, in the heart of each new believer; that repeated new birth is both eternal and timeless, and always located at the body's center.[34] Augustine stresses that the birth of Christ in our hearts at baptism is the birth of a new day (*dies*):

> Ab hodierno die crescunt dies. Crede in Christum et crescit in te
> dies. Credidisti? Inchoatus est dies. Baptizatus es? Natus est
> Christus in corde tuo. Sed numquid Christus natus sic remansit?
> Crevit, ad inventutem pervenit; sed in senectutem non declinavit.
> Crescat ergo et fides tua, vetustatem nesciat.[35]

It is a day that never grows older, as Christ himself never reached old age; likewise, the heart's center of temporal regeneration keeps all believers (like the pearl maidens) forever young.[36] The Fathers also interpreted the Logos' birth from the heart in the light of the several ages of man. History's central event gathered all ages into itself; the conversion of each new Christian re-enacts history's midpoint, producing a decentralized time scheme beginning anew in the individual hearts of a long line of believers.[37] The geometry of the *Pearl* is faithful to medieval Christianity's heart-centered time scheme: the Vineyard parable at the heart of the text, we have seen, simultaneously symbolizes one day, one human life, and all of the ages of history. The pearls on the maidens' hearts, like the laborers' pennies, effect a dispersion of time into a series of new corporeal centers, the reduction of one large concentric scheme into a series of smaller, microcosmic ones.

A good deal of evidence supports the notion that the medievals regarded the Sacred Heart as a kind of symbolic *summa*, a synecdoche for the entirety of Christian theology. Rahner calls Christ's heart a *Monade* which "immer das Gesamtwesen der Kirche des fleischgewordenen Wortes spiegelt."[38] In his interpretation of the special favor whereby the disciple John could lay his head on Christ's breast (John 13:23-25), Augustine remarks on John's access to the most sublime of Christian mysteries residing in the Sacred Heart.[39] Tertullian finds in the shape of the Sacred Heart a symbol for the sum total of God's wisdom, knowledge, and works.[40] Theologians regarded Christ's heart (and the hearts of his followers) as the most intimate point of contact between his human and divine natures, the spatial nexus for both the hypostatic union and the union of the three Persons of the Trinity; it was the corporeal setting for the profoundest mysteries of the faith. Josephus Filograssi calls it the "summa totius mysterii Redemptionis";[41] Leeming writes: "in his Heart is summed up his whole redemptive love and work."[42] There is therefore a sound and extensive theological basis for regarding the heart (and the analogous images of the pearl, rose, and eucharist) as a symbolic condensation of the broadest themes of *Pearl*. The traditional equivalence of Christ's heart with the eucharist, another symbolic *summa*, strengthens this conclusion.

The heart's ability to resume all of Christian theology within itself results from the recapitulatory function that it shares with the head. In *Piers Plowman*, Holy Church's famous discourse on how love works through the power of the Incarnation includes the line "And in the herte, there is the heed" (B. I, 164).[43] The doctrine of the *recapitulatio* therefore constitutes an important component of the *theologia cordis*.[44] As a consequence, the Fathers compare the hierarchy of the church with the rulership exercised by the heart over the body's other members; the spiritual leaders who "head" the church also constitute its heart.[45] One can see in this tradition a general relevance for the special relation of crown to breast pearl noted earlier in *Pearl*, especially in view of the poem's general preoccupation with the status of the head in the mystical body's hierarchy (e.g., lines 475ff.).

The heart also provides a locus for corporeal *recapitulatio* in its function as the site for the mystical body's regeneration: as Christ's heart gave birth to the church, each believer bears the Christ child in his own heart. (We have already seen how the figure of the child corresponds with this point of inside out structure.) A tradition originating with the Gnostic Gospels terms this new life within all Christians the "Logos Child" or "Child of Wisdom"; its conception occurs at baptism.[46] The faithful are occasionally allowed to see this child in

Logos Visions, in which the child is characterized by its surpassing beauty and the dazzling radiance surrounding it.[47] The most outstanding trait of the Logos Child is its wisdom, which inevitably surpasses that of the one privileged to view it; a consequence of bearing this child in one's heart is the believer's ability to appropriate spiritually both its wisdom and its youth (it is always depicted as a newborn infant).[48] Whether or not the *Pearl*-Poet had access to the early texts of this tradition, he is likely to have seen iconography depicting this child within the human heart; many such representations survive from the High Middle Ages.[49] At least tangential influence from this tradition seems possible in this vision poem where the symbolism of the heart provides a background for extensive spiritual instruction offered by the dreamer's very young, radiantly beautiful, and eminently wise daughter.

Having considered some of the theological aspects of the medieval understanding of the heart, we are prepared to look at the heart from a more cosmographic standpoint; the status of this central organ as both microcosm and *Weltbild* bears an affinity to heart and pearl imagery in the text, and lays a foundation for later chapters' discussion of broader microcosmic configurations in *Pearl*.

A starting point for the medievals' conception of the microcosmic heart is the notion that Christians' hearts contain a spiritual ark of the covenant which in turn contains the world.[50] Several exegetes devote attention to the paradoxical expansiveness of this most intimate bodily space. In his commentary on Ps. 118:32, Ambrose writes:

> via sit angustior, cor latius, ut Patris et Filii et Spiritus sancti sustineat mansionem; ne veniat Verbum Dei, et pulset, et videns cordis ejus angustias, dedignetur habitare . . . Non igitur in viis, sed in cordis latitudine sapientia decantatur. In hoc igitur campo interioris hominis, non in angustiis mentis currendum nobis est, ut comprehendamus.[51]

Many church Fathers, including Hilary, Jerome, Augustine, Alcuin, and Peter Lombard, interpret the verse similarly.[52] These commentaries reflect the special role of the human heart in longstanding microcosmic tradition.[53]

And if the heart symbolizes the entire world, then certainly it subsumes the whole body within itself, functioning as a microcosm within a microcosm. Augustine, Anselm, Gregory, and John Chrysostomus all understand the heart as an emblem of the totality of the human personality,[54] and their conception finds its way into Latin and vernacular religious and mystical writings surviving from the eleventh through the thirteenth centuries.[55] The heart of Jesus, as always, is the subject of the most impassioned theological speculation. Richstätter draws this conclusion from his patristic research: "So finden wir den ganzen Christus wieder in der Verehrung seines heiligsten Herzens."[56] Bainvel writes: "Con il sacro Cuore abbiamo tutto Gesú."[57] He explains the significance of the Sacred Heart in terms of the synecdoche, a rhetorical figure whose role in corporeal textuality we have already observed:

> Nel linguaggio abituale, la parola cuore è usata spesso per una figura che i grammatici chiamano sineddoche per disegnare una persona si dice: "E' un gran cuore, è un buon cuore," per dire: "E' una grande, è una bell'anima." E quando diciamo: "Che cuore!" è la persona che designiamo direttamente, non è già il suo cuore. Ciò avviene, naturalmente, nella divozione al sacro Cuore.[58]

In Hayden White's analysis of figurative discourse, we see that this medieval conception of the heart has survived to the present day; he takes the expression "He is all heart" as an archetypical example of synecdochic figuration, stressing its microcosmic implications.[59] Emma Jung sees the Sacred Heart as the Middle Ages' symbol for the Self, the "bewußtseinstranszendente seelische Ganzheit des Menschen."[60] Each human being's heart resumes his entire personality and Christ's heart resumes the whole expression of himself, the entirety of Christian belief.[61]

The *Pearl*-Poet thus draws on an old and wide-ranging tradition when he portrays the breast pearl as a microcosm for both the maiden's body and the entire poem; his center-based corporeal imagery and allusions to the fountain of water and blood underscore his reliance on the heart matrix. Repeatedly he returns to the pearl/heart as the point of closest contact with God and of transformation into God's image (becoming precious pearls).[62]

I have already begun to point out, in preceding chapters, the importance of the heart image in medieval cosmographic representation. The heart bears the same relation to the spatial organization of the universe as the Great Chain of Being; the heart is the *vinculum amoris*.[63] Iconography influenced by the tradition of the Goddess Fortuna often portrays the wheel's spokes emerging from a central figure's heart. In Chaucer's *Troilus*, *rota-rosa* patterning ends with the wish that God's bond of Love might "cerclen hertes alle" (1767). Both Guillaume de Lorris and Jean de Meun mention the heart prominently in allusions to Fortune's Wheel in the *Roman de la Rose*.[64]

Some *Pearl* scholars may still be skeptical about an interpretation that takes the lines "Inmyddeȝ hyr breste watȝ sette so sure" (222) and "even inmyddeȝ my breste it stode" (740) as references to the location of the heart. Though the explicit portrayal of the heart as a central source of fountain imagery and the symbolic equation of pearl and heart via rose and eucharistic imagery in the poem and related tradition already establish the connection, further patristic evidence makes the link especially convincing. In his commentary on verse 1:12 of Canticles, a biblical source important for *Pearl* in many ways, Cassiodorus writes: "Nemo dubitat locum cordis inter ubera esse."[65] At the beginning of Origen's commentary on the same book of the Bible we find a similar assertion: "In praesenti loco quandoquidem amatorium drama est, quod agitur, in uberibus principale cordis intelligamus."[66] Elsewhere in the same commentary Origen bases the connection on the traditional idea, already noted, that the placement of John's head on Christ's breast signified his knowledge of the secrets hidden in the Sacred Heart: "In principale cordis Jesu . . . requievit."[67] The interchangeability of terms for heart and breast is a commonplace in scholarship on the *theologia cordis*. Bauer finds in it the principle, so important throughout *Pearl*, of the equivalence of a vessel and its contents: "Da das Herz wiederum in der Brust seinen Sitz hat, konnte—nach Art der Metonymie—das Gefäß statt des Inhalts, *pectus* statt *cor* Gesetz werden."[68] He cites numerous patristic sources which equate the very same spatial referents—*arca, habitaculum, sedes, mansio, aula, oppidulum, civitas*—with both the heart and the breast, evidence that the plenitude of space resides in both.[69] Kanters remarks on the interchangeability of terms for heart and breast in the writings of Cyprian, Caelius Sedulius, and

Peter Damian.⁷⁰ Von Ertzdorff notes the synonymous use of words for breast and heart in Latin and vernacular medieval literature, tracing the practice back to the equivalence of *cor* and *pectus* in Virgil and Ovid; as in *Pearl*, explicit mention of the heart often gives way to terms for the breast: "Die Prosaschriftsteller lassen den Terminus *cor* zugunsten von *pectus* etwas zurücktreten."⁷¹ Thus tradition ascribes to the breast the heart's capacity to serve as God's habitation, so that Dante is able to pattern an elaborate series of references in *Inferno* 12-13 to the double nature of the breast based, as we can now begin to see, on its participation in the hypostatic potential of the heart.⁷²

Any consideration of the Sacred Heart in cosmographic representation must necessarily come to terms with the influence of medieval *Weltbilder* on the iconography of the Five Wounds. Gray emphasizes the interdependence of the two cults:

> at least three themes . . . are regularly found in the fully developed cult of the Five Wounds. The wounds are (i) a place of refuge, (ii) openings from which the faithful can drink, and (iii) openings which reveal the way to the Sacred Heart of Christ (arcanum cordis). The last of these plays an increasingly important part in the cult. The devotion to the wound in Christ's side gradually becomes the devotion to the heart which was pierced by the soldier's spear until, with St. John Eudes and St. Margaret Mary Alacoque in the seventeenth century, the cult of the Sacred Heart quite overshadows that of the Wounds.⁷³

Gilbert Dolan has found numerous representations from late medieval England displaying the heart together with the other four wounds; the juxtaposition of the two cults has led many scholars to believe that the Sacred Heart made its first appearance in iconography only in conjunction with the wounds.⁷⁴ The central image of the fountain in *Pearl* depends, of course, on the images of both heart and wound (1135-37). Though the poet makes no explicit mention of the other four wounds, his knowledge of the broader tradition has already been suggested by the scholarship on Gawain's pentangle.⁷⁵

Understanding the iconography of the heart against the background of medieval depictions of the Five Wounds clarifies the place of the Sacred Heart within cosmographic representation. Most medieval portrayals of the Sacred

Spatiality of the Heart 143

Heart together with the other wounds evince, I believe, the unmistakable influence of *Weltbild* tradition. No scholar, to my knowledge, has yet remarked on this influence, so it deserves particular emphasis here as evidence for the microcosmic structure of poems, like *Pearl*, containing a spatial and temporal center in the heart. Depictions of the Five Wounds, like many *Weltbilder*, always display a central heart superimposed on the body of a central figure (Christ) and/or enclosing the figure of a small child (the Wisdom Child or Logos Child).[76] The cross, the inevitable nexus of all space and time in *Weltbilder*, appears at the center of depictions of the Five Wounds as well; where its two beams are not recognizable as a literal cross, they are nonetheless indicated by leafy fronds or some other design emerging from the heart to form four right angles.[77] The four wounds in the hands and feet invariably appear at the four corners of such depictions—precisely the location of the four winds (or four gospels, four elements, etc.) in the symmetry of traditional *Weltbilder*; occasionally the wounded heart itself is repeated at the four corners, reflecting the microcosmic relation of center to edge that is so important in *Weltbilder*.[78] The cosmographic significance of this "four and one" arrangement in depictions of the wounds is strengthened by the artists' very consistent use of concentric, circular geometric patterning. The theological prominence of the heart wound is often underscored by a series of comparatively large, concentric circles around it, which are in turn echoed in series of smaller concentric circles around the wounds in Christ's hands and feet.[79] Occasionally even the design of the cross is repeated around the subordinate wounds as well.[80] The pattern corresponds precisely with the "four and one" arrangement of concentric circles in many *Weltbilder*. Also, depictions of the wounds imitate other geometric embellishments found in *Weltbilder*, as when the circumferences of the outer circles interweave with that of the inner one at their point of intersection,[81] or when the artist simplifies the design to a chain of half circles created by the exterior portions of overlapping circles.[82]

In the light of the *Weltbild*-based iconography of Christ's wounds, we can begin better to understand the heart-centered geometry of *Pearl*. The pearl resting over the maiden's heart is the source and dominant center of both her other circular adornments and the other circular structures of the poem. Like the concentrically ringed heart in medieval cosmographic design, it constitutes a spatial and temporal center, a nexus for the poem's complex symbolism. And the image of the crown in *Pearl* provides a further link with the iconography of the wounds; such representations often feature the crown of thorns, either as a central circle around the heart or as a fifth circle at the "head" of the design (corresponding, again, with the "head" circles noticed earlier in cosmographic design).[83] Thus the comparison of one limb's ring with the head's crown in the important *corpus mysticum* passage shows an awareness of the geometric equivalence of encircled body parts paralleling that in renderings of Christ's wounds. Some artists even picture a crown around or above all five wounds, a fact that underscores the basis of the statement "And wolde her coroune3 wern worþe þo fyue" (451; cf. 849) in the geometry of the body.[84] This fundamental pattern of subordinate, concentric circles around a central one also extends itself to the structure of the text, wherein circular stanza groups composed of circular stanzas (arranged, like the wounds, in groups of five) extend the circularity of the Vineyard laborers at the center. This heart-centered "four and one" matrix is especially important to the *Pearl*-Poet, as we will see in the even more explicit influence of the iconography of the wounds on Sir Gawain's pentangle.

The notion of the breast pearl over the heart as a generative center is reinforced by its clear iconographic association with the "nuptial chamber" of the heart. We have already noticed those *Weltbilder* which feature, in the exact center of the dominant figure's breast, a circle whose centripetal relation to surrounding concentric and chained circles bears striking similarity to the geometric position of the breast pearl. Occasionally such circles in turn contain a tiny pair of male and female figures depicted in the early stages of a passionate embrace.[85] This iconographic detail alludes to the tradition of the heart as a nuptial chamber, the innermost space of the body where the sexual union of humanity and divinity produces its hypostatic offspring.[86] The tradition, like so much of *Pearl*'s imagery, originated in commentary on Canticles.[87] Exegetes most often locate this nuptial chamber in the heart or breast of Mary,[88] but the same tradition identifies it with the heart of Christ as well, as in one of the Middle English *Quia amore langueo* poems:

> In my syde I haf made hyr nest,
> loke in me how wyde a wound is here!
> This is hyr chambre, here shall she rest,
> that she and I may slepe in fere.
> Here may she wasshe if any filth were;
> here is socour for all hyr woo.[89]

In both cases the miniature couple in their tiny room reflects the extreme condensation that occurs at the innermost point of Christian space and time; the radical union of opposites that gives birth to the church is portrayed via microcosmic representation of lovers and chamber within the body of each lover. Not surprisingly, then, the nuptial chamber is traditionally linked not only with the heart, but with the womb; commentators frequently speak of the *vulva* or *uterus cordis*.[90] Christ's body, as a consequence, is potentially hermaphroditic, giving birth to the church from his heart as Adam produced Eve from his rib.[91] Traditional associations therefore help us to see the breast pearl as a dense, microcosmic space resonating into larger spaces, a fertile locus of sexual reversibility capable, like the center of a *Weltbild*, of producing infinite pearl-shaped reproductions of itself. The multiple spatial and temporal correlates of heart and womb endow it with the same microcosmic compactness found at the numerological center of those works analyzed by Haubrichs.

Having considered how the heart functions as a spatial and temporal nexus within microcosmic speculation and cosmographic representation, we are prepared to make some broader observations about the nature of this organ's "centeredness." The conception of the heart as the body's main source and center of physical and spiritual energy began with the Greeks, especially the Stoics, and gained even greater acceptance in Roman thought; the notion was transmitted to medieval medical treatises primarily via Cicero and Pliny.[92] Augustine and Gregory place particular importance on the centrality of the heart in their teachings, but the idea was available in Christian writings on the Passion as early as the second century.[93] The Sacred Heart's status as the traditional core of incarnational theology is now widely recognized;[94] from scriptural sources alone the heart emerges as both the center and synecdoche of the body.[95] As a consequence of this tradition, the heart early became the most important medieval symbol of corporeal and spiritual interiority.[96]

Not only is the heart the middle of the body; the heart, as the body's microcosm, itself possesses a center. In one of the lyrics by Walther von der Vogelweide, the speaker's love for his lady moves "mitten in daz herze."[97] Similarly, Durandus allegorizes the triumphal cross at the center of many cathedrals as an admonition to love Christ in the middle of our hearts.[98] Augustine tells Christians that God's presence in their bodies is "corde tuo interior," leading him to address God in his *Confessions* thus: "Tu autem eras interior intimo meo et superior summo meo."[99] The heart, therefore, reflects the paradoxical inside out geometry of Christian space as depicted in medieval *Weltbilder*. As in *Pearl*, the circumference is contained by the center; the heart is "an internal landmark acquiring a universal spatial meaning."[100]

Multiple exegetical resonances of architectural space in the symbol of the heart also contribute to the plenitude of space associated with the breast pearl. The Fathers describe the heart variously as a house, chamber, closet, shrine, cloister, or tent, equipped with door and key, walls and ceiling, and furniture (normally a seat or throne).[101] The metaphor stems from the tradition, originating with Paul's epistles to the Corinthians and Ephesians, of believers' hearts as Christ's habitation.[102] Augustine understands the water and blood emerging from Christ's heart as the sacraments "quibus aedificatur Ecclesia."[103] Exegetes therefore equate the heart with the church and, by extension, with the tabernacle, the Holy of Holies, the ark of covenant, and Solomon's Temple.[104] It is also called both a treasure-house[105] and, in courtly lyrics, a prison.[106]

Earlier I presented evidence for the commonplace association of heart and altar. Rabanus Maurus allegorizes the dimensions of the heart/altar in a way that recalls allegorical handling of the dimensions of the heart conceived as the ark of the covenant.[107] The altar is the heart/hearth of a building conceived corporeally. And the altar vessels, which share many of the same allegorical meanings with the altar itself, are also traditionally linked with the heart—especially the chalice,[108] paten,[109] incense burners,[110] wine and water containers,[111] and the altar's cloth covering.[112] Similarly, the breast pearl at the heart of *Pearl* resumes the dimensions of the multiple enclosures depicted in the poem, including the textual superstructure whose dimensions imitate those of the New Jerusalem.

Spatiality of the Heart 147

Finally, the doctrine of the *verbum cordis* identifies the heart itself as a book or text. Replacing the Old Law written on tables of stone, God has inscribed the law of grace on the *tabulae cordis* (2 Cor. 3:3; cf. Deut. 4:1).[113] The liquid outpouring of the New Testament from Christ's heart supersedes the water that issued from the rock struck by Moses.[114] Hildebert of Lavardin produced an elaborate book metaphor in his commentary on Deut. 4:1, preparing for a transition in later tradition from the phrase *tabulae cordis* to *liber cordis*.[115] Augustine and St. Thomas were major expositors of the *verbum cordis* doctrine, and their teachings originated in turn in Greek speculation about the birth of the Logos in the human heart.[116] The *verbum* resides *in medio cordis* (Ps. 39:9), and the outpouring of water and blood is allegorized as Christian teaching.[117] The doctrine endowed medieval manuscripts themselves with a new corporeality; as we have noticed, scribal rubrication reminded exegetes of the heart and four limbs' bleeding wounds.

The heart, then, is the point of maximum verbal condensation within the entire textuality of the incarnational body. As a consequence, literary texts which contain a numerological or symbolic heart may be said to possess an epitome of their total meaning at that central locus. A text's heart, as indicated by Geoffrey's phrase *intrinseca linea cordis*, is the moment of greatest symbolic "thickening," the place where the text becomes most self-reflexive, structurally folding in on itself. Literature composed according to the law of grace no longer derives its meaning and validity from stone tables exterior to themselves; instead, its meaning originates in the *tabulae cordis* at its core. The pearl symbol at the heart of *Pearl*, the precious stone bearing "in scrypture" (in writing) the names of the children of Israel on the gates of Jerusalem (1039), is a text within a text.[118]

I must conclude this chapter by pointing out that the *Pearl*-Poet's attention to traditional corporeal centers did not limit itself to heart/womb and head. Another important image of bodily centrality is evoked by the author's use of the word "naule," again in stanza thirty-nine's crucial *corpus mysticum* description:

>   Al arn we membreȝ of Jesu Kryst;
>   As heued and arme and legg and naule
>   Temen to hys body ful trwe and tryste . . .   (458-60)

Despite one scholar's insistence that the word be rendered "nail" (as in "fingernail" and "toenail"), philologists have generally agreed with Gollancz' suggestion that the meaning "navel" (OE *nafela*) was intended by the poet; thus Gordon and Hillmann accept the rendering by Gollancz in their own glosses.[119] But no one has yet attempted to supply a reason for this odd reference to that particular body part, a reference which must be especially crucial given the thematic importance of this passage to the poem's overall handling of corporeal theology.

A rather convincing explanation, I believe, is suggested by the widespread medieval tradition of the navel as a corporeal and geographic center roughly equivalent to both heart and womb. As I mentioned earlier, the navel often constitutes the midpoint of circles inscribed around the human body in medieval iconography.[120] De Bruyne notes that the head, arms, and legs often provide points of contact with the circular circumference of such representations; these five body parts provide an iconographic basis, he says, for the tradition of the pentagonal man (a variant of the *homo quadratus*).[121] Like the *Weltbild*-based pentangle which in *Sir Gawain* represents *trauþe*, this key figure in *Pearl* represents *courtayse* as a principle of cosmic order. We have already seen how often such geometrically inscribed human figures occur at the core of medieval pictures of the cosmos, underscoring the relation of microcosm to universe. Given the prominence of body-based circular geometry in the microcosmic configurations of *Pearl*, line fifty-nine's reference both to the traditional five peripheral body parts and the navel at the center should probably be understood in this light. The microcosmic relation of part to whole, as we have seen, is a fundamental theme of this passage; just as a ring on the arm or finger signifies its share in the kingship of the crowned head, so too all of the pearl maidens bear the crown of Christ. Like the circle appearing on the central figure's breast in medieval iconography, the navel is a round center and geometric core in microcosmic representation.[122] The poet's reference to the navel in this passage provides more evidence for the iconographic influence which we already noticed in his descriptions of the pearls at the center of each maiden's breast.

Like the other traditional "centers" which influenced the poet, the navel constitutes both a corporeal and a geographic midpoint. It is a generative core of the body, associated with both penis and vagina/womb in classical and Jewish teaching.[123] It was the most intimate point of contact between human and divine flesh at the birth of Christ, and is therefore an appropriate image in this description of bodily connections within the *corpus mysticum*: "Ryȝt so is vch a Krysten sawle / A longande lym to þe Mayster of myste" (461-62). As multiple geographic centers bearing typological relation to the body's midpoint, Jerusalem, the Earthly Paradise, and Mt. Zion are all linked with the navel in Christian tradition.[124] In religious architecture, the navel (like the heart and womb) is associated with the altar,[125] and some sources also call the navel the foundation stone of the world, comparing it to the cornerstone of sacred buildings.[126] We have already seen how the symbolism of the altar parallels structures of centrality in *Pearl*. The idea that the symmetrical structure of texts forms itself around a central "navel" is an old one; Haubrichs cites Justinian's application of the metaphor to the crucial middle section of his numerologically symmetrical codification of Roman law.[127] One is reminded again of Freud's notion of the "navel" of a dream, the locus (like the symbol of the pearl in *Pearl*'s dream vision) where the dream's entire symbolism coheres most densely.[128] The reference to the navel in *Pearl*, consistent with the way the poem represents space in its plenitude, reaches potentially from the initial, paradisaical depiction of the *erber grene* to the final vision of New Jerusalem on a mountaintop.

Notes

1. See Ch. G. Kanters, *Le Coeur de Jésus dans la Littérature Chrétienne des douze premiers siècles* (Brussels: Beyaert, 1930) 13-14; Jean V. Bainvel, *La divozione al S. Cuore di Gesu: La sua dottrina e la sua storia*, 2nd ed., Biblioteca Ascetica 4 (Milano: Società Vita e Pensiero, 1922) 175ff., 190ff. Augustinus Bea et al. have edited a convenient collection of articles on the Sacred Heart entitled *Cor Jesu* (Freiburg: Herder, 1959); my study draws from the following contributions to this anthology: Luigi Ciappi, "La SS. Trinità e il Cuore SS. di Gesù" 115-48; Herman Michel Diepen, "L'Esprit du Coeur de Jésus" 149-90; Josephus Filograssi, "De obiecto cultus SS. Cordis Jesu in Litteris Encyclicis 'Haurietis aquas'" 95-114; Franz Lakner, "Das Rundschreiben Pius XII 'Haurietis aquas' und der Kult des Unbefleckten Herzens Marias" 721ff.; Joseph Lécuyer, "Le Sacré-Coeur et le Corps Mystique du Christ" 191-240; Bernard Leeming, "Consecration to the Sacred Heart" 595-656; Hugo Rahner, "Mirabilis Progressio" 21-58; David Michael Stanley, "'From his Heart will flow rivers of living water' (Jn. 7,38)" 507-42; and Sebastian Tromp, "SS. Cor Jesu et Ecclesia, Corpus et Sponsa Salvatoris," 241-68. In addition, the following includes some of the major studies of the *theologia cordis*: *Le Coeur*, Les études carmélitaines 29 (Paris: Desclée, 1950); Von Ertzdorff, "Herz," and "Die Dame im Herzen und das Herz bei der Dame: Zur Verwendung des Begriffs Herz in der höfischen Liebeslyrik des 11. und 12. Jahrhunderts," *Zeitschrift für deutsche Philologie* 84 (1965): 6-46; D. Gray, "The Five Wounds of Our Lord," *Notes and Queries* ns 10 (1963): 50-51, 82-89, 127-34, 163-68; P. Josef Hättenschwiller, S. J., *Führer durch die neuere deutsche Herz-Jesu-Literatur* (Innsbruck: Rauch, 1932); Ch. G. Kanters, *De Godsvrucht tot het Heilig Hart van Jesus in de vroegere Staten der Nederlanden (XII-XVII. eeuw)* ('s-Hertogenbosch: Mosman, 1929); Bertrand de Margerie, S. J., "Le coeur de Marie, coeur de l'Église," *Ephemerides mariologicae* 16 (1966): 189-227; Hugo Rahner, "Flumina de ventre Christi: Die patristische Auslegung von Joh 7,37.38" and "Die Gottesgeburt: Die Lehre der Kirchenväter von der Geburt Christi aus dem Herzen der Kirche und der Gläubigen," *Symbole der Kirche: Die Ekklesiologie der Väter* (Salzburg: Müller, 1964) 13-90, 177-235 ("Flumina" first appeared in *Biblica* 22 (1941): 269-302, 367-403); Karl Richstätter, *Herz-Jesu-Verehrung*, and *Das Herz des Welterlösers in seiner dogmatischen, liturgischen, historischen und aszetischen Bedeutung* (Freiburg: Herder, 1932); Sebastian Tromp, "De nativitate Ecclesiae ex corde Iesu in Cruce," *Gregorianum* (1932), and *De virgine deipara Maria corde Mystici*. For an excellent study of the theology of the heart in medieval literature, see Giuseppe Mazzotta, *The World at Play in Boccaccio's Decameron* (Princeton: Princeton UP, 1986).

2. Cf. von Ertzdorff, "Dame im Herzen" 6ff.

3. Cf. Bainvel 84ff., 95ff.

4. Gray examines the tradition of the five wounds of Christ as fountains at considerable length, citing some Middle English sources which use the same word *welle* (131-32, 163-64, 168, and passim). For further discussion of the heart as this fountain's source and of the four rivers of paradise, see von Ertzdorff, "Herz" 288ff. and Lécuyer, 208ff.

5. Cf. also ll. 17, 51, 174, 176, 682.

6. See chapter nine.

7. Rahner "Flumina" 198-99 and passim.
8. "Flumina" 234.
9. Lakner passim.
10. Kanters, *Coeur de Jésus* 187. Richstätter, *Herz-Jesu-Verehrung* 68.
11. See the *Summi Regis cor aveto*, composed in the twelfth century by Hermann Joseph (cited in Richstätter, *Herz-Jesu-Verehrung* 40ff.). Lydgate's *A Seying of the Nightingale* advises the reader to devote himself to the five wounds thus: "Make of þees fyue, in þyn hert a roose / And let it þeer contynuelly abyde"; another poet in the same century likens the wounds to "the rede rose roddy in apparence." Mechtild's *Liber Specialis Gratiae* states, "ecce rosa pulcherrima habens quinque folia exivit de corde Dei totum pectus ejus cooperiens," and pictures the wounds "circumposita gemmis pretiosis." (These latter citations are from Gray 85; he also describes iconographic depictions on 164.) Cf. Kanters, *Coeur de Jésus* 174-78 and passim.
12. Reproduced by Richstätter, *Herz-Jesu-Verehrung* 121. E. Jung takes this round figure containing the image of the cross as a representation of the moon, identifying a second appearance of the same figure here as the sun (106). But while round hosts were often stamped with the shape of a cross, I have seen no depictions of the sun or moon featuring this design.
13. Leeming 611; he bases his observations on iconographic research by Dom Gilbert Dolan.
14. Richstätter, *Herz-Jesu-Verehrung* 49ff., 98ff.; *Herz des Welterlösers* 83ff. See Gregory, *Moralia in Job* 25 (*PL* 76.328).
15. Op. 38, 193-95 (cited in Sauer 99; cf. 164).
16. *PL* 202.1136D-1137A. For more information on the equation of the eucharist and Sacred Heart see Bern. Hardy Welzel, S.J., *Herz Jesu und Eucharistie* (München: Ars Sacra, 1952); Holböck 1; Bainvel 50; Lécuyer 211, 227; Leeming 648ff.; de Lubac 217; de Margerie 207.
17. *Epist.* 70.13, 16 (*PL* 16.1237, 1238).
18. *Comm. in Luc.* 10 (*CSEL* 32.4.464ff.).
19. Richstätter cites (in modern translation) a thirteenth-century German mystical text entitled "Die Lilie" which illustrates how a transformed heart transforms the whole person: "Nimm dies Herz of Christ und lege es an dein Herz, damit du diesem Herzen werdest gleich." *Herz-Jesu-Verehrung* 67.
20. *Comm. in Apoc.* 12.5, cited in Rahner, "Gottesgeburt" 71.
21. Bernard of Clairvaux, Sermo 6 in *Vigil. Nat.* (*PL* 183.112); Haymo of Halberstadt, *Comm. in Apoc.* 3.12 (*PL* 117.1081); Richard of St. Victor, *De superexc. bapt. Christi* (*PL* 196.1017). For other sources of the same idea, see Rahner, "Gottesgeburt" 67-79.
22. Richstätter, *Herz-Jesu-Verehrung* 68.
23. See William Billyng, *The Five Wounds of Christ* (early fifteenth century), ed. W. Bateman (Manchester: n.p., 1814); cited in Gray 164. Billyng addresses the Sacred Heart thus:
    O truest tabernacle of alle the towrys
    Comlyest closet, encensed alle with spyces
    Most plesaunte pa ra dyse most ryalle in honoure. . . .
24. Richstätter, *Herz-Jesu-Verehrung* 68.
25. Augustine, Sermo 246 (*PL* 33.1154). Cf. Rahner, "Gottesgeburt" 49; Piehler 158.
26. See Billyng's passage above; Bauer, *Claustrum Animae* passim.
27. L. Johnson 156, 180-84; Wilson 12.
28. "The *Pearl*-Poet as Bezalel," *Mediaeval Studies* 35 (1973): 413-32.
29. See especially commentary on the *cultor vineae* of the Fig Tree parable in the *Glossa ordinaria* (*PL* 114.302). Cf. Stephen A. Barney, "The Plowshare of the Tongue: The Progress of a Symbol from the Bible to *Piers Plowman*," *Mediaeval Studies* 35 (1973): 261-93; Lakner 735; Kanters 181ff.
30. Quoted in Richstätter, *Herz-Jesu-Verehrung* 62-63.

31. *Analecta hymnica medii aevi*, ed. Clemens Blume and Guido M. Dreves, 55 vols. (Leipzig: Reisland, 1886-1922) 50: 72.

32. Cited in Filograssi 114. Cf. Lécuyer 194; Leeming 622.

33. Peck 69.

34. Rahner, "Gottesgeburt" 60-61.

35. Sermo 370.4 (*PL* 39.1659).

36. John K. Crane writes, "Besides the idea of spiritual purification around which Baptism is conceived, present also is the Christian belief that man's body is, at that very moment, returned to pre-lapsarian perfection." "Four Levels of Time in *Sir Gawain and the Green Knight*," *Annuale Medievale* 10 (1969): 67.

37. Rahner, "Gottesgeburt" 79-80.

38. "Mirabilis progressio" 25.

39. Augustine writes in *In Evang. S. Joannis* 18.5 (*PL* 35.1535-36): "Joannes evangelista inter consortes et comparticipes suos alios evangelistas, hoc praecipuum et proprium donum accepit a Domino (super cujus pectus in convivio discumbebat (*Joan.* 13, 25), ut per hoc signi ficaret quia secreta altiora de intimo ejus corde potabat)." Again, in *Sermo* 120 (*PL* 38.676) he links the opening of John's Gospel with John's access to the secrets of Christ's *pectus*: "Evangelii Joannis principium, *In principio erat Verbum*. Sic coepit, hoc vidit, et transcendens universam creaturam, montes, aera, coelos, sidera, Sedes, Dominationes, Principatus, Potestates, omnes Angelos, omnes Archangelos, transcendens omnia, in principio Verbum vidit, et bibit. Super omnem creaturam vidit, de pectore Domini bibit. Ipse est enim Joannes evangelista sanctus, quem praecipue diligebat Jesus; ita ut super pectus ejus recumberet (*Joan.* 13:23, 25). Ibi erat hoc secretum, ut inde biberetur, quod in Evangelio ructuaretur." I discuss the traditional equivalence of heart and breast below.

40. *De carnis resurr.* 6 (*PL* 2.802).

41. Filograssi 112; cf. 95-97.

42. Leeming 647. Cf. Diepen 158, 161, 176, 178.

43. All citations from the B Text of *Piers Plowman* are taken from the edition by A. V. C. Schmidt (New York: Dutton, 1978). Leeming discusses how the "fulness of the Godhead" resides in the Sacred Heart (622). Cf. Lakner 740-41.

44. Cf. Lécuyer 214; Rahner, "Flumina" 211; Scharl 43-44.

45. See Hesychius of Jerusalem, *De titulis Psalmorum*, in *Ps. 39.24* (published among the works of Athanasius, *PG* 27.805). Cf. Theodoret (*PG* 83.590); and the citation from Procopius of Gaza in Kanters 87. Rahner also remarks on the exalted position of the heart within the "Hierarchie der Andachten" ("Mirabilis progressio" 26).

46. For a general discussion of the Logos Child and Logos Visions, see Rahner, "Gottesgeburt" 19-62. Cf. also A. Harnack, *Die Bezeichnung Jesu als 'Knecht Gottes' und ihre Geschichte in der alten Kirche*, Sitzungsberichte der Berliner Akademie der Wissenschaften (1926).

47. Rahner, "Gottesgeburt" 24.

48. Rahner, "Gottesgeburt" 21.

49. See reproductions in Richstätter, *Herz-Jesu-Verehrung* facing 88, 168, 184.

50. See Ohly, "Cor amantis non angustam," *Schriften* 139.

51. *PL* 15.1316.

52. Hilary (*PL* 9.531); Jerome (*PL* 26.1262); Augustine (*PL* 37.1527); Alcuin (*PL* 100.601); Peter Lombard (*PL* 191.1060). Cf. Ohly, "Cor amantis" 139-40.

53. Meyer discusses the neoplatonic conception of the world as a stream flowing eternally out of God, a notion that no doubt contributed to the medievals' understanding of the birth of the church from Christ's side (45). Maimonides, the great Jewish philosopher whose writings influenced Christian scholastics, believed that the universe's outer sphere corresponded with the

human heart (Conger 43, cf. 25). The tradition has persisted into more modern times. The Tate Gallery in London possesses an anonymous seventeenth-century British painting entitled "William Style of Langly" (Accession No. T2308) in which a gentleman is depicted pointing at a heart resting on the floor; contained within this heart is an image of the globe, and an inscription above the heart reads "Microcosmus Microcosmi non impletur Megacosmo." Also, a colleague reports having frequently seen popular icons of the Virgin featuring a globe at the center of her heart in the homes of Puerto Rican immigrants living in Chicago.

54. Cited in von Ertzdorff, "Herz" 272-73; Kanters, *Coeur de Jésus* 20-21.
55. See von Ertzdorff, "Herz" esp. 6ff., 277ff., 287-89.
56. *Herz des Welterlösers* 47.
57. Bainvel 157. Cf. 107-08: "La vita di Nostro Signore può così concentrarsi tutta nel cuore; in tutti i suoi stati posso studiare quanto vi ha di più profondo, di più intimo, di più personale. Gesù si riassume tutto e si esprime nel sacro Cuore."
58. Bainvel 107.
59. *Metahistory: The Historical Imagination in Nineteenth-Century Europe* (Baltimore: Johns Hopkins UP, 1973) 35-36.
60. E. Jung 103ff.
61. Bainvel 159.
62. See Rahner, "Gottesgeburt" 84-85 for Eckhart's "Auffassung vom Herzen als dem lebensspendenden Mittelpunkt des Menschen, als dem heimlichen, abgrundtiefen Ort der Begegnung mit dem Göttlichen." Von Ertzdorff discusses the "Verwandlung der Welt durch die Freude im Herzen" in the lyrics of Bernart of Ventadorn ("Dame im Herzen" 38-39).
63. Cf. Filograssi 101.
64. See lines 4590-99, 5614-21. All *Roman de la Rose* citations are taken from the edition by Félix Lecoy, 3 vols. (Paris: Champion, 1965-70).
65. *PL* 70.1060.
66. *Origenis opera*, ed. D. A. B. Calliau, 7 vols. (Paris: Mellier, 1842) 4: 390; cited in Kanters, *Coeur de Jésus* 36.
67. Cited in Kanters, *Coeur de Jésus* 35-36. Cf. Augustine, *In Evang. S. Joannis* 18.5: "Secreta altiora de intimo ejus cordis potabat"; cf. *PL* 35.1535.
68. Bauer 54. On 105 he asserts that "*cor* und *pectus* als Bildworte weitgehend gleichbedeutend sind." Cf. 337ff.
69. Bauer 106-07; cf. both my preceding treatment of spatial plenitude in the heart and the discussion of architectural metaphors for the heart below.
70. Of Cyprien's *Liber de bono pat.* 3, Kanters writes: "Il ressort clairement de ce texte que les mots *poitrine* et *coeur* y sont synonymes" (22-23). With reference to Peter Damian's *Epist. IIe ad Leonem IX* (*PL* 144.209), he notes: "Je me permets d'insister sur l'observation suivante: La lettre de saint Pierre Damien, dans laquelle la poitrine humaine est synonyme de coeur physique au sens que nous venons de voir, est de nature à insinuer quelle signification doit être donnée au mot poitrine en maint endroit analogue dans les écrits des Pères et des Docteurs de l'Église" (128; cf. 77-78, 161-62). To his citations we can add one from Lactantius, *De opificio Dei* 12 (*PL* 7.58): "ad nutrimenta nascentis fontibus lacteis fecundum pectus exuberat. Nec enim decebat aluid quam ut sapiens animal a corde alimoniam duceret."
71. "Herz" 258-59.
72. See Sauer 51-52; Singleton, "Campi semantici" 11-22.
73. Gray 85-86.
74. "Devotion to the Sacred Heart in Medieval England," *Dublin Review* 120 (1897). Dolan claims, however, to have discovered representations of the heart alone which antedate those displaying it together with the other wounds. Cf. Leeming 610.
75. For bibliographical references on this point see chapter eight.

76. See the reproductions in Richstätter, *Herz-Jesu-Verehrung* 57, 89, 105, 121. Richstätter reproduces only German designs, but Dolan has established the existence of many similar representations in medieval England as well.
77. See reproductions in Richstätter *Herz-Jesu-Verehrung* 105.
78. Richstätter *Herz-Jesu-Verehrung* 121. Cf. E. Jung 105-06; Beer, *Die Rose* figs. 45, 51; figures in Bober, "Illustrated Schoolbook" 68, 79; A. R. Bayley, "The Five Wounds," *Notes and Queries* 171 (1936): 266.
79. Gray remarks on the comparatively large size of the center wound (166).
80. Richstätter *Herz-Jesu-Verehrung* 57, 89.
81. Richstätter *Herz-Jesu-Verehrung* 89.
82. Richstätter *Herz-Jesu-Verehrung* 57.
83. Richstätter *Herz-Jesu-Verehrung* 57, 89, 345.
84. See Gray 50-51.
85. See especially the drawings by Opicinus de Canistris reproduced by Salomon.
86. Richstätter writes: "Das Herz des Herrn ist hypostatisch auf das innigste mit der Gottheit des Gottessohnes und seiner ewigen Liebe verbunden" (*Herz des Welterlösers* 9). Cf. Filograssi 111-12.
87. Cant. 4:19 says, "Vulnerasti cor meum, soror mea sponsa; vulnerasti cor meum." Cassiodorus writes: "Vulnerasti cor meum, id est: tuo amore fecisti ut ego in cruce vulnerarer" (*PL* 70.1076). Cf. Kanters 91-92.
88. For references to appropriate commentaries, see Tromp, *Corpus Christi quod est Ecclesia* 1: 24ff.; J. M. Bover, "Tamquam sponsus procedens de thalamo suo," *Estudios Eclesiásticos* 4 (1925): 59-73.
89. *Political, Religious, and Love Poems*, ed. Frederick J. Furnivall, Early English Text Society os 15 (London: Trübner, 1866) 155.
90. For the *vulva cordis*, see Tertullian, *Adv. Praxeam* 7 (*PL* 2.161); Cyprian, *Test.* 2.3 (*CSEL* 3.64). The *uterus cordis* is mentioned by Ambrose, *De Noe* 6.14 (*CSEL* 32.1.423), and *De virgin.* 3.1.3 (*PL* 16.221); Gregorius of Elvira, *De fide orthod.* 2 (*PL* 20.35); *Altercat. Simonis et Theoph.* (*CSEL* 45.8). See also Augustine, *Sermo* 189.3 (*PL* 38.1006); Rupert of Deutz, *In libros Reg.* 3.14 (*PL* 167.1157); Hugh of St. Victor, *De B. Mariae virginitate* 2 (*PL* 176.872).
91. See Carolyn Bynum, *Jesus as Mother: Studies in the Spirituality of the High Middle Ages* (Berkeley: U of California P, 1982) esp. 114, 119-20, 125, 132-33. Cf. Brown, *Love's Body* 73, 130-31.
92. See Pliny, *Historia naturalis* 11.69; Lactantius, *De opificio Dei* 12.6 (*CSEL* 27.44). Cf. von Ertzdorff, "Herz" 258; Bauer 53-54; Rahner, "Gottesgeburt" 14; E. Sperka, "Cor und Pectus: Untersuchungen zum Leib-Seele-Problem bei den Römern," diss., U Tübingen, 1953.
93. Von Ertzdorff, "Herz" 264-65; Kanters, *Coeur de Jésus* 33ff. Leeming remarks on early iconography showing the heart fixed to the center of the cross (611).
94. See Richstätter, "Zentrale Stellung der Herz-Jesu-Verehrung," *Herz des Welterlösers* 81ff; *Le Coeur* 9ff.
95. "Das Herz ist in biblischer Sicht nicht ein bevorzugtes Organ zum Empfang religiöser Erfahrungen, neben dem es noch andere geistige Zentren gibt oder geben kann; sondern der in ihm, gleichsam wie in einem Punkt, zusammengezogene Mensch in seiner geistig-geschöpflichen Gesamtheit." Von Ertzdorff, "Herz" 251.
96. Rahner provides ample documentation of what he calls the "Geschichte der Innerlichkeit" associated with the heart in "Gottesgeburt" 15-16, 87. Bauer discusses the same tradition in his chapter entitled "Deus Internus" 42-61; cf. 218-19. Von Ertzdorff terms this conception of the heart "das geistige Innen," tracing its influence in both religious and courtly texts: see especially "Herz" 262, 298-99; "Dame im Herzen" 13, 45.

97. Lyric 43.4, l. 4, cited in von Ertzdorff, "Dame im Herzen" 42.
98. Cited in Sauer 131. Cf. the "innerster Schoß des Herzens" as discussed in Rahner, "Flumina" 198; cf. Richstätter, *Herz-Jesu-Verehrung* 43.
99. *Enarrat. in Psalmos* 74.9 (*PL* 36.952); *Confessiones* 3.6.11. Cf. Richstätter, *Herz-Jesu-Verehrung* 20.
100. Bloomer and Moore 39; cf. wounding as the act of turning the body inside out and its relation to the heart in Scarry, *Body in Pain* 202-3, 349.
101. Ohly, "Cor amantis" 130; Gray 85. For references to the door of the heart, see von Ertzdorff "Dame im Herzen" 39-40, and the quotations from Walter Hilton in Leeming 607-08. Bauer provides an especially thorough study of this tradition in his section entitled "Das Herz als Haus," esp. 174-79. Cf. C. L. Powell, "The Castle of the Body," *Studies in Philology* 16 (1919): 197-98; Kanters *Coeur de Jésus* 94.
102. See esp. Augustine, *De magistro* 1.2 (*PL* 32.1195; cf. 1216).
103. *De civ. Dei* 22.17 (*PL* 41.778-79). Cyprien writes similarly: "Lex christianorum crux est sancta Christi Filii Dei vivi, dicente aeque propheta: lex tua in medio ventris mei. Percussus in lateris ventre, de latere sanguis et aqua mixtus profusus affluebat, unde sibi ecclesiam sanctam fabricavit, in quam legem passionis suae consecrabat, dicente ipso: Qui sitit veniat et bibat qui credit in me. Sicut scriptum est, flumina de ventre eius fluebant aquae vivae." *De mont. Sina et Sion* 9 (in Hartel's edition of Cyprien's works, 3.3.115), cited in Lécuyer 209.
104. Richstätter, *Herz-Jesu-Verehrung* 68. Cf. quotations from "Billyng's Five Wounds" in Gray 85. The allegorical conception of the heart as the ark of the covenant is especially important. Albertus Magnus and Ambrose support the eucharistic resonances already noted in the heart symbol by comparing it with the manna-filled ark (see citations in Richstätter, *Herz-Jesu-Verehrung* 98-99). According to Origen and Hugh of St. Victor, believers "build" the three levels of scriptural allegory in their hearts as an analogue to the three dimensions of the ark (*In Gen., hom.* 2.6, cited in Spitz 206n). Cf. Sauer 164; Ohly, "Cor angustam" 138-39.
105. Kanters, *Coeur de Jésus* 150 and passim; Leeming 609; Richstätter, *Herz-Jesu-Verehrung* 90. It is therefore a fitting receptacle for the pearl.
106. Von Ertzdorff, "Dame im Herzen" 34-35.
107. *In libros IV Reg.* 3.7 (*PL* 109.180); cf. other patristic citations in Bauer 108-09.
108. Richstätter, *Herz-Jesu-Verehrung* 39-40, 43; E. Jung 106. For a general consideration of the heart conceived as a vessel, see Morse, *Pattern of Judgment* 14-16 and passim; von Ertzdorff, "Dame im Herzen" 39.
109. Durandus and Innocent III, in Sauer 199.
110. Durandus and Sicardus, in Sauer 207; Mechthild von Magdeburg, in Richstätter, *Herz-Jesu-Verehrung* 81, 148.
111. Isidore of Seville, *Etymologiae* 20.5 (*PL* 82.716).
112. Durandus, Sicardus, and Innocent III, cited in Sauer 180.
113. Cf. Mersch, "Le Christ, l'homme et l'universe" 143.
114. Origen, *Hom. in Exod.* 11.2 and Caesarius, *Sermo* 103.3; cited in Rahner, "Flumina" 225.
115. *PL* 171.815ff.; see Curtius 311, 318-20.
116. Augustine, *Sermo* 119.7 (*PL* 38.675); Aquinas, *Summa* 1ª, q. 27, a. 1, c - q. 34, a. 1, c. Cf. Rahner, "Gottesgeburt" 15-16.
117. Rahner, "Flumina" 189-91, 220-21.
118. For more on the self-reflexive nature of the *verbum cordis*, see Gadamer 397: "So ist dieses innere Wort der Spiegel und das Bild des göttlichen Wortes." Scarry explains how humans project their heart into the perceived center of cultural and artistic artifacts, including literary artifacts (*Body in Pain* 281-82 and passim). Cf. Bainvel 77-81.

119. Israel Gollancz, *Pearl* (London: Nutt, 1891). See Daniel M. Murtaugh, "*Pearl* 462: 'Þe mayster of myste,'" *Neophilologus* 55 (1971): 191-93; Jefferson B. Fletcher, "The Allegory of the *Pearl*," *Journal of English and Germanic Philology* 20 (1921) 1-2.

120. See Singer fig. 7, and several of the diagrams in Wittkower, *Architectural Principles*. Cf. Fowler 260-68.

121. De Bruyne 343ff.

122. For a brief reference to the round shape of the navel, see W. W. Roscher, *Neue Omphalosstudien*, Abhandlungen der königlichen Sächsischen Gesellschaft der Wissenschaften, Philologische-historische Klasse 31.1 (Leipzig, 1915) 5.

123. Roscher 10n; Brown, *Love's Body* 60.

124. Urban II stated that "Hierusalem umbilicus est terrarum, terra prae ceteris fructifera, quasi alter Paradisus deliciarum" (quoted in Petrus Cellensis, *Epistolae*, PL 202.595). Cf. Roscher 10, 13-20, 72; E. Jung 341-43; Eliade, *Images et Symboles* 55. For Mt. Zion as the navel of the earth, see Roscher 72-75; Eliade, *Images et Symboles* 54-55.

125. Roscher 10, 16-18 and passim.

126. Roscher 16-18 and 73-74; many of his sources are Jewish. See also Brown, *Love's Body* 60; E. Jung 341-43.

127. Haubrichs 100-01.

128. Cf. the medieval conception of man as *nodus et vinculum* of the universe.

Chapter Eight

"AYQUERE HIT IS ENDELEZ" PENTANGLE AND TEXT IN *SIR GAWAIN AND THE GREEN KNIGHT*

One of the fundamental presuppositions of this study's interpretive *modus operandi* is its applicability to a broad range of creative artifacts. My opening chapters defined the corporeal matrix of certain kinds of architectural and iconographic production and attempted an overview of body-based structures in several texts; they laid the groundwork for the more exhaustive probing of *Pearl* that followed. Neither of the final chapters will attempt as thorough an interpretation as the chapters devoted to *Pearl*. Rather, my inquiry from this point on will restrict itself to preliminary exploration of corporeal symmetries and poetic nuclei in two of the poet's other works, *Sir Gawain* and *Patience*. My brief discussion of each of the following texts will focus primarily on how the body matrix manifests itself; structural similarities among these texts by the same poet will be underscored as a confirmation of the theory's general validity. These chapters are intended as an indication of the direction that further studies based on the same theoretical framework should take.

A few remarks on *Cleanness* are called for before I begin discussion of *Sir Gawain* and *Patience*. Scholarship on *Cleanness* already points so strongly in the direction of the body matrix presented elsewhere that an outline of relevant findings should suffice. Charlotte Morse and others devote considerable attention to the way the image of the vessel functions as a governing theme;[1] that image connects images of the heart and body with the poem's other spaces (including, as in *Pearl*, clothing)[2] in a way that suggests the fundamental equivalence of a plenitude of spaces, and the harmony between container and contained. Attempts to grasp the overall structure of the text confirm our findings elsewhere; the "Christ event in the center"[3] creates a textual vortex recalling the center of Christian history. Diagrammatic representations of the poem's structure by Morse and by Clark and Wasserman suggest concentric layers of space around a core.[4] What is generally missing in such studies is recognition of the primacy of the body as a textual matrix, and of parallels with body-based structures in architecture and iconography; the body is treated as one vessel among many.

Sir Gawain is the only work by this poet in which Leyerle claims to have found a poetic nucleus; it suggests itself, therefore, as a fruitful subject for the kind of inquiry I have been conducting. Leyerle finds a nucleus in the poem's frequent repetition of *gomnez*, a Middle English word denoting various kinds of "games." He argues that this key word functions as a thematic, centripetal core for the several interlocking games constituting the narrative's basic structure: the Beheading Game, The Temptation, The Hunts, and The Exchange of Winnings. The structure of the poem, he argues, reflects the shape of creation; the poet, as *homo ludens*, imitates God's primordial "play":

> The analysis of play in terms of the form that it creates has special significance for literature; the opening words of the gospel according to John, *in principio erat verbum*, indicate that the primal act of creation was verbal. . . . the poet's creation of verbal order out of his perception of the randomness and mutability of the world repeats the divine act and is serious in its form and playful in the doing.[5]

The Incarnation thus stands, according to Leyerle, at the center of the poem's order of words. And, like *Pearl*'s link words, *Sir Gawain*'s key word *gomnez* exhibits the hypostatic cohabitation of double meaning: Middle English *gome* is also cognate with Latin *homo*.

We can expand considerably on Leyerle's insight by juxtaposing it with what we know about corporeal, microcosmic aesthetic form; he appears to be eagerly in pursuit of the body-based "shape of creation" we have already noticed in other texts. Previous chapters would suggest that if *Sir Gawain* does contain a poetic nucleus, it may well be represented by a compact symbol uniting the main structural and thematic features of the text with an emblem of the microcosm linked explicitly to the hierarchy of corporeal organization. If we assume that that emblem is also characterized by self-reflexivity and a dense and paradoxical implosion of meaning, we may again feel justified in following the beaten paths of scholarly controversy to find it. In *Sir Gawain* criticism, of course, such a course leads us inevitably to the pentangle. My analysis will once again begin at this structural center and move outwards.

A good deal of evidence associates the pentangle with the body of man (*gome*) at the poem's nucleus; as Leyerle observes, the poet himself calls the pentangle design a *gomen* (661).[6] In medieval numerology, five is the number of man as three is the number of God. Roger Lass notes the pentangle's resonances of the many pentads characterizing the human body: "the five senses, the five bones of the skull, the five metacarpal bones and five fingers of each hand, the five metatarsals and five toes of each foot, the five sensory orifices of the face."[7] Thus when Gawain falls short of the ideal represented by the pentangle, a design whose interdependence of parts and whole admits of no flaw, he receives an analogous corporeal "flaw" on his neck; he wears the green girdle (a "transformation" of the pentangle) as a sign of that flaw. The pentangle also represents broader human characteristics. In scholastic philosophy, it became a common symbol for the rational soul. Dante employs it with this sense in the *Convivio*, and Otfrid relies on this tradition in his use of five as a principle of textual structure.[8]

The iconography of the pentangle forms a distinct strand of traditional representations of microcosm and cosmos. Commonly, both a pentangle and the human body are inscribed within a circle taking as its midpoint the navel or genitals.[9] The body's special relation to the geometry of the circle has already been discussed. The pentangle shows how the circle arises from the five points formed at the intersection of arms, legs, and head with the circle itself; these same five points are the furthest tips of the pentangle star. Gawain, says de Bruyne, is the ideal pentagonal man. De Bruyne does not specifically recognize Gawain's status as a microcosm within the poem, but the microcosmic features of the pentagonal man are important evidence for the present interpretive framework; the pentagonal man recapitulates a number of universal "fives":

> Cinq est le nombre de la sphère terrestre, embrassant les cinq essences des choses, les cinq zones élémentaires, les cinq parties de l'harmonie musicale, les cinq genres d'êtres vivants (plantes, poissons, oiseaux, animaux, hommes): or, l'homme reproduit en tant que microcosme, le grand univers.[10]

The tradition of the pentagonal man is linked with the iconography of bodies inscribed within circles, and thus with the *Pearl* text as well, whose circular geometry relies at every point on the numerological significance of five and the corporeality of both the text and the characters depicted. Both *Pearl*-Poet texts emerge, ultimately, from the same poetic nucleus.

As in *Pearl*, the location of the poem's central symbol on the garment of the hero reinforces both its microcosmic status and the emblematic value of clothing as a bodily extension. Gawain bears the pentangle on "schelde and cote" (637), just as the pearl maidens bear a large pearl in the center of their breasts. Several scholars have seen in the description of Gawain's arming a revelation of the *interioris hominis proprietates* via the *homo exterior*.[11] The relation of armor to the body of the knight parallels the relation of holy vesture to the body of a priest; the Incarnation effects the sacramental equivalence of clothing and body.[12] Clothing creates a "second body," whereby the ornamentation of the enclosure epitomizes the character of the enclosed.[13]

The "bond" and "chain" nuclei that Leyerle finds in Chaucer's work can also be applied to *Sir Gawain*'s central symbol. The pentangle, like the poem's analogous images of the love knot and green girdle, is a microcosmic *Weltenverknotung*, a miniature representation of the Great Chain of Being: Gawain's failure disrupts the cosmic order emblemized by the symbol that he wears. As John Burrow convincingly shows, both the pentangle and the entire poem center on *trauþe*, which I take as a virtue that aligns chivalric idealism with the structure of the cosmos.[14] And the pentangle also resonates with the microcosmic significance of the heart, the other poetic nucleus explored in Leyerle's "The Heart and the Chain" article, via its traditional connection with Christ's five wounds; oddly enough, Leyerle does not appear to have noticed the heart nucleus in *Sir Gawain*. The five wounds are one of the series of five groups of "fives" mentioned explicitly in the pentangle description (642), and Richard Green has presented evidence for a traditional connection between the pentangle and Christ's wounds.[15] The image of the heart, as we have seen, is implicit in any reference to the wounds; in the poem, the many occurrences of *hert* make it a key facet of Gawain's characterization.[16] Like Gawain's pentangle, representations of the five wounds frequently appear on shields.[17] Wound imagery, of course, plays a very significant role in the Beheading Game and in related descriptive details throughout the poem.[18]

The pentangle image thus draws on the same tradition of *Weltbild* iconography as the five wounds. R. Lass has shown how medieval understanding of the pentangle's numerology emphasized the relation of five to one: the pentangle evokes both numbers simultaneously.[19] In our analysis of *Pearl*, we noticed that the relationship between the four outer wounds and the central heart wound (depicted as four small circles clustered around a large one) was based on the geometry of medieval *Weltbilder*.[20] The ability for one pearl maiden to equal five maidens (or for one crown to equal five) and for five angles to equal one pentagonal figure parallels the concentric equivalence of a *Weltbild*'s central circle with the group of five circles to which it belongs. The plenitude of the center and heart projects its own unity into layers of concentric enclosure.

Thus, the pentangle constitutes an extremely dense, microcosmic emblem at the core of *Sir Gawain*'s symbolism. Based on the body as *minor mundus*, the pentangle itself contains five parts which reiterate the structure of the whole: it is a group of five fives, a microcosm enclosing five microcosms. In this way it resembles drawings of the pentagonal man wherein the five senses, fingers, and toes create microcosmic subgroups at the five extremities (head, arms, and legs; the five fingers are one of the five pentangle groups, line 641). It is also structurally reminiscent of the ritual of consecration described by Moessel: a series of four crosses at each extremity of a large fifth cross traced over a church altar.[21] Thus the pentangle functions within *Sir Gawain* much like the numerological microcosms within microcosms that Haubrichs discovered in Otfrid and in Carolingian symmetrical poetry. Haubrichs lays particular emphasis on the "pentagonale Grundform" of the *Liber Evangeliorum*, finding its basis both in the shape of the cross and in the microcosmic relation between the world's five zones and man's five senses (another of the groups in the pentangle):

> Die Fünfzahl ist Sinnbild der Welt und ihrer fünf Zonen. In Handschriften von Isidors 'De natura rerum' sind diese fünf Zonen als gleichmäßige Fünfteilung eines Kreises, also in pentagonaler Form dargestellt.
> Wie aber die Fünfzahl die Ordnung des *Makrokosmus* repräsentiert, so auch den *Mikrokosmus*, der analog in der Fünfteilung seiner Sinne angeschaut werden kann: "Mundi figuram quinque zone continent, / Sensusque nostri dividuntur quinquies." Der Mensch in der Sündhaftigkeit seines Fleisches ist das verkleinerte Abbild des "mundus peccatus." Erlösungsbedürftiger Mensch und heilsverlorener Kosmos gehören zusammen.[22]

Isidore's geometric representation of this concept (reproduced by Haubrichs 361) shows a five-part circle surrounded by a five-part concentric ring, the latter containing five circles; like Gawain's pentangle, it represents microcosms within microcosms in a scheme based on the number five.[23]

As the heart and microcosm of the text, the pentangle implodes *Sir Gawain*'s overarching plot structures and thematic concerns. It is the *gome* that knots together the story's several games; Gawain's *trauþe*, epitomized by the emblem on his shield, is tried at each stage.[24] Howard finds the poem to be ordered by the pentangle and girdle's "centripetal force," applying Northrop Frye's term in the same way we have used it to describe the pearl symbol.[25] But can we describe the relationship between text and symbolic nucleus in even more precise terms? In *Pearl*, as in many of the texts analyzed in chapter four, the poem's central symbol pointed us towards a specific moment or scene where theme and structure dramatically "thickened" like the geometry at the center of a *Weltbild* or the symbolic network closest to an altar. In *Sir Gawain*, the web of four interlocking games reaches its densest texture in Fitt 3. Here the rapid alternation between The Temptation in the bedroom and The Hunts on the field provides the basis for The Exchange of Winnings in intervening scenes set in the castle hall; Gawain's faithfulness to the terms of the latter game, in turn, determines the outcome of The Beheading Game.[26] Nowhere else in the story do the games interweave themselves so tightly. That this point of greatest density does not, as in *Pearl*, occur at the numerological center of the poem should not bother us; Haubrichs has found many poems whose structural nexus is deliberately off center.[27]

The tight web of games in Fitt 3, always explicitly tied to the heart-based symbol of the pentangle and girdle, resembles the way that the interlocking games of *hert-huntying* and chess weave together most closely in John of Gaunt's speech at the center of the *Book of the Duchess*.[28] Fitt 3 is the heart of the poem and, as such, displays the heart's peculiar spatial and temporal dimensions; at this point in the text, space and time fold in on themselves, resulting in thematic thickening and narrative repetition.

The dramatic alternation among private (bedroom), public (hunting ground), and intermediate (castle hall) spaces highlights the tension between inside and outside, enclosure and enclosed that always characterizes the point of maximum interiority in Christian space. Henry L. Savage has already established the parallels between stages of the "hunt" both in the bedroom and on the field;[29] the Exchange of Winnings scenes occur in an intermediate, transitional space. Within the structure of incarnational space, what happens within is always tied to what happens without; hence, in the *Perceval/Parzival* myth, the Fisher King's wounded and sinful genitalia extend their sterility to the entire kingdom. As so often occurs in medieval romance, the bedroom is here conceived as the castle's core, the estate's procreative center. (A striking parallel from a more modern era is the layout of Versailles, where Louis XIV's bed constitutes the geometric hub at which all the lines of the castle, grounds, and city converge.[30]) The proper use to which the genitals should or should not be put is, of course, at the crux of The Temptation; the womb is the bedroom's implicit center and also the interlocking games' most intimate point of spatial contact with the heart/womb at the center of the microcosmic pentangle. Faithfulness to the wounds and heart/womb of Christ presupposes an honorable relation to the womb that first enclosed Him. The fundamental equivalence of pentangle and Virgin as pictured on opposing sides of Gawain's shield establishes the link between spatial patterning in both symbol and narrative.

The peculiar configurations of the text's spatial center in Fitt 3 correspond with the concentric spatial and temporal rings created at the text's edge. The opening lines begin in the far historical and geographic distance, at Troy, and zoom in step by step towards the setting of the story: Rome, Tuscany, Lombardy, Britain, Arthur's court. The concluding lines enact a compact mirror image of the opening: Arthur's court, Britain (via allusion again to "Brutus"), Troy. "Siþen þe sege and þe assaut" in the first line anticipates "After þe segge and þe asaute" in the line preceding the final bob and wheel. Dale Randall has shown how the correspondence of beginning and ending elements fits into a careful symmetrical pattern: the three days of Fitt 3 form a geometrical center preceded by a pattern of narration (opening lines, challenge made on New Year's Day, ride to seek the chapel) that is inverted in the Fitt 4 (ride to seek the chapel, challenge fulfilled on New Year's Day, closing lines). Dale Randall's observation about the structure of Fitt 3 supports the microcosmic quality we have already noticed in it:

> Of particular interest is the way in which suspense is built by breaking each hunting episode into two parts which are placed on either side of an episode that occurs back at the castle, thus giving each major subdivision of this central portion of the romance an inner and wave-length dynamic of its own.[31]

Fitt 3 repeats and condenses the frame structure of the entire poem at its center in a manner strikingly similar to the numerological microcosms discovered by Haubrichs at the center of Latin and German texts. The relation of part to whole in the textual superstructure thus resembles that in *Pearl*. When Gawain's integrity is measured by the ideal of the pentangle, he is judged against a series of heroes (Aeneas, Romulus, Tirius, Brutus) within the traditional microcosmic scheme of Christian history and geography. The *Gawain*-Poet, as J. K. Crane points out, presupposes the fundamental equivalence of time and space in this poem about the establishment of an *axis mundi*: he depicts "the microcosmic cosmogonic moment of the birth of a nation."[32] Gawain's greatest test occurs at the very center of the poem's space and time, but its ramifications and consequences reach to the edge of the text and far beyond. We have already seen in *Troilus and Criseyde* how the innermost space of the womb constitutes a temporal and spatial nexus at the center of successive layers of architectural, textual, and cosmic space, as well as the similar status of the *Mons veneris* as a locus of sexual and textual unity in Spenser. This elaborate microcosmic structure surrounding depictions of sex occurs frequently in medieval literature.

Several scholars have commented on the interaction of circular and linear time schemes in *Sir Gawain*, a framework that again resembles *Pearl*'s microcosmic textual structure. Morton Bloomfield writes: "Cyclic time or the time of nature is superimposed on linear time or the time of history, in order to contrast the two and to point up Gawain's dilemma."[33] Robert Margeson notes that while Gawain perceives the shape of his quest as linear, both the Green Knight and the court affirm its essential circularity.[34] In this respect both Gawain and *Pearl*'s dreamer begin their quest with the same misconceptions about the spatial and temporal configurations of the Christian universe; both must finally acknowledge their capacity for error and their consequent new vision of a cosmos shaped according to the dictates of grace.[35]

The structure of the text returns us to the structure of the pentangle. Shoaf writes:

> If the lel *layk of luf* is a lettrure *of armes* and if the pentangle is a figure of which *vche lyne vmbelappez and* loukez *in oþer*, the poem itself is a "stori stif and stronge, / With *lel letteres loken*" (34-35; emphasis added). The poem, like the *layk of luf*, being a lettered thing, is also a *lettrure*, or 'learning'; moreover, its letters are *lel* just like the *layk of luf*; finally, the *lel letteres* of the poem are *locked* just like the lines of the pentangle. Hence the form of the poem repeats itself in the pentangle and the *lettrure of armes*: the poem analyzes its own form . . . [36]

The pentangle acts as a text within a text, the point where the poem begins to comment on itself. It is the *tabulae cordis* within the poem's body, a microcosm of the five wounds within a manuscript penned with Christ's blood.[37] Its self-reflexivity is implicit in its numerology; the pentangle, like the pearl, is both the origin and consummation of its own meaning:

> Cinq est un nombre merveilleux et circulaire puisque se multipliant, il revient sans cesse à lui même . . . . Or, c'est là une parenté avec la cause première, qui subsiste toujours en elle-même, et dont l'homme est l'image et la ressemblance.[38]

Penetrating to the interior of the pentangle, we find the greatest mysteries of the Christian faith.[39]

Like the sacramental quality of the pearl symbol, the pentangle proves capable of transforming itself into other shapes whose meaning derives from their relation to it. The inadequacy of the green girdle emerges by way of contrast with the emblem on Gawain's shield; the pentangle's knot is *endeles*, but the ends of the girdle must be *samned* by hand.[40] Analogous with the body's image in medieval cathedrals and *Weltbilder*, the symbol at the center of *Sir Gawain* disperses itself throughout the textual macrocosm. Like the many pearls on the Pearl Maiden's clothing which extend the symbolism of the one on her breast, Gawain's pentangle is reiterated in the several knots adorning his chivalric gear (2376, 2487). When he adopts the girdle as a permanent feature of his attire, the rest of Arthur's court follows suit; the sign extends itself to the entire body politic, just as all the virgins in *Pearl* bear the same chief adornment as the Pearl Maiden.[41]

Notes

1. *The Pattern of Judgment in the* Queste *and* Cleanness (Columbia: U of Missouri P, 1978). T. D. Kelly and John T. Irwin also focus on the image of the vessel in "The Meaning of *Cleanness*: Parable as Effective Sign," *Mediaeval Studies* 35 (1973): 232-60.

2. See Earl G. Schreiber, "The Structures of *Clannesse*," *The Alliterative Tradition in the Fourteenth Century* 134.

3. See diagram in Morse *Pattern* 132. She calls this moment "the pivot around which the rest of the poem turns" in "The Image of the Vessel in *Cleanness*," *University of Toronto Quarterly* 40 (1971): 202.

4. "*Purity*: The Cities of the Dove and the Raven," *American Benedictine Review* 29 (1978): 284-306.

5. "The Game and Play of Hero," *The Concept of the Hero in the Middle Ages and Early Renaissance*, ed. Christopher Reagan (Albany: State U of New York P, 1975) 78; see also 50ff., 76ff.

6. "Game" 57.

7. "Man's Heaven: The Symbolism of Gawain's Shield," *Mediaeval Studies* 28 (1966): 356.

8. *Convivio* 4.7.14, cited in Gerald Morgan, "The Significance of the Pentangle Symbolism in *Sir Gawain and the Green Knight*," *Modern Language Review* 74 (1979): 772-73. Cf. Haubrichs 167.

9. See Lass 356-57, and the frontispiece to both volumes of Moessel's work.

10. De Bruyne 350-51. He cites St. Hildegard, a source whose ideas figure prominently in my previous chapters, as an important writer linking the number five with microcosmic speculation. Cf. Howard, "Structure and Symmetry in *Sir Gawain*," in Sir Gawain *and* Pearl: *Critical Essays*, ed. Robert J. Blanch (Bloomington: Indiana UP, 1966) 197-98.

11. See Stephanie J. Hollis, "The Pentangle Knight: *Sir Gawain and the Green Knight*," *Chaucer Review* 15 (1981): 272-73. R. A. Shoaf writes: "It is as if in bearing the shield a knight would become the shield." *The Poem as Green Girdle: Commercium in Sir Gawain and the Green Knight* (Gainsville: UP of Florida, 1984) 71.

12. St.-Jacques 154-56; Burrow 38-39; Howard, "Structure and Symmetry" 197-98. Cf. my earlier discussion of priestly vestments and the symbolism of vesture in *Pearl* and, in that connection, the article by Finkelstein.

13. See Kamper, *Wiederkehr* 20 on armor as a *Zweitkörper*. Cf. Douglas M. Moon, "Clothing Symbolism in *Sir Gawain and the Green Knight*," *Neuphilosophische Mitteilungen* 66 (1965): 334-47; Moon writes: "It has been shown that in each of its appearances, the article in question symbolically reflects the moral position of the person who wears it" (347).

14. *A Reading of Sir Gawain and the Green Knight* (London: Routledge, 1965); he elaborates on this important foundation to his interpretation throughout the book. Cf. Hieatt, "*Sir Gawain*: Pentangle, *luf-lace*, Numerical Structure," *Silent Poetry*, ed. Alastair Fowler (London: Routledge, 1970) 123-24; R. E. Kaske, "Sir Gawain and the Green Knight," *Medieval and Renaissance*

Studies, ed. George Mallary Masters, Proceedings of the Southeastern Institute of Medieval and Renaissance Studies, Summer 1979 (Chapel Hill: U of North Carolina P, 1984) 24-25.

15. "Gawain's Shield and the Quest for Perfection," in Blanch anthology 188-89. Another scholar notes, in connection with the wounds reference here: "Devotion to the Five Wounds was the most popular of all Catholic devotions during the fourteenth and fifteenth centuries." J. R. F., "The Five Wounds," *Notes and Queries* 171 (1936): 335.

16. See lines 120, 371, 467, 1594, 1781, 1855, etc. Cf. J. R. F. 335-36, on the image of the heart in the context of the wounds reference here; also Hollis 227-28, 281.

17. See Gray 50 (notes 2 and 5) and 88.

18. See Paul F. Reichardt, "Gawain and the Image of the Wound," *PMLA* 99 (1984): 154-61.

19. "Man's Heaven: The Symbolism of Gawain's Shield," *Mediaeval Studies* 28 (1966): 354-60; cf. Green 186-87.

20. See A. R. Bayley, "The Five Wounds," *Notes and Queries* 171 (1936): 266; figures in Bober, "Illustrated Schoolbook" 68, 79; Beer, *Die Rose* figs. 45, 51.

21. Moessel 2: 154-55; cf. my discussion of this ritual in chapter two.

22. Haubrichs 362. He supports his assertions with generous citations from Isidore, Martianus Capella, and Alcuin. Cf. also his notes on the symbolism of the number five in medieval architecture (361). The resonances of the cross in the pentangle symbol, of course, contribute to its function as a spatial and temporal center in the poem. For further discussion of the traditional link between cross and pentangle, see Hopper 121-25; Cowen 95.

23. One might also argue that the group of five virtues symbolized by the last point of Gawain's pentangle bears a special microcosmic relation to the rest of the pentangle akin to that of head to body. More than one scholar has observed how this group, mentioned as a sort of climactic finale in the description, distinguishes itself from the others. R. E. Kaske suggests that *pité*, the final virtue which "passez alle poyntez" (654), epitomizes both the group to which it pertains and all five groups symbolized by the pentangle ("Sir Gawain" 34). If we accept Kaske's suggestion, *pité* would appear to function as a microcosm within a microcosm, recapitulating the entire pentangle much as the head recapitulates the body. The possibility is strengthened if, as Kaske also suggests, the final group consists of those virtues which Gawain must draw on at Bercilak's castle in order to avoid losing his head. See also Morgan 775, 778-79. In any case, the special relation of head to heart that we have seen in theological sources, *Weltbilder*, the symbolism of *Haupt-* and *Kreuzaltäre* in Gothic architecture, and the geometry of crowns and breast pearls in *Pearl* appears to hold in *Sir Gawain* as well. Gawain's success in upholding the ideal of the pentangle, with its resonances of the theology of the heart, has a direct bearing on the outcome of the Beheading Game. Put another way, the wound on his neck is the consequence of Gawain's flawed allegiance to Christ's wounds.

24. Leyerle, "Game" 59.

25. "Structure" 195-96.

26. Again I follow the classification and terminology for the games used by Leyerle "Game" 50.

27. Cullmann notes that when we speak of the middle of Christian time, the "middle" does not create two exactly equivalent halves, but should be considered "im Sinne des entscheidenden Einschnitts" (13n).

28. See my discussion of this speech in chapter four.

29. "The Significance of the Hunting Scenes in *Sir Gawain and the Green Knight*," *Journal of English and Germanic Philology* 27 (1928): 1-15. Although some of the details of Savage's interpretation remain controversial, his theory has met with general acceptance in its broadest outlines.

30. See Bloomer and Moore, passim, for Versailles' bed-centered plan in the context of body-based architecture.

31. "A Note on Structure in *Sir Gawain and the Green Knight*," *Modern Language Notes* 72 (1957): 161-63. Cf. Howard, who remarks on the "recapitulation" of the opening series of events at the poem's end (*Three Temptations* 267-68). Clark and Wasserman make similar observations about *Sir Gawain*'s opening in "The Pearl Poet's City Imagery," *Southern Quarterly* 16 (1978): 302. On 306 they remark on the alternation between interior and exterior spaces: "*Patience* and in particular *Sir Gawain and the Green Knight* take their chief characters outside in order that they may be brought back inside, wiser and chastened."

32. Crane 71; cf. 73, 77. Crane's very general discussion does not address the issue of textual microcosmic structure or the nexus of the pentangle. Cf. Johnson 92-93.

33. "*Sir Gawain and the Green Knight*: An Appraisal," *PMLA* 77 (1961): 18.

34. "Structure and Meaning in *Sir Gawain and the Green Knight*," *Papers on Language and Literature* 13 (1977): 16-24. Cf. Arnold F. Soucy, "Linear Pattern within the Cyclical Patterns of *Sir Gawain and the Green Knight*," diss., U of Minnesota, 1972.

35. Both poems also appear to draw on the tradition of sin as a "breaking" of the perfect circle, as when Adam's bite marred the circularity of the forbidden fruit. Gawain's refusal to acknowledge the gift of the girdle to his host breaks the perfect circularity of the pentangle. Nelson argues that *Pearl*'s famous missing line (472) also creates a deliberate flaw in the poem's round structure (33).

36. Shoaf 74.

37. Cf. Reichardt, passim.

38. De Bruyne 349n, based on Macrobius, *Somnium Scipionis* 1.6.

39. "Das Innere des Pentagramms enthält große Mysterien." Moessel 2: 168.

40. A. Kent Hieatt, "*Sir Gawain*: Pentangle, *luf-lace*, Numerical Structure," *Silent Poetry* 120-21.

41. The juxtaposition of the Virgin and the pentangle on opposing sides of the same shield suggests another way of seeing transformation symbolism in this central image. Mary and the pentangle apparently figure as two aspects of the same symbol, much as *rota* and *rosa* represent two transformations of the same poetic nucleus in *Troilus*; the two images at the core of both poems rest back to back, interpenetrating the same plane, as in a rose-wheel window. The pentangle, based on the microcosmic symbolism of Christ and the five wounds, is also a theological coordinate of the Virgin: both Christ and Mary give birth to the church, and the bodies of both are allegorized as the *corpus mysticum*. The number five is as closely linked in tradition with Mary as with Christ's wounds; her five joys are one of the pentangle groups. This interpretation of the shield's double symbolism seems especially likely in view of the way that both rose and Wheel of Fortune images cohabit the poetic nucleus of *Pearl*—an indication that the *Pearl*-Poet was as intrigued by the structural paradox of the rose-wheel as was Chaucer. The pentangle, of course, draws on the same tradition of cosmographic representation as both the rose and the Wheel of Fortune. The peculiar duality of the shield, understood in this light, may be understood to bear a specific structural relation to Gawain's interlocking series of games. The conflict between a knight's duties to his lady and to "chivalry" (his lord, hunting, military prowess, etc.) is a classic thematic nucleus of medieval romance. Fitt 3 dramatizes the conflict by its self-conscious series of movements from outer to inner spaces: We associate the outer space with Gawain's lord/host, the inner with the lady. The depiction of Mary on the inside of the shield, together with the more explicitly chivalric emblem of the pentangle on the outside, thus functions as a symbolic condensation of both the delicate balance of loyalties tested in the interlocking games and the way interior and exterior spaces underscore the interdependence of those games in Fitt 3. Another deployment of the conflict between duty to lady and lord/chivalry as a poetic nucleus and basis for bipartite structure occurs in *Parzival*. *Parzival*'s Book 4 features a tightly structured alternation among bedroom, battle, and intermediate spaces which dramatizes the same conflict of duties in a manner that is strikingly similar to *Sir Gawain*.

Chapter Nine

"HELLEN WOMBE"
THE HEART OF *PATIENCE*

The striking similarities in the spatial organization of *Pearl* and *Sir Gawain* tempt one to rummage further in the *Pearl*-Poet opus. *Patience* suggests itself as the next scholarly port of call, if for no other reason than the preponderance of references to the heart and the interpretations already proposed by scholars who take the "virtues of the heart" as the poem's controlling theme. Given the heart-based symbolism and structure of *Pearl* and *Sir Gawain*, it would indeed be surprising if the poem where that organ makes its most conspicuous thematic appearance did not share the other two texts' corporeal spatiality.

Certain formal parallels among the three poems suggest themselves immediately. Verbal echoes linking the first and last lines of all three presuppose a shared reliance on the geometry of the circle. I have already noted how the word *poynt* in the first and last lines of *Patience* appears to rely on the same geometric tradition as the *poynt determynable* at the center of *Pearl*. Eldredge's comments on the *poynt* indicate that the poem may develop a spatial theme that is consistent with microcosmic theory:

> A point occupies no space, theoretically, and yet it can be located in space. It is, in effect, the non-dimensional space occupied by an attitude of mind—the quiet sufferance of whatever God sends. God may require something definite, such as running to Rome on his errand (52), or his demands may be less dramatically specific, such as enduring poverty without complaint (35). Whatever he demands, patience is that kind of trust and acceptance that relies confidently on a God who will never ask what is not to a man's ultimate good. Thus man's appropriate response to the vastness of the cosmos is not to seek shelter but rather to be a point.[1]

Line 68 links the words *poynt*, *place*, and *hert*, suggesting a very well-defined spatial sense in this poem's preoccupation with the interiority of the heart: "þat in þat place, at þe poynt, I put in þi hert." In fact, there is an implicit *poynt* in the poem's central whale episode, akin to the explicit *poynt* at the center of *Pearl*; Friedman has shown in commentaries by Gregory and Jerome how the image of the hook in this biblical tradition evoked the "punctus" of God's divinity.[2] There is every reason to believe, as Anderson notes in his gloss on *poynt*, that the poet employs his word in a rather unusual sense in the poem.[3] The circularity created by the interlocking of the poem's first and last lines, together with the theological connection with the *punctus* at the text's center, suggests that *Patience*, like *Sir Gawain* and *Pearl*, structures itself according to the traditional corporeal geometry of the *minor mundus*. The parallel with *Pearl* is supported by the occurrence of "displese" in the first and last lines of *Patience*, a verbal link whose literal meaning recalls the similar placement of "pay."

Scholarship on the poem to date reveals an incipient awareness of corporeal spatiality, but lacks both the extensive patristic grounding necessary to place the poem within its traditional framework and any extended description of spatial parallels with the poet's other works. Thus Enoch Padolsky correctly identifies the heart as a governing image, but fails to notice its microcosmic structural implications.[4] Clark and Wasserman draw on a wider knowledge of the theology of the vessel, but stop short, among other things, of applying the broad traditions of the *theologia cordis* and microcosmic speculation.[5] Studies of the poem's opening Beatitudes passage, in particular, suffer from incomplete acquaintance with aspects of Christianity's theology of the heart underlying the deliberate repetition of "hert" at that point.[6] Eldredge goes the furthest towards defining the poem's cosmic spatial frame, but does not provide the traditional background necessary for a thoroughgoing "medieval" reading. None of these studies apply a systematic knowledge of Gothic architecture, cosmographic iconography, or mystical geometry; their combined contribution to our understanding of the complex thematic patterns in the poem is, however, considerable.

Having speculated on the structural implications of the word echoes at the poem's two "edges," we would do well to consider the textual center in some detail; the spatial configurations at the poem's middle are especially complex and provide a point of orientation for consideration of its other spaces. Following the lines of the text to its exact numerical center (265-66), we find Jonah in the whale's mouth, just on the verge of being swallowed (as described in the lines immediately following):

> And þrwe in at hit þrote with-outen þret more,
> As mote in at a munster dor, so mukel wern his chawleȝ.
> He glydes in by þe giles þurȝ glaymande gletteȝ . . . (267-69)

It is surely no coincidence that the numerical center of the text coincides so precisely with the protagonist's passage into the most interior of the poem's depicted spaces. And the numerological correspondence is supported by the exegetical tradition surrounding Matthew 12:40: "sicut enim fuit Ionas in ventre ceti tribus diebus et tribus noctibus, sic erit Filius hominis in corde terrae tribus diebus et tribus noctibus." The *venter ceti* prefigures the *cor terrae*; Jonah's entry into the belly of the whale is the typological coordinate of the Harrowing, whereby Christ descended into the "heart of the earth." Malcolm Andrew has already explored other figural resonances of the Harrowing throughout the poem; whether or not we agree with all of the details of his interpretation, this numerological correspondence provides especially striking evidence for some such reading of the poem.[7] As I noted earlier, Christ's Harrowing at the heart of the earth during the three days following his Atonement constitute a nexus for Christian time and space analogous to the birth of the church from his own heart. Just as Christ endows salvation history with a new center from his position at the center of the Ptolomaic universe, so too the swallowing of Jonah marks the spatial and numerological midpoint of *Patience*. Jonah's sojourn in the belly of the whale marks the time of his conversion, the moment when he, like all new Christians, appropriates the new spatial and temporal sense of the Incarnation.

Friedman has pointed out how the imagery in Jonah's prayer from the whale's belly (282-87) highlights the contrast between a wrathful Old Testament Jehovah and the merciful Father of the New Law, remarking that "the Old Law prophet metaphorically turns to the values of the New in his trouble, and generalizes the contrast of mercy and wrath."[8] In *Patience*, as in Christian figural history, this central event marks a point of textual *recapitulatio*, encapsulating the core themes and structures of the poem. The heart/belly at the center of *Patience* endows the rest of the text with its own peculiar stamp, just as the *minor mundus* in Christ's body determined the shape of creation from the heart of creation itself. As Bachelard, in a similar context, writes: "Nous allons voir comment une image très particulière peut commander l'espace, donner sa loi à l'espace."[9]

The passage that surrounds this crucial textual moment establishes the poet's full awareness of the spatial tradition in which he writes. Jonah calls to God out of "hellen wombe" (306); he lies in the "warlowes gutteȝ" (258) which "stank as þe deuel" (274) and "sauoured as helle" (275). Jonah finds himself in cramped quarters linked not only with hell but with the image of the heart: "þou dipteȝ me of þe depe se in-to þe dymme hert" (308).[10] His spiritual condition is characterized by references to his own heart (283, 300). Clearly, what is at issue at this "heart" of the poem is the necessity for a change in Jonah's heart, the same change that will be required of the Ninevites (368). The importance of this explicitly corporeal transformation is prepared for as early as the opening paraphrase of the Beatitudes (where "hert" occurs four times) and sustained via repeated mention of this central organ throughout the poem.[11]

In addition to his frequent mention of the heart, the poet underscores the interiority of this middle space in *Patience* by simultaneous reference to all of the other traditional corporeal centers; each of them is a center whose special relation to the macrocosm outside the body we have already noted. The belly (*maw*, 255, 299; *gutteȝ*, 258; *stomak*, 274; *gut*, 280; *bouel*, 298) is one of the "plusieurs milieux intérieurs concentriques" which "n'est encore, tout intérieur qu'il est, que le milieu extérieur."[12] Traditional usage associates the stomach and the heart even outside of commentary on the Jonah story.[13] The comparison between the "wombe of þat fissche" (262) and "hellen wombe" evokes another classic corporeal center in connection with the common image of the macrocosm as a giant body with its womb in hell. And Jonah's search, within the whale's stomach, "in vche a nok of his nauel" (278), alludes to a bodily center whose prominent appearance in *Pearl*'s *corpus mysticum* passage we have already seen; Anderson correctly glosses *nauel* as the "interior" or "bowels" of the whale. Thus within a short, numerically central passage, we find allusions to the heart, womb, and navel familiar as the midpoint of medieval *Weltbilder*'s concentrically-inscribed bodies and as universal axes in Christian geography. All three bear allegorical equivalence with the belly of the whale. The appearance of these images is especially significant in view of the deployment of all three as points of spatial convergence in *Pearl* and of the similar occurrence of two of the images (heart and womb) in *Sir Gawain*.

We have already noticed in medieval architecture and iconography, as well as in numerous texts, how often a structural core is characterized by the overlay of multiple meanings; the references to all of the body's traditional axes at the numerical core of *Patience* is therefore significant not only because the body parts alluded to are themselves centers, but because these centers are so tightly juxtaposed at this particular point. And the poet reinforces this sense of spatial and allegorical convergence in other ways as well. Looking again at the key passage following the poem's center from this standpoint, the lines "And þrwe in at hit þrote with-outen þret more, / As mote in at a munster dor, so mukel wern his chawleȝ" must certainly give us pause. The famous *munster dor* reference, of course, draws on the commonplace comparison between the whale's mouth and the gates of hell familiar to everyone from records of the sets used in cycle plays, encyclopedias, bestiaries, and medieval iconography; the line is consistent with the poem's other resonances of the Harrowing,[14] and is supported by other architectural references in the passage (*rode*, 270; *halle*, 272; *bour*, 276; *nok*, 278; *hyrne*, 289). But its appearance at this key textual midpoint imparts an important spatial dimension to the poem. Based on the introductory line, "I herde on a halyday, at a hyȝe masse" (9), Friedman suggests that we experience the entire poem as if spoken "within the confines of a church";[15] the entire text, we have seen, shares with *Pearl* and *Sir Gawain* the geometry of Gothic architecture. But here at the middle of the text we find the protagonist crossing the threshold of a cathedral—precisely at the moment he is in the belly of a whale conceived allegorically as hell. That *Patience*'s most striking image of ingress occurs at this most interior point of its textual space, that the cathedral's resonances of paradise should be so radically juxtaposed with the "ramel ande myre" (279) of hell, should come as no surprise to those familiar with the paradoxical symbolism of medieval geometry. The center of a circle contains its circumference. At the Harrowing that Jonah's story prefigures, the vast circle of the Empyrean contained in the *maior mundus* of Christ's body was juxtaposed with the universe's center in hell, effecting so drastic a change in the shape of creation that even the most cramped core of hell could partake of the broadest dimensions of heaven. The belly of the whale is a cathedral contained within the architecture of the poem; like the *tabulae cordis*, it is a heart-shaped text contained within the heart-based symbolism of the entire text. Thus the structure of the center of *Patience* is inside out in much the same way that *Pearl*'s row of Vineyard workers inverts the textual frame into an upside-down body of Christ, and that Dante's *Inferno* features an inverted body of Christ radiating around Satan's upside-down body in the *lago del cor*. In *Patience*, this traditional inversion is further reinforced by a telling detail in the description of Jonah's passage through the whale's throat: he glides in "hele ouer hed" (head over heels). His inverted posture can leave no doubt about the transformational quality of this spatial transition.[16] Again, this spatial inversion at the threshold of a belly figuring as both heart and *munster* derives from medieval conceptions of the heart as a microcosmic building within the temple of the body (as discussed earlier); at the moment of each new convert's reenactment of the Harrowing, God's Spirit enters his body through the "door of the heart," transforming the structure of his belief from the inside.[17] Jonah's conversion inside the whale, like the conversion of all believers, dictates the shape of his story as it recapitulates the Harrowing's transformation of Old Covenant time and space. The geometry of the poem's centermost image, the "mote in at a munster dor," contrasts Jonah's tiny frame with the whale/cathedral's cavernous opening; Jonah slides in easily, "with-outen þret more," because the whale's jaws are so "mukel." The word *mote* is familiar from the poet's careful puns in *Pearl*: one of its meanings is "spot, speck," allowing it to participate in the geometry of contraction evoked by the *spot* and *poynt* marking *Pearl*'s edges and middle. In *Patience*, the *mote* at the middle and the *poynt* at each edge create a textual superstructure akin to *Pearl*'s; the midpoint of both evokes the circumference. And both poems' numerical centers share the same preoccupation with the paradoxical geometry of grace. Just as "euer þe lenger þe lasse, þe more" (600) provides a quantitative index to *Pearl*'s structure and main theme, so the *mote* that finds itself contained by the vastness of the church at the door to hell's confinement figures forth both the shape of *Patience* and its protagonist's most difficult lesson. The spatial didactic of both poems is rooted in an identical geometrical principle. *Pearl*'s dreamer, after trying to leap across the stream into the Empyrean, realizes that God's expansiveness was available all along at the *spot* where he began; for him, like the Vineyard laborers at the poem's center, *more* and *lasse* were equal. Jonah, attempting to escape rather than pursue God, learns the opposite lesson based on the same geometry. No matter where he goes, the *poynt* he occupies will always be encompassed by the great circumference of God's rulership, just like a *mote* disappearing into a whale's mouth. "Pacience is a noble poynt, þaȝ hit displese oft": when Jonah acquires the patience necessary to submit to the limits of the *poynt*, he discovers in it the scope of God's provision for him—the *nexus mysteriorum* of the heart. Just as *trothe* in *Sir Gawain* and the key themes of the Vineyard in *Pearl* find their most concise expression in the geometry of the pentangle and circle, here the poetic nucleus of the heart defines the key virtue of patience via the geometry of the point.

Two *Patience* studies provide evidence for the uniquely transformational quality of this moment through analysis of narrative perspective. Considering lines 298-304, Clark and Wasserman write:

> The evolution of narrative voice from the finite to the omniscient over the course of these four stanzas takes the reader from cognition of simple inclusion (that is, a knowledge of the area or interior of the circle, as is shown in the first stanza) to an awareness of the infinite area which lies beyond the circumference of that circle (as is presented in the fourth stanza). . . . The detached narrator is now able to see both the outside and the inside of the whale simultaneously, so that the shift in narrative perspective demonstrates the internal reorientation from the finite, man-centered world to the infinite, God-centered universe which has taken place within Jonah.[18]

A. C. Spearing remarks on how the peculiar sense of perspective achieved here effectively draws both reader and poet into the whale's belly (a perspective also achieved by the nuclear image in *Pearl*): "The poet has gone with Jonah inside the fish, and we follow with him the headlong, uncontrolled journey, coming to a sudden stumbling halt in the fish's belly."[19]

The core space of *Patience* also creates a matrix for understanding the structure of the poem's other spaces; drawing on the body-based geometry of center and circumference, it effects a textual *plenitudo*, a fundamental equivalence of all microcosmic enclosures within a poem whose overarching geometry implodes at its center. In this respect all three poems rely on the centripetal theology and geometry of the heart. Akin to how the interchangeability of *more* and *lasse* in the circular pearl equates every *spot* in *Pearl* with its central Vineyard, and how the geometry of the pentangle/girdle creates a spatial axis in *Sir Gawain*'s Fitt 3, *Patience*'s ship and *wodbynde* provide enclosures for Jonah whose figural significance derives from their structural resemblance to the stomach/*cor terrae* at the center. The heart, the key image in the theology of the vessel, projects its own dimensions into each of a succession of enclosed spaces.

A fundamental resemblance between the whale and the ship is unmistakeable; the ship is a classic figure for the church, and is therefore inevitably compared with the whale/cathedral. Jonah's journey within the whale is likened to sailing in an image that William Vantuono derives from the Latin *De Iona*: "Ande as sayled þe segge, ay sykerly he herde / Þe bygge borne on his bak and bete on his sydes" (301-02).[20] In both ship and whale Jonah finds an interior shelter where he can sleep; the poet compares these two shelters explicitly:[21]

> With þat he hitte to a hyrne and helde hym þer-inne,
> Þer no de-foule of no fylþe watȝ fest hym aboute;
> Þer he sete also sounde, saf for merk one,
> As in þe bulk of þe bote þer he by-fore sleped. (289-92)

This *hyrne* in the whale recalls a reference to "vche hyrne" of the ship (178), creating a parallel between enclosures which themselves contain inner enclosures to shelter the sleeping protagonist.

The description of the *wodbynde*, Jonah's third shelter for sleep, also contains details that recall the central space of the whale. Each is equipped with a door (*munster dor*, 268; *nos*, 451), and just as the cathedral-like whale is "brod as a halle" (272), the *wodbynde* is also a "brod . . . house" with what appears to be a vaulted roof: "For hit watȝ brod at þe boþem, boȝted on lofte, / Happed vpon ayþer half, a house as hit were" (449-50).[22] The *bour* (437) that Jonah builds rests under the *wodbynde* provided by God and thus figures, like the *hyrne* in both ship and whale, as a container within a container; the term designating this structure recalls the *bour* (276) within the whale.

Thus an obvious series of verbal echoes and structural parallels establishes a relationship between the central whale enclosure and the two peripheral spaces that strongly resembles how *Pearl*'s central Vineyard projects its dimensions into the two principal enclosures of the *erber grene* and New Jerusalem. The parallel even extends itself to *Sir Gawain*, where the bedroom in which Gawain sleeps constitutes an inner shelter within each of the three days' layered narrative frames. The tripartite scheme of all three poems bases itself on the image of the body contained within the multiple sub-layers of each principal space. In *Patience*, Jonah's three nights within the whale's belly enact a temporal recapitulation of his three total sleeping enclosures; the shelter-within-a-shelter of ship and *wodbynde*, in turn, reiterate the microcosmic configuration of the belly/heart. Jonah himself is a container at the center of all of these containers, one in whom the Word of God is "loke" (350), and the frame for the inmost center of his own heart;[23] he is the *mote* from which each far *poynt* of the poem derives its dimensions.

The *poynt* of *Patience*, like the main themes of *Pearl* and *Sir Gawain*, is man's all-consuming need to understand the geometry of grace, to submit to the spatiality of the heart. Christ allowed his infinite expansiveness to be compassed by the finite dimensions of the human womb and the ultimate constriction of the *cor terrae* in order that he might undo the Old Covenant's material order; his triumphal re-emergence prefigures the *kosmogonia* of every believer's conversion. Jonah fails to shelter himself from God because he misconstrues the shape of creation. His three attempts to burrow himself more deeply "within" culminate, paradoxically, in his violent expulsion into exterior space. Enfolding himself in sleep within the innermost recesses of ship, whale, and *bour*, he is nonetheless cast overboard, vomited out, exposed again to the elements. The more resolutely he pursues the shelter of a center, the more inexorably he finds himself propelled to the periphery; his each act of seclusion becomes, willy-nilly, a recapitulation.

Notes

1. "Sheltering Space and Cosmic Space in the Middle English *Patience*," *Annuale Mediaevale* 21 (1981) 132; cf. David Williams, "The Point of *Patience*," *Modern Philology* 68 (1970): 127-36. In this connection cf. Gilligan, "Neoplatonic Cosmology," passim.
2. Friedman 107.
3. *Patience* (Manchester: Manchester UP, 1969).
4. "Steering the Reader's Heart in *Patience*," *University of Ottawa Quarterly* 53 (1983): 169-80.
5. "The Virtues of the Heart: The Beatitudes in *Patience*," *Journal of the Rocky Mountain Medieval and Renaissance Association* 2 (1981): 51-59.
6. In addition to Clark and Wasserman, "Virtues," see Jay Schleusener, "*Patience*, Lines 35-40," *Modern Philology* 67 (1969): 64-66.
7. See Petrus Chrysologus, Sermo 37 (*PL* 52.304) and the *Glossa ordinaria*'s commentary on this passage, both cited in Malcolm Andrew, "Jonah and Christ in *Patience*," *Modern Philology* 70 (1973): 230; cf. also references to glosses by Jerome, Haymo of Halberstadt, and Rupert of Deutz by Joseph B. Zavadil, "A Study of Meaning in *Patience* and *Cleanness*," diss., Stanford U, 1962, 26ff, and citations from Hugh of St. Cher and Ps.-Augustine in Friedman 106. We have already remarked on the *lago del cor* at the center of Dante's *Inferno*; see also the *cor terrae* in Gregory (*PL* 76.672) and in Bonaventure, *In Hexaemeron* 1.24, *Opera omnia* (ed. Quaracchi, 5.333). Bonaventure exploits the geometry of center and circumference explicitly in a description of Christ's penetration to the earth's *cor* and *venter* that bears particular relevance to the spatiality of the whale episode: "Non solum venit ad superficiem terrae, sed in profundo centri, et, in ventre centri, in corde terrae, salutem operatus est: quia per crucifixionem anima sua ad infernum descendit, et restauravit coelestium sedium vacationes. In hoc profundo medio salus est, quia recedens a medio humilitatis, damnatur."
8. Friedman 125. On 103-04 he quotes Adam of St. Victor's synopsis of the book of Jonah; Adam describes the withering of the flower of Synagoga and the blooming of the flower of Ecclesia that occurs within the space of the whale's stomach.
9. Bachelard 188.
10. Malcolm Andrew and Ronald Waldron translate this line: "You plunged me into the dim heart of the deep sea." *The Poems of the Pearl Manuscript*, York Medieval Texts, 2nd ser. (London: Arnold, 1978).
11. In fact, there is good reason to believe that the repetition of "hert" in the Beatitudes paraphrase, together with a circular effect achieved by verbal echoes at the beginning and end of the passage, can be taken as a species of textual *recapitulatio* at that point. Several medieval commentators interpreted the Beatitudes as a microcosmic parallel of the first week of creation (e.g., Bonaventure, *De sex alis Seraphim*), and Haubrichs finds a similar textual structure based on the microcosmic significance of the Beatitudes in Otfrid (204-05). The circular structure of the Beatitudes passage has already provoked some scholarly comment (Vantuono 419-20; Burrow

Patience 181

156-57). The Beatitudes passage may stand in a microcosmic relation to the theme and structure of the entire *Patience* text akin to the recapitulatory status of *Pearl*'s *erber grene*, Holy Church's speech in *Piers Plowman*, and other such introductory microcosms; again, these moments of textual ingress resemble the Gothic portal's *pars pro toto* relation to its architectural superstructure.

12. Mersch, *Le Christ, l'homme et l'universe* 59-60.

13. See Rahner, "Flumina" passim. See also Prudentius, *Apoth.* 583, and Augustine ("Venter interioris hominis conscientia cordis est," *PL* 35.1643), cited in Curtius 137. Zara Zaddy discusses Old French *ventre* and Latin *venter* as traditional locations for the heart in "Chrétien de Troyes and the Localisation of the Heart," *Romance Philology* 12 (1958/59): 257-58. The modern English word "ventricle," of course, conceives of the heart's chambre as a small stomach. One could argue that the poet's recourse to these several terms as references to the same corporeal space merely reflects the semantic interchangeability of the words themselves. But even this phenomenon of linguistic overlap itself probably reflects the perceived congruence of multiple bodily centers. Iconographic representations of geometrically inscribed bodies feature very separate traditions emphasizing a midpoint in the navel, heart, and womb; the interchangeability of these centers in no way precludes the separate existence of each such tradition. The poet's allusion to all of these traditions in such a short central passage is unlikely to have occurred merely by coincidence, especially in light of the explicit figural relation among the images understood as part of the poem's overall spatial dynamics.

14. See Malcolm Andrew, "*Patience*: The 'Munster Dor,'" *English Language Notes* 14 (1977): 164-67.

15. Friedman 102-03.

16. Visually it also parallels the way that Virgil and Dante (in the *Inferno*), travelling at their exit from hell towards a point on the earth diametrically opposing their point of entry, find themselves positioned upside-down. Clark and Wasserman speculate that a probable pun on "rode" (27) creates a secondary meaning of "rood," in addition to the more obvious "road." They add that this pun "converts the whale into an altar upon which Jonah places himself" ("Jonah and the Whale" 18n). While I see no compelling evidence for the pun here, I have already noted how the medievals regarded the swallowing of the eucharist as a reenactment of the Harrowing. Whether or not resonances of an altar can be construed from this passage, the symbolic equivalence of a cathedral with the whale's belly here supports the possibility of eucharistic associations. Further, the dense overlay of several allegorical resonances here resembles the altar's simultaneous evocation of multiple sacred spaces (as noted in chapter two); the altar, as we have noted, was often regarded as the heart of the Gothic cathedral.

17. As we have seen, the images of the door and gate also depend on the symbolism of the heart in *Pearl*.

18. "Jonah and the Whale" 11-12.

19. Gawain-*Poet* 83-84.

20. "The Structure and Sources of *Patience*," *Mediaeval Studies* 34 (1972): 413.

21. Cf. Eldredge 122; Clark and Wasserman, "Jonah and the Whale" 7.

22. Cf. Eldredge 129.

23. Many of the occurrences of *hert* in *Patience* refer to Jonah's own heart: e.g., ll. 283, 300.

BIBLIOGRAPHY

This list contains the most important works consulted, but it does not constitute a complete bibliography of the subject. Each first reference in the notes provides reasonably full bibliographical information for the work cited; this list is intended as an aid to the reader who has trouble locating a first note reference. This list does not, however, always provide individual references to articles when several are cited from the same anthology. To conserve space, some sources infrequently cited in the notes are also not repeated here. Please note that *CSEL*, *PG*, *PL*, and *PMLA* have been substituted for *Corpus scriptorum ecclesiasticorum latinorum*, *Patrologia graeca*, *Patrologia latina*, and *Publications of the Modern Language Association of America*.

Ackerman, Robert W. "Gawain's Shield: Penitential Doctrine in *Sir Gawain and the Green Knight*." *Anglia* 76 (1958): 254-65.
---. "The Pearl-Maiden and the Penny." *Romance Philology* 17 (1964): 614-23. Rpt. in Conley 149-62.
Adamus Scotus. *De tripartito tabernaculo una cum pictura*. *PL* 198.609-796.
Adler, A. "The Topos *Quinque Linea Sunt Amoris* Used by Ronsard in *Amours* (1552), CXXXVI." *Bibliothèque d'Humanisme et Renaissance* 15 (1953): 220-25.
Adolf, Helen. "Der Eingang zu Wolframs *Parzival*." *Neophilologus* 22 (1936-37): 110-20, 171-85, 181-85.
Alanus de Insulis. *Distinctiones*. *PL* 210.687-1011.
---. *De planctu naturae*. *PL* 210.429-82.
Alcuin. *Expositio in Psalmos poenitentiales*. *PL* 100.569-638.
Allcroft, A. H. *The Circle and the Cross*. 2 vols. London: Macmillan, 1927-30.
Allen, Hope Emily, ed. *English Writings of Richard Rolle*. Oxford: Clarendon, 1931.
Allen, Judson B. "Commentary as Criticism: Formal Cause, Discursive Form, and the Late Medieval Accessus." *Acta Conventus Neo-Latini Lovaniensis: Proceedings of the First International Congress of Neo-Latin*

Studies, Louvain, 23-28 August 1971. Ed. J. IJsewijn and E. Kessler. München: Fink, 1973. 29-48.
---. "Langland's Reading and Writing: *Detractor* and the Pardon Passus." *Speculum* 59 (1984): 342-59.
Allers, Rudolf. "Microcosmus: From Anaximandros to Paracelsus." *Traditio* 2 (1944): 319-407.
Ambrose. *De virginibus*. *PL* 16.187-232.
Anderson, J. J., ed. *Patience*. Manchester: Manchester UP, 1969.
---. "The Prologue of *Patience*." *Modern Philology* 63 (1966): 283-87.
Andrew, Malcolm. "Jonah and Christ in *Patience*." *Modern Philology* 70 (1973): 230-33.
---. "*Patience*: The *Munster Dor*." *English Language Notes* 14 (1977): 164-67.
---, and Ronald Waldron, eds. *The Poems of the* Pearl *Manuscript*. York Medieval Texts, 2nd ser. London: Arnold, 1978.
Anger, Joseph. *La doctrine du Corps Mystique de Jésus-Christ d'après les principes de la théologie de Saint-Thomas*. Paris: Beauchesne, 1946.
Arnheim, Rudolf. *The Dynamics of Architectural Form*. Berkeley: U of California P, 1977.
Athanasius. *De titulis Psalmorum*. *PG* 27.591-1344.
Auerbach, Erich. *Mimesis: The Representation of Reality in Western Literature*. Trans. Willard R. Trask. Princeton: Princeton UP, 1968.
---. *Scenes from the Drama of European Literature*. New York: Meridian, 1959.
Augustine. *De civitate Dei*. *PL* 44.
---. *The Confessions of St. Augustine*. Trans. Edward B. Pusey. Harvard Classics 7. New York: Collier, 1909.
---. *In Evangelium S. Joannis*. *PL* 35.1379-1976.
---. *De magistro*. *PL* 32.1193-1220.
---. *In Psalmos*. *PL* 36-37.
---. *Sermones dubii*. *PL* 39.1639-1720.
---. *Sermonum classes quatuor*. *PL* 38.23-1484.
Austin, H. D. "Number and Geometrical Design in the Divine Comedy." *The Personalist* 14 (1935): 310-30.
Bachelard, Gaston. *La poétique de l'espace*. Paris: PU de France, 1957.
Baeumker, Clemens, ed. *Liber XXIV Philosophorum*. *Beiträge zur Geschichte der Philosophie des Mittelalters* (1928): 207-14.
Bainvel, Jean V. *La divozione al S. Cuore di Gesu: La sua dottrina e la sua storia*. 2nd ed. Biblioteca Ascetica 4. Milano: Società Vita e Pensiero, 1922.
Baird, Joseph L. "Maskele3, Makele3: Poet and Dreamer in the *Pearl*." *American Notes and Queries* 12 (1973): 27-28.
Baltrusaitis, Jurgis. "Cercles astrologiques et cosmographiques à la fin du moyen-âge." *Gazette des beaux-arts* 21 (1939): 65-84.

Barney, Stephen A. "The Plowshare of the Tongue: The Progress of a Symbol from the Bible to *Piers Plowman*." *Mediaeval Studies* 35 (1973): 261-93.
---. "Troilus Bound." *Speculum* 47 (1972): 445-58.
Barthes, Roland. *Image, Music, Text*. Ed. and trans. Stephen Heath. New York: Hill, 1977.
---. *Le plaisir du texte*. Paris: du Seuil, 1973.
Batts, Michael Stanley. "Numerical Structure in Medieval Literature, with a Bibliography." *Formal Aspects of Medieval German Poetry*. Ed. S. N. Werbow. Austin: U of Texas P, 1969.
Bauer, Gerhard. *Entstehungsgeschichte*. München: Fink, 1973. Vol. 1 of *Claustrum Animae: Untersuchungen zur Geschichte der Metapher vom Herzen als Kloster*. 1 vol. to date.
Bayley, A. R. "The Five Wounds." *Notes and Queries* 171 (1936): 266.
Bazin, Germain. "En quête du sentiment courtois." *Le Coeur*. Études carmélitaines 29. Paris: Desclée, 1950.
Bea, Augustinus, et al., eds. *Cor Jesu*. Freiburg: Herder, 1959.
Beer, Ellen J. "Nouvelles réflexions sur l'image du monde dans la cathédrale de Lausanne." *Revue de l'art* 10 (1970): 57-62.
---. *Die Rose der Kathedrale von Lausanne und der Kosmologische Bilderkreis des Mittelalters*. Bern: Benteli, 1952.
Bennett, J. A. W., ed. *The Parlement of Foules*. Oxford: Clarendon, 1957.
Benoît, P. "Corps, tête, et plérôme dans les épîtres de la captivité." *Revue biblique* 63 (1956): 5-44.
Bense, Max. *Raum und Ich: Eine Philosophie über den Raum*. München: Oldenbourg, 1943.
Benz, Ernst. *Ecclesia spiritualis: Kirchenidee und Geschichtstheologie der franziskanischen Reformation*. Stuttgart: Kohlhammer, 1934.
Bernard of Claivaux. *Sermones de Sanctis*. PL 183.359-536.
Bernardo, Aldo. "Flesh, Spirit, and Rebirth at the Center of Dante's *Comedy*." *Symposium* 19 (1965): 335-51.
Biblia Sacra cum glossis, interlineari et ordinaria, et Moralitatibus Nicolai Lyrani. Venice: n.p., 1588.
Binswanger, Ludwig. "Das Raumproblem in der Psychopathologie." *Ausgewählte Vorträge und Aufsätze*. Pfullingen: Neske, 1954.
Bishop, Ian. Pearl *in Its Setting: A Critical Study of the Structure and Meaning of the Middle English Poem*. Oxford: Blackwell, 1968.
---. "The Significance of the *Garlande Gay* in the Allegory of *Pearl*." *Review of English Studies* ns 8 (1957): 12-21.
Blanch, Robert J., ed. Sir Gawain and the Green Knight *and* Pearl: *Critical Essays*. Bloomington: Indiana UP, 1966.
Blanchot, Maurice. *L'espace litteraire*. 4th ed. Paris: Gallimard, 1955.
Blenkner, Charles Louis. "The Pattern of Traditional Images in *Pearl*." *Studies in Philology* 68 (1971): 26-49.

---. "The Theological Structure of *Pearl.*" *Traditio* 24 (1968): 43-75. Rpt. in Conley 220-71.
Bloomer, Kent C., and Charles W. Moore. *Body, Memory and Architecture.* New Haven: Yale UP, 1977.
Bloomfield, Morton W. "*Sir Gawain and the Green Knight*: An Appraisal." *PMLA* 77 (1961): 7-19.
Bober, Harry. "An Illustrated School-Book of Bede's 'De Natura Rerum.'" *Journal of the Walters Art Gallery* 19-20 (1956-57): 65-97.
---. "*In Principio.* Creation Before Time." *De Artibus Opuscula XL, Essays in Honor of Erwin Panofsky.* Ed. Millard Meiss. Zurich: Buehler, 1960. 13-28.
Borroff, Marie. "*Pearl*'s 'Maynful Mone': Crux, Simile, and Structure." *Acts of Interpretation: The Text in Its Contexts, 700-1600. Essays on Medieval and Renaissance Literature in Honor of E. Talbot Donaldson.* Ed. Mary J. Carruthers and Elizabeth D. Kirk. Norman, OK: Pilgrim, 1982.
Braun, Joseph. *Der christliche Altar in seiner geschichtlichen Entwicklung.* 2 vols. München: Koch, 1924.
---. *Das christliche Altargerät in seinem Sinn und seiner Entwicklung.* München: Hueber, 1932.
Bronfen, Elisabeth. *Der literarische Raum: Eine Untersuchung am Beispiel von Dorothy M. Richardsons Romanzyklus Pilgrimage.* Studien zur englischen Philologie N.F. 25. Tübingen: Niemeyer, 1986.
Brown, Carleton. "The Author of *The Pearl*, Considered in the Light of his Theological Opinions." *PMLA* 19 (1904): 115-45. Published separately, Baltimore: MLA, 1904.
---. Rev. of "*The Pearl*: An Interpretation," by Robert Garrett. *Modern Language Notes* 34 (1919): 42-45.
Brown, Norman O. *Life Against Death: The Psychoanalytic Meaning of History.* London: Routledge, 1959.
---. *Love's Body.* New York: Random, 1966.
Brownlee, Kevin. "Reflections in the *Miroer aus amoreus*: The Inscribed Reader in Jean de Meun's *Roman de la Rose.*" *Mimesis: From Mirror to Method, Augustine to Descartes.* Ed. John D. Lyons and Stephen G. Nichols. Hanover: UP of New England, 1982. 60-70.
Burke, Kenneth. *A Grammar of Motives.* New York: Braziller, 1955.
Burrow, John. *A Reading of Sir Gawain and the Green Knight.* London: Routledge, 1965.
Bynum, Carolyn. *Jesus as Mother: Studies in the Spirituality of the High Middle Ages.* Berkeley: U of California P, 1982.
Carruthers, Mary J. "Time, Apocalypse, and the Plot of *Piers Plowman.*" *Acts of Interpretation: The Text and Its Contexts. Essays on Medieval and Renaissance Literature in Honor of E. Talbot Donaldson.* Ed. Mary J. Carruthers and Elizabeth D. Kirk. Norman, OK: Pilgrim, 1982. 175-88.

Cassiodorus. *Expositio in Cantica Canticorum*. *PL* 70.1055-106.
---. *Expositio in Psalterium*. *PL* 70.9-1056.
Chapman, C. O. "Numerical Symbolism in Dante and the *Pearl*." *Modern Language Notes* 54 (1939): 256-59.
Chrysostomus, Joannes. *Opus imperfectum in Matthaeum*. *PG* 56.601-946.
Clare of Assisi. *The Legends and Writings of Saint Clare of Assisi*. Trans. Ignatius Brady. St. Bonaventure, NY: Franciscan Institute, 1953.
Clark, S. L., and J. N. Wasserman. "Jonah and the Whale: Narrative Perspective in *Patience*." *Orbis Litterarum* 35 (1980): 1-19.
---. "The Pearl Poet's City Imagery." *Southern Quarterly* 16 (1977-78): 297-309.
---. "*Purity*: The Cities of the Dove and the Raven." *American Benedictine Review* 29 (1978): 284-306.
---. "The Spatial Argument of *Pearl*: Perspectives on a Venerable Bead." *Interpretations: Studies in Language and Literature* 11 (1979): 1-12.
---. "The Virtues of the Heart: The Beatitudes in *Patience*." *Journal of the Rocky Mountain Medieval and Renaissance Association* 2 (1981): 51-59.
Le Coeur. Les études carmélitaines. Paris: Déclee de Brouwer, 1950.
Conger, G. P. *Theories of Macrocosms and Microcosms in the History of Philosophy*. 1922. New York: Russell, 1967.
Conley, John. *The Middle English* Pearl: *Critical Essays*. Notre Dame: U of Notre Dame P, 1970.
Cook, Eleanor, et al., eds. *Centre and Labyrinth: Essays in Honor of Northrop Frye*. Toronto: U of Toronto P, 1983.
Cornélis, H. *The Resurrection of the Body*. Trans. M. Joselyn. Notre Dame: Fides, 1964.
Cornelius, Roberta D. *The Figurative Castle: A Study of the Medieval Allegory of the Edifice with Especial Reference to Religious Writings*. Diss. Bryn Mawr, 1930.
Courcelle, Pierre. "Tradition platonicienne et traditions chrétiennes du corps-prison." *Revue des études latines* 43 (1966 for 1965): 406-43.
Cowen, Painton. *Rose Windows*. Golborne: Thames, 1979.
Crane, John Kenny. "Four Levels of Time in *Sir Gawain and the Green Knight*." *Annuale Medievale* 10 (1969): 65-80.
Crawford, John F., ed. *The Pearl*. San Francisco: Grabhorn, 1967.
Critchlow, Keith, Jane Carroll, and Llewylyn Vaughan Lee. *Chartre Maze: A Model of the Universe and the Journey of the Soul*. Cambridge: n.p., 1975.
Cross, James Edwin. "Aspects of the Macrocosm and Microcosm in Old English Literature." *Comparative Literature* 14 (1962): 1-22.
Culler, Jonathan. *On Deconstruction: Theory and Criticism After Structuralism*. London: Routledge, 1983.

Cullmann, Oscar. *Christus und die Zeit: Die urchristliche Zeit- und Geschichtsauffassung.* Zürich: Evangelischer, 1946.

Curtius, Ernst Robert. *European Literature and the Latin Middle Ages.* Trans. Willard R. Trask. Bollingen Series 36. New York: Pantheon, 1953.

Dahl, Murdoch E. *The Resurrection of the Body.* Naperville, IL: Allenson, 1962.

Daniélou, J. "The Problem of Symbolism." *Thought* 25 (1950): 423-40.

Davenport, W. A. *The Art of the* Gawain-*Poet.* London: Athalone, 1978.

Davis, Norman. "A Note on *Pearl.*" *Review of English Studies* ns 17 (1966): 403-05; 18 (1967): 294. Rpt., with additional material, in Conley 325-34.

---. "Two Unprinted Dialogues in Late Middle English, and their Language." *Revue des langues vivantes* 35 (1969): 461-72.

Davlin, Sister Mary Clemente, O.P. "*Petrus, Id Est, Christus*: Piers the Plowman as 'the Whole Christ.'" *Chaucer Review* 6 (1972): 290-92.

De Bruyne, Edgar. *Études d'esthétique médiévale.* 3 vols. Recueil de travaux publiés par la faculté de philosophie et lettres 97-99. Brussels: De Tempel, 1946.

De Lubac, Henri. *Corpus mysticum.* 2nd ed. Paris, 1949.

---. *Histoire et esprit: l'intelligence de l'Écriture d'après Origène.* Paris: Montaigne, 1930.

De Man, Paul. *Blindness and Insight: Essays in the Rhetoric of Contemporary Criticism.* New York: Oxford UP, 1971.

De Margerie, Bertrand, S. J. "Le coeur de Marie, coeur de l'Église." *Ephemerides mariologicae* 16 (1966): 189-227.

Dempf, Alois. *Sacrum Imperium: Geschichts- und Staatsphilosophie des Mittelalters und der politischen Renaissance.* München: Oldenbourg, 1929.

Derrickson, Ann. "The Pentangle: Guiding Star for the *Gawain*-Poet." *Comitatus* 11 (1980): 10-19.

Donner, Morton. "Word Play and Word Form in *Pearl.*" *Chaucer Review* 24 (1989): 166-82.

Dunlap, Louse. "Vegetation Puns in *Pearl.*" *Mediaevalia* 3 (1977): 173-88.

Durling, Robert M. "'Io son venuto': Seneca, Plato, and the Microcosm." *Dante Studies* 93 (1975): 95-129.

Eckhardt, Caroline D., ed. *Essays in the Numerical Analysis of Medieval Literature.* Lewisburg, PA: Bucknell UP, 1979.

Eggers, Hans. "Strukturprobleme mittelalterlicher Epik, dargestellt am *Parzival* Wolframs von Eschenbach." *Euphorion* 47 (1953): 260-70.

Eldredge, Laurence. "Sheltering Space and Cosmic Space in the Middle English *Patience.*" *Annuale Mediaevale* 21 (1981): 121-33.

---. "The State of *Pearl* Studies since 1933." *Viator* 6 (1975): 171-94.

Eliade, Mircea. *Das Heilige und das Profane: Vom Wesen des Religiösen.* Rowohlts deutsche Enzyklopädie 31. Reinbek bei Hamburg: Rowohlt, 1957.

---. *Images et Symboles: essais sur le symbolisme magico-religieux*. Paris: Gallimard, 1952.
---. *Le mythe de l'éternel retour: archétypes et répétition*. 3rd ed. Paris: Gallimard, 1949.
---. "Psychologie et histoire des religions. A propos du symbolisme du centre." *Eranos-Jahrbuch* 19 (1950): 252-82.
Emert, Joyce Rogers. "*Pearl* and the Incarnate Word: A Study in the Sacramental Nature of Symbolism." Diss. U of New Mexico, 1969.
Engelhardt, George J. "The Predicament of Gawain." *Modern Language Quarterly* 16 (1955): 218-25.
Faral, Edmond, ed. *Les arts poétiques du XIIe et du XIIIe siècle*. Paris: Champion, 1924.
Ferster, Judith. "Reading Nature: The Phenomenology of Reading in the *Parliament of Fowls*." *Mediaevalia* 3 (1977): 189-213.
Finkelstein, Dorothee M. "The *Pearl*-Poet as Bezalel." *Mediaeval Studies* 35 (1973): 413-32.
Finlayson, John. "*Pearl*: Landscape and Vision." *Studies in Philology* 71 (1974): 314-43.
Fisher, John H. "Wyclif, Langland, Gower, and the *Pearl* Poet on the Subject of Aristocracy." *Studies in Medieval Literature: In Honor of Professor Albert Croll Baugh*. Ed. MacEdward Leach. Philadelphia: U of Pennsylvania P, 1961. 139-57.
Fleming, John V. "The Centuple Structure of the *Pearl*." *The Alliterature Tradition in the Fourteenth Century*. Ed. Bernard S. Levy and Paul E. Szarmach. Kent, OH: Kent State UP, 1981. 81-98.
---. *The Roman de la Rose: A Study in Allegory and Iconography*. Princeton: Princeton UP, 1969.
Fletcher, Jefferson B. "The Allegory of the *Pearl*." *Journal of English and Germanic Philology* 20 (1921): 1-21.
Foucault, Michel. *Les mots et les choses: une archéologie des sciences humaines*. Paris: Gallimard, 1966.
Fowler, Alastair, ed. *Silent Poetry: Essays in Numerological Analysis*. New York: Barnes, 1970.
---. *Spenser and the Numbers of Time*. London: Routledge, 1964.
Fowler, David C. *The Bible in Middle English Literature*. Seattle: U of Washington P, 1984.
Frank, Erich. *St. Augustine and Greek Thought*. Cambridge: Augustinian Society, 1942.
Frank, Joseph. "Spatial Form: An Answer to the Critics." *Critical Inquiry* 4 (1977): 231-52.
---. "*Spatial Form in Modern Literature*," *Sewanee Review* 53 (1945). Rpt. (revised) in *The Widening Gyre* (New Brunswick: Rutgers UP, 1963).

Frappier, J. "Le Graal et l'hostie." *Les Romans du Graal aux XIIe et XIIIe siècles: Strasbourg, 29 mars - 3 avril 1954.* Colloques internationales du Centre national de la recherche scientifique. Sciences humaines 3. Paris: Centre national de la recherche scientifique, 1956.

Freccero, John. "Dante's Ulysses: From Epic to Novel." *Concepts of the Hero in the Middle Ages and the Renaissance.* Papers of the Fourth and Fifth Annual Conference of the Center for Medieval and Early Renaissance Studies, State U of New York at Binghamton, 2-3 May 1970, 1-2 May 1971. Ed. Norman T. Burns and Christopher J. Reagan. Albany: State U of New York P, 1975. 101-19.

---. "Paradiso X: The Dance of the Stars." *Dante Studies* 86 (1968): 85-111.

Freud, Sigmund. *The Interpretation of Dreams.* London: Hogarth, 1900. Vols. 4 and 5 of *The Standard Edition of the Complete Psychological Works of Sigmund Freud.* Ed. James Strachey. 24 vols. 1900-1.

Friedman, John B. "Figural Typology in the Middle English *Patience*." *The Alliterative Tradition in the Fourteenth Century.* Ed. Bernard Levy and Paul Szarmach. Kent, OH: Kent State UP, 1981.

Fritz, Donald W. "*The Pearl*: The Sacredness of Numbers." *American Benedictine Review* 31 (1980): 314-34.

Frye, Northrop. *Anatomy of Criticism.* Princeton: Princeton UP, 1957.

---. *Fearful Symmetry: A Study of William Blake.* Princeton: Princeton UP, 1947.

---. *The Great Code: The Bible and Literature.* New York: Harcourt, 1982.

---. *The Secular Scripture: A Study of the Structure of Romance.* Cambridge: Harvard UP, 1976.

Gadamer, Hans-Georg. *Wahrheit und Methode.* 3rd ed. Tübingen: Mohr, 1972.

Gaerte, W. "Kosmische Vorstellungen im Bilde prähistorischer Zeit: Erdberg, Himmelsberg, Erdnabel und Weltströme." *Anthropos* 9 (1914): 956-79.

Galpin, Stanley Leman. "Fortune's Wheel in the *Roman de la Rose.*" *PMLA* 24 (1909): 332-42.

Garrett, Robert Max. "*The Pearl*: An Interpretation." *University of Washington Publications in English* 4 (1918): 1-45. Published separately: Seattle: U of Washington, 1918.

Gatta, John, Jr. "Transformation Symbolism and the Liturgy of the Mass in *Pearl.*" *Modern Philology* 71 (1974): 243-56.

Gelley, Alexander. "Metonymy, Schematism and the Space of Literature." *New Literary History* 11 (1980): 469-87.

Gilbert, Allan H. "Spirit and Flesh in Dante's *Commedia.*" *Italica* 42 (1965): 8-20.

Ginsberg, Warren. "Place and Dialectic in *Pearl* and Dante's *Paradiso.*" *English Literary History* 55 (1988): 731-53.

Godfrey of St. Victor. *Microcosmus.* Ed. P. Delhaye. Lille: Gembloux, 1951.

Goldin, Frederick. *The Mirror of Narcissus in the Courtly Love Lyric.* Ithaca, NY: Cornell UP, 1967.
Gordon, E. V., ed. *Pearl.* Oxford: Oxford UP, 1953.
Götz, Walter. *Dasein und Raum: Philosophische Untersuchungen zum Raum.* Frankfurt: Klostermann, 1977.
Graber, Rudolf. *Christus in seinen heiligen Sakramenten.* München: Kösel, 1940.
Gray, D. "The Five Wounds of Our Lord." *Notes and Queries* ns 10 (1963): 50-51, 82-89, 127-34, 163-68.
Green, Richard Hamilton. "Gawain's Shield and the Quest for Perfection." *English Literary History* 29 (1962): 121-39. Rpt. in Blanch 86-97.
Greene, Thomas. *The Descent from Heaven: A Study in Epic Continuity.* New Haven: Yale UP, 1963.
Gregory the Great. *Moralia in Job.* PL 75.499-1162, 76.9-782.
Gross, Laila. "Telescoping in Time in *Sir Gawain and the Green Knight.*" *Orbis Litterarum* 24 (1969): 130-37.
Haines, Victor Yelverton. "Hony soyt qui mal pence: Can the Reader Sin?" *University of Ottawa Quarterly* 53 (1983): 181-88.
Hall, Edward T. *The Hidden Dimension: Man's Use of Space in Public and Private.* London: Bodley Head, 1969.
Hamilton, Marie Padgett. "The Meaning of the Middle English *Pearl.*" *PMLA* 70 (1955): 805-24. Rpt. in Blanch 37-59, and Vasta 117-45.
Hammerle, Karl. "*The Castle of Perseverance* and *Pearl.*" *Anglia* 60 (1936): 401-02.
Hankins, J. E. "Spenser and the Revelation of St. John." *PMLA* 60 (1945): 364-81.
Harnack, A. "Die Bezeichnung Jesu als 'Knecht Gottes' und ihre Geschichte in der alten Kirche." *Sitzungsberichte der Berliner Akademie der Wissenschaften* (1926).
Hättenschwiller, P. Josef, S.J. *Führer durch die neuere deutsche Herz-Jesu-Literatur.* Innsbruck: Rauch, 1932.
Haubrichs, Wolfgang. *Ordo als Form: Strukturstudien zur Zahlenkomposition bei Otfrid von Weissenburg und in karolingischer Literatur.* Hermaea, Germanistische Forschungen N.F. 27. Tübingen: Niemeyer, 1969.
Haymo of Halberstadt. *Commentaria in Apocalypsim.* PL 117.937-1220.
Heidegger, Martin. "Bauen Wohnen Denken." *Vorträge und Aufsätze.* Pfullingen: Neske, 1954. 145-62.
---. *Sein und Zeit.* Tübingen: Niemeyer, 1953.
Hieatt, A. Kent. *Short Time's Endless Monument: The Symbolism of the Numbers in Edmund Spenser's "Epithalamion."* New York: Columbia UP, 1960.
---, and Constance Hieatt. "'The Bird with Four Feathers': Numerical Analysis of a Fourteenth-Century Poem." *Papers on Language and Literature* 6 (1970): 18-38.

Hieatt, Constance. "*Pearl* and the Dream-Vision Tradition." *Studia Neophilologica* 37 (1965): 139-45. Rpt. (revised) in *The Realism of Dream Visions: The Poetic Exploitation of the Dream Experience in Chaucer and his Contemporaries*. De Proprietatibus Litterarum, Series Practica 2. The Hague: Mouton, 1967.

Hilary. *In Psalmos*. PL 9.917-1078.

Hildebert of Lavardin. *Sermones*. PL 171.339-968.

Hildegard of Bingen. *Lieder*. Ed. Pudentiana Barth and Joseph Schmidt-Görg. Salzburg: Müller, 1969.

Hill, John M. "Middle English Poets and the World: Notes Towards an Appraisal of Linguistic Consciousness." *Criticism* 16 (1974): 153-69.

Hillmann, Sister Mary Vincent. "Some Debatable Words in *Pearl* and Its Theme." *Modern Language Notes* 60 (1945): 241-48. Rpt. in Conley 9-17.

---. The Pearl: *Mediaeval Text with a Literal Translation and Interpretation* (Notre Dame: U of Notre Dame P, 1961).

Hocke, Gustav René. *Die Welt als Labyrinth*. Reinbek bei Hamburg: Rowohlt, 1961.

Hoffman, Stanton de Voren. "The *Pearl*: Notes for an Interpretation." *Modern Philology* 58 (1960): 73-80. Rpt. in Conley 86-102.

Holböck, Ferdinand. *Der eucharistische und der mystische Leib Christi in ihren Beziehungen zueinander nach der Lehre der Frühscholastik*. Roma: Officium libri catholici, 1941.

Hollis, Stephanie J. "The Pentangle Knight: *Sir Gawain and the Green Knight*." *Chaucer Review* 15 (1981): 267-81.

Holtz, William. "A Reconsideration of Spatial Form." *Critical Inquiry* 4 (1977): 271-83.

Hope, Emily Allen. *English Writings of Richard Rolle*. Oxford: Clarendon, 1931.

Hopper, Vincent Foster. *Medieval Number Mysticism*. New York: Columbia UP, 1938.

Howard, Donald R. "Structure and Symmetry in *Sir Gawain*." *Speculum* 39 (1964): 425-33. Rpt. in Blanch 195-208.

---. *The Three Temptations: Medieval Man in Search of the World*. Princeton: Princeton UP, 1966.

Hugh of St. Cher. *Opera omnia in universum Sanctum Scripturam (Postillae in totam Bibliam)*. Venice: n.p., 1669.

Hugh of St. Victor. *De arca Noe morali*. PL 176.618-680.

---. *De B. Mariae virginitate*. PL 176.857-76.

Huisman, J. A. *Neue Wege zur dichterischen und musikalischen Technik Walthers von der Vogelweide, mit einem Exkurs über die symmetrische Zahlenkomposition im Mittelalter*. Studia Litteraria Rheno-Traiectina 1. Utrecht: Kemink en Zoon, 1950.

Huppé, Bernard F. "Petrus id est Christus: Word Play in *Piers Plowman, the B Text*." *English Literary History* 17 (1950): 163-90.
Idiart, P. *Études sur le Sacrement de l'Ordre*. Paris: du Cerf, 1957.
Innocent III. *Sermones*. PL 217.309-690.
Isidore of Seville. *Etymologiae*. PL 82.9-728.
Jakobson, Roman and Morris Halle. *Fundamentals of Language*. Janua Linguarum, Ser. Minor. 1. 'S-Gravenhage: Mouton, 1956.
James, John. *Chartres: The Masons Who Built a Legend*. London: Routledge, 1982.
Jeffrey, David L., ed. *By Things Seen: Reference and Recognition in Medieval Thought*. Ottawa: U of Ottawa P, 1979.
Johnson, Lynn Staley. *The Voice of the Gawain-Poet*. Madison: U of Wisconsin P, 1984.
Johnson, Wendell Stacy. "The Imagery and Diction of *The Pearl*: Toward an Interpretation." *English Literary History* 20 (1953): 161-80. Rpt. in Conley 27-49.
Jordan, Robert. *Chaucer and the Shape of Creation*. Cambridge: Harvard UP, 1967.
Journet, Charles. *L'église du verbe incarné: essai de théologie spéculative*. Bibliothèque de la revue thomiste 3. Paris: Desclée, 1951.
Jung, C. G. *Modern Man in Search of a Soul*. Trans. W. S. Dell and Cary F. Baynes. New York: Harcourt, 1933.
Jung, Emma. *Die Graalslegende in psychologischer Sicht*. Studien aus dem C. G. Jung-Institut Zürich 12. Zürich: Rascher, 1960.
Kamper, Dietmar, and Volker Rittner. *Zur Geschichte des Körpers*. München: Hanser, 1976.
---, and Christoph Wulf. *Der andere Körper*. Edition Corpus: Alltagswissen, Körpersprache, Ethnomedizin 1. Berlin: Mensch und Leben, 1984.
---. *Das Schwinden der Sinne*. Frankfurt: Suhrkamp, 1984.
---. *Die Wiederkehr des Körpers*. Frankfurt: Suhrkamp, 1982.
Kanters, Ch. G. *Le Coeur de Jésus dans la littérature chrétienne des douze premiers siècles*. Brussels: Beyaert, 1930.
---. *De Godsvrucht tot het Heilig Hart van Jesus in de vroegere Staten der Nederlanden (XII - XVII eeuw)*. 'S-Hertogenbosch: Mosman, 1929.
Kantorowicz, Ernst H. *The King's Two Bodies: A Study in Mediaeval Political Theology*. Princeton: Princeton UP, 1956.
Kaske, Carol V. "Mount Sinai and Dante's Mount Purgatory." *Dante Studies* 89 (1971): 1-18.
Kaske, R. E. "Holy Church's Speech and the Structure of *Piers Plowman*." *Chaucer and Middle English Studies in Honour of Rossel Hope Robbins*. Ed. Beryl Rowland. London: Allen, 1974. 320-27.
---. "Langland on the Incarnation." *Review of English Studies* ns 16 (1965): 349-63.

---. "Langland's Walnut-Simile." *Journal of English and Germanic Philology* 58 (1959): 650-4.
---. "Sir Gawain and the Green Knight." *Medieval and Renaissance Studies.* Ed. George Mallary Masters. Proceedings of the Southeastern Institute of Medieval and Renaissance Studies, Summer 1979. Chapel Hill: U of North Carolina P, 1984. 24-44.
---. "The Speech of 'Book' in *Piers Plowman.*" *Anglia* 77 (1959): 117-44.
---. "Two Cruxes in *Pearl*: 596 and 609-10." *Traditio* 15 (1959): 418-28.
Katzenellenbogen, Adolf. *The Sculptural Programs of Chartres Cathedral: Christ, Mary, Ecclesia.* Baltimore: Johns Hopkins UP, 1959.
Kean, P. M. "Numerical Composition in *Pearl.*" *Notes and Queries* 210 (1956): 49-51.
---. *The Pearl: An Interpretation.* New York: Barnes, 1967.
Kellog, Alfred L. "Note on Line 274 of the *Pearl.*" *Traditio* 12 (1956): 406-07. Rpt. as "*Pearl* and the Augustinian Doctrine of Creation," in Conley 335-37.
Kelly, T. D. and John T. Irwin. "The Meaning of *Cleanness*: Parable as Effective Sign." *Mediaeval Studies* 35 (1973): 232-60.
Kermode, Frank. *The Sense of an Ending: Studies in the Theory of Fiction.* New York: Oxford UP, 1967.
Kestner, Joseph. *The Spatiality of the Novel.* Detroit: Wayne State UP, 1978.
Kitzinger, Ernst. "World Map and Fortune's Wheel: A Medieval Mosaic Floor in Turin." *Proceedings of the American Philosophical Society* 117 (1973): 344-73.
Klenke, M. Amelia. "Chrétien's Symbolism and Cathedral Art." *PMLA* 70 (1955): 223-43.
Knightly, William J. "*Pearl*: The hy3 seysoun." *Modern Language Notes* 76 (1961): 97-102.
Koestler, Arthur. *Janus: A Summing Up.* London: Pan, 1979.
Köhler, Erich. *Ideal und Wirklichkeit in der höfischen Epik: Studien zur Form der frühen Artus- und Graldichtung.* Tübingen: Niemeyer, 1970.
Kolve, V. A. *The Play Called Corpus Christi.* London: Arnold, 1966.
König-Hartmann, Daniela, and Harro Schweizer. "Kommentierte Bibliographie zu psychologischen Arbeiten über die kognitive und sprachliche Verarbeitung räumlicher Beziehungen (Laufende Thematische Bibliographie, Stand Oktober 1982)." *Linguistische Berichte* 85 (June 1983): 102-13; 86 (Aug. 1983): 107-26; 87 (Oct. 1983): 99-120.
Krautheimer, Richard. "Introduction to an 'Iconography of Mediaeval Architecture.'" *Journal of the Warburg and Courthauld Institutes* 5 (1942): 1-33.
---. "Sancta Maria Rotunda." *Arte del primo millenio.* Atti del II° convegno per lo studio dell'arte del'alto medio evo tenuto presso l'università di Pavia

nel Settembre 1950. Ed. Edoardo Arslan. Torino: Viglongo, 1954. 21-27.
Kubler, George. *The Shape of Time: Remarks on the History of Things*. New Haven: Yale UP, 1962.
Lactantius. *Divinarum Institutionum libri septem*. PL 6.
---. *De opificio Dei*. PL 7.9-78.
Ladner, Gerhart B. *Ad Imaginem Dei: The Image of Man in Medieval Art*. Wimmer Lecture 16. Latrobe, PA: Archabbey, 1965.
Lass, Roger. "Man's Heaven: The Symbolism of Gawain's Shield." *Mediaeval Studies* 28 (1966): 354-60.
Lecoy, Félix, ed. *Le Roman de la Rose par Guillaume de Lorris et Jean de Meun*. 3 vols. Paris: Champion, 1965-70.
---. "Urzeit und Endzeit." *Eranos-Jahrbuch* 17 (1949): 11-51.
Lesser, George. *Gothic Cathedrals and Sacred Geometry*. 2 vols. London: Tirauti, 1957.
Lewis, C. S. *Allegory of Love*. 1936. New York: Oxford UP, 1958.
---. *The Discarded Image: An Introduction to Medieval and Renaissance Literature*. Cambridge: Cambridge UP, 1964.
---. *Miracles: A Preliminary Study*. 1947. London: Collins, 1974.
Leyerle, John. "The Game and Play of Hero." *The Concept of the Hero in the Middle Ages and Early Renaissance*. Ed. Christopher Reagan. Albany: State U of New York P, 1975. 49-81.
---. "The Heart and the Chain." *The Learned and the Lewed: Studies in Chaucer and Medieval Literature*. Ed. Larry D. Benson. Cambridge: Harvard UP, 1974. 113-45.
---. "The Rose-Wheel Design and Dante's *Paradiso*." *University of Toronto Quarterly* 46 (1977): 280-308.
Liebschuetz, H. *Das allegorische Weltbild der Hl. Hildegard von Bingen*. Studien der Bibl. Warburg 16. Leipzig: Teubner, 1930.
Lorenz, S. "Das Unendliche bei Nicolaus von Kues." *Philosophisches Jahrbuch* 40 (1927): 57-84.
Lotman, Jurij. *The Structure of the Artistic Text*. Trans. Ronald Vroon. Michigan Slavic Contributions 7. Ann Arbor: U of Michigan P, 1977.
Lovejoy, Arthur O. *The Great Chain of Being: The Study of the History of an Idea*. Cambridge: Harvard UP, 1936.
Löwith, Karl. *Meaning in History*. Chicago: U of Chicago P, 1949.
Luttrell, C. A. "*Pearl*: Symbolism in a Garden Setting." *Neophilologus* 49 (1965): 160-76. Rpt. in Conley 297-324.
Lyons, John D., and Stephen G. Nichols, Jr., eds. *Mimesis: From Mirror to Method, Augustine to Descartes*. Hanover: UP of New England, 1982.
Macrae-Gibson, O. D. "*Pearl*: The Link-Words and the Thematic Structure." *Neophilologus* 52 (1968): 54-64. Rpt. in Conley 203-19.

Madaleva, Sister M. *Pearl: A Study in Spiritual Dryness*. 1925. New York: Phaeton, 1968.
Mahl, Mary R. "The Pearl as the Church." *English Record* 17 (1966): 27-29.
Mahnke, Dietrich. *Eine neue Monadologie*. Berlin: Reuther, 1917.
---. *Unendliche Sphäre und Allmittelpunkt: Beiträge zur Genealogie der mathematischen Mystik*. Deutsche Vierteljahrschrift für Literaturwissenschaft und Geistesgeschichte 23. Tübingen: Niemeyer, 1937.
Mâle, Émile. *L'art religieux du XIIIe siècle en France: Études sur l'iconographie du moyen âge et sur ses sources d'inspiration*. 6th ed. Paris: Colin, 1925.
Margeson, Robert W. "Structure and Meaning in *Sir Gawain and the Green Knight*." *Papers on Language and Literature* 13 (1977): 16-24.
Marsh, John. *The Fulness of Time*. London: Nisbet, 1952.
Maslow, Abraham. *Religions, Values, and Peak Experiences*. New York: Viking, 1971.
---. *Toward a Psychology of Being*. 2nd ed. New York: Van Nostrand, 1963.
Mazzotta, Giuseppe. *Dante, Poet of the Desert*. Princeton: Princeton UP, 1979.
---. *The World at Play in Boccaccio's Decameron*. Princeton: Princeton UP, 1986.
McCarthy, Sister Mary Frances, S. N. D. "Architectonic Symmetry as a Principle of Structure in the *Nibelungenlied*." *Germanic Review* 41 (1966): 157-69.
McGalliard, John C. "Links, Language, and Style in *The Pearl*." *Studies in Language, Literature, and Culture of the Middle Ages and Later: Studies in Honor of Rudolph Willard*. Ed. E. Bagby Atwood and Archibald A. Hill. Austin: U of Texas P, 1969. 279-99.
McLuhan, Marshall, and Harley Parker. *Through the Vanishing Point: Space in Poetry and Painting*. New York: Harper, 1969.
Mendillo, Louise Dunlap. "Word Play in *Pearl*: Figures of Sound and Figures of Sense." Diss. U of California (Berkeley): 1976.
Mersch, Émile, S. J. *Le Christ, l'homme et l'univers. Prolégomènes à la théologie du corps mystique*. Museum Lessianum section théologique 57. Brussels: Desclée, 1962.
---. *The Whole Christ*. Trans. John R. Kelly. London: Dobson, 1949. Trans. of *Le corps mystique du Christ, études de théologie historique*. 2 vols. Louvain: Museum Lessianum, 1933.
---. *Morale et corps mystique*. 4th ed. Museum Lessianum, section théologique 34 and 47. Brussels: Desclée, 1955.
---. *Theology of the Mystical Body*. Trans. C. Follert. St. Louis: Herder, 1951.
Mersmann, E. "Die Bedeutung des Rundfensters im Mittelalter." Diss. U Wien, 1944.

Meyer, Adolf. *Wesen und Geschichte der Theorie vom Mikro- und Makrokosmus*. Berner Studien zur Philosophie und ihrer Geschichte 25. Bern: Sturzenegger, 1900.
Meyer, Herman. "Raumgestaltung und Raumsymbolik in der Erzählkunst." *Studium Generale* 10 (1957): 620-30.
Milroy, James. "*Pearl*: The Verbal Texture and the Linguistic Theme." *Neophilologus* 55 (1971): 195-208.
Mitchell, W. J. T. "Spatial Form in Literature: Towards a General Theory." *Critical Inquiry* 6 (1980): 539-67.
Moessel, Ernst. *Die Proportion in Antike und Mittelalter*. 2 vols. München: Beck, 1926.
---. *Urformen des Raumes als Grundlagen der Formgestaltung*. München: Beck, 1931.
Moon, Douglas M. "Clothing Symbolism in *Sir Gawain and the Green Knight*," *Neuphilologische Mitteilungen* 66 (1965): 334-47.
Moorman, Charles. *The* Pearl-*Poet*. Twayne English Authors Series. New York: Twayne, 1968.
---. "The Role of the Narrator in *Pearl*." *Modern Philology* 53 (1955): 73-81. Rpt. in Conley 103-21.
Moran, Dennis William. "Style and Theology in the Middle English *Pearl*: Patterns of Change and Reconciliation." Diss. U of Notre Dame, 1976.
Morgan, Gerald. "The Significance of the Pentangle Symbolism in *Sir Gawain and the Green Knight*." *Modern Language Review* 74 (1979): 769-90.
Morse, Charlotte C. *The Pattern of Judgment in the* Queste *and* Cleanness. Columbia: U of Missouri P, 1978.
---. "The Image of the Vessel in Cleanness." *University of Toronto Quarterly* 40 (1971): 202-16.
Müller, Werner. *Kreis und Kreuz: Untersuchungen zur sakralen Siedlung bei Italikern und Germanen*. Deutsches Ahnenerbe 2.10. Berlin: Widukind, 1938.
Mura, Ernest. *Le corps mystique du Christ: sa nature et sa vie divine*. Paris: Blot, 1947.
Murtaugh, Daniel M. "*Pearl* 462: 'þe mayster of myste.'" *Neophilologus* 55 (1971): 191-93.
Muscatine, Charles. "The Emergence of Psychological Allegory in Old French Romance." *PMLA* 68 (1953): 1160-82.
Nardi, Bruno. "Il Mito dell' Eden." *Saggi di filosofia dantesca*. Biblioteca pedagogica antica e moderna italiana e straniera. Milano: Società anonima Dante Alighieri, 1930. 347-74.
Nelson, Cary Robert. *The Incarnate Word: Literature as Verbal Space*. Urbana: U of Illinois P, 1973.
Niebuhr, Reinhold. *Faith and History*. New York: Scribner's, 1951.

Niederer, Arnold. "Zur Ethnographie und Soziographie nichtverbaler Dimensionen der Kommunikation." *Zeitschrift für Volkskunde* 71 (1975): 1-20.

Norberg-Schultz, Christian. *Genius Loci: Toward a Phenomenology of Architecture.* New York: Rizzoli, 1980.

Norton-Smith, John. *Geoffrey Chaucer.* London: Routledge, 1974.

Oakden, James P. "The Liturgical Influence in *Pearl*." *Chaucer und seine Zeit: Symposion für Walter F. Schirmer.* Ed. Arno Esch. Tübingen: Niemeyer, 1968. 337-53.

Oettermann, Stephan. *Zeichen auf der Haut: Die Geschichte der Tätowierung in Europa.* Frankfurt: Syndikat, 1979.

Ohly, Friedrich. *Schriften zur mittelalterlichen Bedeutungsforschung.* Darmstadt: Wissenschaftliche, 1977.

Ong, Walter J. "Wit and Mystery: A Revaluation of Medieval Latin Hymnody." *Speculum* 22 (1974): 310-41.

Padolsky, Enoch D. "Steering the Reader's Heart in *Patience*." *University of Ottawa Quarterly* 53 (1983): 169-80.

Panofsky, Erwin. *Gothic Architecture and Scholasticism.* Latrobe, PA: Archabbey, 1951.

Payen, Jean-Charles. "L'espace et le temps dans *Le Roman de la Rose*." *Études de langue et de littérature françaises offertes à André Lanly.* Ed. Charles Brucker, et al. Nancy: U Nancy, 1980. 287-99.

Peck, Russell A. "Number as Cosmic Language." *By Things Seen.* Ed. David L. Jeffrey. Ottawa: U of Ottawa P, 1979.

Peter Damien. *Epistolae.* PL 144.203-498.

Peter Lombard. *Commentaria in Psalmos.* PL 191.61-1296.

Petroff, Elisabeth. "Landscape in *Pearl*: The Transformation of Nature." *Chaucer Review* 16 (1981): 181-93.

---. "Psychological Landscape in Fourteenth-Century Poetry and Painting." Diss. U of California (Berkeley), 1972.

Petrus Cellensis. *Epistolae.* PL 202.405-636.

Petrus Chrysologus. *Sermones.* PL 52.183-680.

Picard, Max. *Die Welt des Schweigens.* Zürich: Reutsch, 1948.

Piehler, Paul. *The Visionary Landscape: A Study in Medieval Allegory.* London: Arnold, 1971.

Pilch, Herbert. "The Middle English *Pearl*: Its Relation to the *Roman de la Rose*." Trans. Heide Hyprath. In Conley 163-84. Trans. of "Das mittelenglische Perlengedicht: Sein Verhältnis zum *Rosenroman*." *Neuphilologische Mitteilungen* 64 (1964) 427-46.

Poirion, Daniel. "Guillaume de Lorris, alchimiste et géomètre." *L'information littéraire: revue paraissant cinq fois par an* 36 (1984): 6-11.

Pollmann, Leo. *Chrétien de Troyes und der Conte du Graal. Beihefte zur Zeitschrift für Romanische Philologie* 110. Tübingen: Niemeyer, 1965.

Poulet, Georges. *Études sur le temps humain.* Edinburgh U Publications, Language and Literature 1. Edinburgh: Edinburgh UP, 1949.
---. *La distance intérieur.* Paris: Plon, 1952.
---. *Les métamorphoses du cercle.* Paris: Plon, 1961.
Powell, C. L. "The Castle of the Body." *Studies in Philology* 16 (1919): 197-205.
Press, John. *The Fire and the Fountain.* London: Oxford UP, 1955.
Ps.-Ambrose. *De sacramentis. PL* 16.417.
Puech, Henri-Charles. "La Gnose et le Temps." *Eranos-Jahrbuch* 20 (1951): 57-113.
Quispel, Gilles. "Zeit und Geschichte im antiken Christentum." *Eranos-Jahrbuch* 20 (1951): 115-40.
Qvarnström, Gunnar. *Dikten och den nya vetenskapen: Det astronautiska motivet.* Acta Reg. Soc. Humaniorum Litterarum Lundensis 60. Lund: Gleerup, 1961.
Rabanus Maurus. *Allegoriae in Scripturam Sanctum. PL* 112.849-1088.
---. *In libros IV Regum. PL* 109.9-280.
Rahner, Hugo. "Flumina de ventre Christi: die patristische Auslegung von Joh. 7, 37.38." *Biblica* 22 (1941): 269-302, 367-403. Rpt. in *Symbole der Kirche* 177-235.
---. *Griechische Mythen in christlicher Deutung.* 3rd ed. Zürich: Rhein, 1966.
---. *Symbole der Kirche: Die Ekklesiologie der Väter.* Salzburg: Müller, 1964.
Randall, Dale. "A Note on Structure in *Sir Gawain and the Green Knight.*" *Modern Language Notes* 72 (1957): 161-63.
Rathofer, Johannes. *Der Heiland: Theologischer Sinn als tektonische Form.* Köln: Böhlau, 1962.
Raw, Barbara. "As Dew in Aprille." *Modern Language Review* 55 (1960): 411-14.
Reichardt, Paul F. "Gawain and the Image of the Wound." *PMLA* 99 (1984): 154-61.
Reiss, Edmund. *The Art of the Middle English Lyric: Essays in Criticism.* Athens: U of Georgia P, 1972.
---. "Number Symbolism and Medieval Literature." *Medievalia et Humanistica* ns 1 (1970): 161-74.
Richard of St. Victor. *De superexcellenti baptismo Christi. PL* 196.1011-18.
Richstätter, Karl. *Das Herz des Welterlösers in seiner dogmatischen, liturgischen, historischen und aszetischen Bedeutung.* Freiburg: Herder, 1932.
---. *Die Herz-Jesu-Verehrung des deutschen Mittelalters.* 2nd ed. Regensburg: Kösel, 1924.
Ritter, A., ed. *Landschaft und Raum in der Erzählkunst.* Darmstadt: Wissenschaftliche, 1975.

Robertson, D. W. "The Doctrine of Charity in Mediaeval Literary Gardens." *Speculum* 26 (1951): 24-49.
---. "The 'Heresy' of *The Pearl*." *Modern Language Notes* 65 (1950): 152-55. Rpt. in Conley 291-96.
---. "The Pearl as a Symbol." *Modern Language Notes* 65 (1950): 155-61. Rpt. in Conley 18-26.
Robinson, F. N., ed. *The Works of Geoffrey Chaucer*. 2nd ed. Boston: Houghton, 1957.
Robinson, J. A. T. *The Body: A Study in Pauline Theology*. Naperville, IL: Allenson, 1957.
Robson, Charles Alan. "The Technique of Symmetrical Composition in Medieval Narrative Poetry." *Studies in Medieval French Presented to Alfred Ewert*. Ed. E. A. Francis. Oxford: Oxford UP, 1961. 26-75.
Roheim, G. *Animism, Magic and the Divine King*. London: Knopf, 1930.
Roscher, W. W. *Neue Omphalosstudien*. Abhandlungen der königlichen Sächsischen Gesellschaft der Wissenschaften, Philologische-historische Klasse 31.1. Leipzig: Teubner, 1915.
Røstvig, Maren Sofie. "Numerical Composition in *Pearl*: A Theory." *English Studies* 48 (1967): 326-32.
Rudolfsky, Bernard. *Architecture without Architects: An Introduction to Non-Pedigreed Architecture*. 5th ed. New York: Museum of Modern Art, 1964.
Rupert of Deutz. *In Genesim*. PL 167.199-566.
---. *In libros Regum*. PL 167.1059-1272.
Rupp, Henry R. "Word-Play in *Pearl*, 277-78." *Modern Language Notes* 70 (1955): 558-59.
Rust, E. C. *The Christian Understanding of History*. London: Lutterworth, 1947.
Ryding, William W. *Structure in Medieval Narrative*. The Hague: Mouton, 1971.
Rykwert, Joseph. *On Adam's House in Paradise: The Idea of the Primitive Hut in Architectural History*. New York: Museum of Modern Art, 1972.
St.-Jacques, Raymond. "Langland's Christ-Knight and the Liturgy." *Revue de l'Université d'Ottawa* 37 (1967): 146-58.
Salomon, Richard. *Opicinus de Canistris: Weltbild und Bekenntnisse eines avignonesischen Klerikers des 14. Jahrhunderts*. Studies of the Warburg Institute 1ab. London: Warburg Institute, 1936.
Salter, Elizabeth. "Medieval Poetry and the Figural View of Reality." *Proceedings of the British Academy* 54 (1970 for 1968): 73-92.
Sanchis, Dominique. "Le symbolisme communautaire du temple chez saint Augustin." *Revue d'ascétique et de mystique* 37 (1961): 3-30, 137-47.
Sappok, Christian. *Die Bedeutung des Raumes für die Struktur des Erzählwerks*. München: Sagner, 1970.

Sauer, Joseph. *Symbolik des Kirchengebäudes und seiner Ausstattung in der Auffassung des Mittelalters.* 2nd ed. 1924. Münster: Mehren, 1964.

Savage, Henry L., ed. *St. Erkenwald: A Middle English Poem.* 1926. Hamden, CT: Archon, 1972.

---. "The Significance of the Hunting Scenes in *Sir Gawain and the Green Knight.*" *Journal of English and Germanic Philology* 27 (1928): 1-15.

Scarry, Elaine. *The Body in Pain: The Making and Unmaking of the World.* New York: Oxford UP, 1985.

---. "The Well-Rounded Sphere: The Metaphysical Structure of *The Consolation of Philosophy.*" *Essays in the Numerical Analysis of Medieval Literature.* Ed. Caroline Eckhardt. Lewisburg, PA: Bucknell UP, 1979.

Scharl, Emmeran. *Recapitulatio Mundi: Rekapitulationsbegriff des heiligen Irenäus und seine Anwendung auf die Körperwelt.* Freiburger Theologische Studien 60. Freiburg: Herder, 1941.

Schleusener, Jay. "*Patience*, Lines 35-40." *Modern Philology* 67 (1969): 64-6.

Schleusener-Eichholz, Gudrun. *Das Auge im Mittelalter.* München: Fink, 1985.

Schmitz, Hermann. *Der Leib, Der Leib im Spiegel der Kunst,* and *Der leibliche Raum.* Vol. 2 and 3 of *System der Philosophie.* 3 vols. Bonn: Bouvier, 1965-67.

Schreiber, Earl G. "The Structures of *Clannesse.*" *The Alliterative Tradition in the Fourteenth Century.* Ed. Bernard S. Levy and Paul E. Szarmach. Kent: Kent State UP, 1981. 131-52.

Schultz, James A. *The Shape of the Round Table: Structures of Middle High German Arthurian Romance.* Toronto: U of Toronto P, 1983.

Schumacher, Fritz, ed. *Lesebuch für Baumeister: Äußerungen über Architektur und Städtebau.* 2nd ed. Berlin: Henseel, 1947.

Schweizer, Harro, ed. *Sprache und Raum: Psychologische und linguistische Aspekte der Aneignung und Verarbeitung von Räumlichkeit; Ein Arbeitsbuch für das Lehren von Forschung.* Stuttgart: Metzler, 1985.

Sedlmayr, Hans. *Die Entstehung der Kathedrale.* 1950. Afterword. Graz: Akademische, 1976.

Seward, Barbara. "Dante's Mystic Rose." *Studies in Philology* 52 (1955): 515-23.

Shoaf, R. A. *The Poem as Green Girdle:* Commercium *in* Sir Gawain and the Green Knight. Gainesville: UP of Florida, 1984.

Sicardus Cremonensis. *Mitrale, sive Summa de officiis.* PL 213.9-436.

Singer, Charles J. "The Scientific Views and Visions of St. Hildegard." *Studies in the History and Method of Science.* Ed. Charles J. Singer. Vol. 1. New York: Arno, 1975. 37ff. 2 vols.

Singleton, Charles. "Campi semantici dei canti XII dell'*Inferno* e XIII del *Purgatorio.*" *Miscellanea di studi danteschi.* Genova: Bozzi, 1966. 11-22.

---. *Commedia: Elements of Structure*. Dante Studies 1. Cambridge: Harvard UP, 1954.
Smitten, Jeffrey R., and Ann Daghistany, eds. *Spatial Form in Narrative*. Cornell UP, 1981.
Sneyders de Vogel, K. "'Le cercle dont le centre est partout et la circonférence nulle part' et le *Roman de la Rose*." *Neophilologus* 16 (1931): 246-49; 17 (1932): 211-12.
Soergel, Gerda. *Untersuchungen über den theoretischen Architekturentwurf von 1450-1550 in Italien*. Diss. U Köln, 1958. München: n.p., 1958.
Soucy, Arnold Francis. "Linear Pattern within the Cyclical Patterns of *Sir Gawain and the Green Knight*." Diss. U of Minnesota, 1972.
Spearing, A. C. *The Gawain-Poet: A Critical Study*. Cambridge: Cambridge UP, 1970.
---. *Medieval Dream Poetry*. Cambridge: Cambridge UP, 1976.
---. "Symbolic and Dramatic Development in *Pearl*." *Modern Philology* 60 (1962): 1-12. Rpt. in Conley 122-48.
Spencer, Sharon. *Space, Time and Structure in the Modern Novel*. New York: New York UP, 1971.
Sperka, E. "*Cor* und *Pectus*: Untersuchungen zum Leib-Seele-Problem bei den Römern." Diss. U Tübingen, 1953.
Spitz, Hans Jörg. *Die Metaphorik des geistigen Schriftsinns: Ein Beitrag zur allegorischen Bibelauslegung des ersten christlichen Jahrtausends*. Münstersche Mittelalter-Schriften 12. München: Fink, 1972.
Spraycar, Rudy S. "Dante's *lago del cor*." *Dante Studies* 96 (1978): 1-19.
Stanbury, Sarah. "Space and Visual Hermeneutics in the *Gawain*-Poet." *The Chaucer Review* 21 (1987): 476-89.
Stern, Milton R. "An Approach to the *Pearl*." *Journal of English and Germanic Philology* 54 (1955): 684-92. Rpt. in Conley 73-85.
Stiller, Nikki. "The Transformation of the Physical in the Middle English *Pearl*." *English Studies* 63 (1982): 402-09.
Strachan, L. R. M. "The Five Wounds." *Notes and Queries* 171 (1936): 266.
Ströker, Elisabeth. *Philosophische Untersuchungen zum Raum*. Frankfurt: Klostermann, 1977.
Taylor, Jerome and A. H. Nelson. *Medieval English Drama: Essays Critical and Contextual*. Chicago: U of Chicago P, 1972.
Tertullian. *Adversus Praxeam*. PL 2.153-96.
---. *De carnis resurrectio*. PL 2.791-886.
Theodoret. *De providentia*. PG 83.355-774.
Thomas Aquinas. *Opera omnia*. Ed. S. E. Fretté and P. Maré. 34 vols. Paris: Vivès, 1874-89.
Tillich, Paul. *The Interpretation of History*. New York: Scribner's, 1936.
Tinkle, Theresa. "The Heart's Eye: Beatific Vision in *Purity*." *Studies in Philology* 85 (1988): 451-70.

Tristman, Richard. "Some Consolatory Strategies in *Pearl.*" *The Middle English Pearl: Critical Essays.* Ed. John Conley. Notre Dame: U of Notre Dame P, 1970. 272-87.

Tromp, Sebastian. *Corpus Christi quod est Ecclesia.* 4 vols. Roma: U Gregoriana, 1946-60. Vol. 1: *Introductio generalis.* Trans. by A. Condit as *The Body of Christ Which Is the Church.* New York: Vantage, 1960. Vol. 2: *De Christo capite mystici corporis.* Vol. 3: *De spiritu Christi anima.* Vol. 4: *De virgine deipara Maria corde Mystici.*

Trower, Katherine Bache. "Temporal Tensions in the *Visio* of *Piers Plowman.*" *Mediaeval Studies* 35 (1973): 389-412.

Tzonis, Alexander and Liane Lefairre. "The Mechanical vs. the Divine Body." *Journal of Architectural Education* 29 (1975): 4-7.

Van Baak, J. J. *The Place of Space in Narration: A Semiotic Approach to the Problem of Literary Space.* Studies in Slavic Literature and Poetics 3. Amsterdam: Rodopi, 1983.

Van der Leeuw, Gerardus. *"In dem Himmel ist ein Tanz": Über die religiöse Bedeutung des Tanzes und des Festunges.* Trans. Clercq van Weel. Der Tempel des Leibes 1. München: Dornverlag, 1931.

Vantuono, William. "The Structure and Sources of *Patience.*" *Mediaeval Studies* 34 (1972): 401-21.

---. "A Triple-Three Structure for *Cleanness.*" *Manuscripta* 28 (1984): 26-32.

Vasta, Edward. "*Pearl*: Immortal Flowers and the Pearl's Decay." *Journal of English and Germanic Philology* 66 (1967): 519-31. Rpt. in Conley 185-202.

---, ed. *Middle English Survey: Critical Essays.* Notre Dame: Notre Dame UP, 1965.

Velte, Maria. *Die Anwendung der Quadratur und Triangulatur bei der Grund- und Aufrißgestaltung der gotischen Kirchen.* Basler Studien zur Kunstgeschichte 8. Basel: Birkhäuser, 1951.

Vinaver, Eugène. *The Rise of Romance.* New York: Oxford UP, 1971.

Vloberg, Maurice. *L'Eucharistie dans l'art.* Grenoble: Arthaud, 1946.

Von Ertzdorff, Xenja. "Die Dame im Herzen und das Herz bei der Dame. Zur Verwendung des Begriffs Herz in der höfischen Liebeslyrik des 11. und 12. Jahrhunderts." *Zeitschrift für deutsche Philologie* 84 (1967): 6-46.

---. "Das Herz in der lateinisch-theologischen und frühen volkssprachigen religiösen Literatur." *Beiträge zur Geschichte der deutschen Sprache und Literatur* 84 (1962): 249-301.

Von Simson, Otto. *The Gothic Cathedral: Origins of Gothic Architecture and the Medieval Concept of Order.* Bollingen Series 48. New York: Pantheon, 1956.

Wasserman, Julian N. "The Edifice Complex: The Metaphor of the City in *Purity* and *Patience.*" Diss. Rice U, 1975.

Watts, Alan W. *The Book: On the Taboo Against Knowing Who You Are.* New York: Collier, 1967.
Watts, V. E. "*Pearl* as a *Consolatio.*" *Medium aevum* 32 (1963): 34-36.
Wellek, René. "*The Pearl*: An Interpretation." *Prague Studies in English* 4 (1933): 1-33. Rpt. in Blanch 86-97.
---, and Austin Warren. *Theory of Literature.* 3rd ed. New York: Harcourt, 1962.
Welzel, Bern. *Herz Jesu und Eucharistie.* München: Ars Sacra, 1952.
Wetherbee, Winthrop. "The Descent from Bliss: *Troilus* III. 1310-1582." *Chaucer's "Troilus": Essays in Criticism.* Ed. Stephen A. Barney. London: Scolar, 1980. 297-317.
White, Hayden. *Metahistory: The Historical Imagination in Nineteenth-Century Europe.* Baltimore: Johns Hopkins UP, 1973.
---. *Tropics of Discourse: Essays in Cultural Criticism.* Baltimore: Johns Hopkins UP, 1978.
Williams, David. "The Point of *Patience.*" *Modern Philology* 68 (1970): 127-36.
Wilson, Edward. *The Gawain Poet.* Medieval and Renaissance Authors Series. Leiden: Brill, 1976.
---. "Word Play and the Interpretation of *Pearl.*" *Medium aevum* 40 (1971): 116-34.
Wimsatt, James I. *Allegory and Mirror: Tradition and Structure in Middle English Literature.* New York: Pegasus, 1970.
Wittig, Susan. *Stylistic and Narrative Structures in Middle English Romances.* Austin: U of Texas P, 1978.
Wittkower, Rudolf. *Architectural Principles in the Age of Humanism.* Columbia University Studies in Art History and Archaeology 1. New York: Random, 1965.
Wood, Ann Douglas. "The *Pearl*-Dreamer and the *Hyne* in the Vineyard Parable." *Philological Quarterly* 52 (1973): 9-19.
Zadavil, Joseph B. "A Study of Meaning in *Patience* and *Cleanness.*" Diss. Stanford U, 1962.
Zaddy, Zara P. "Chrétien de Troyes and the Localisation of the Heart." *Romance Philology* 12 (1958/59): 257-58.

INDEX

Ackerman, Robert 88
Alanus de Insulis 11, 54
Albertus Magnus 9, 19, 123, 134, 135
Alcuin 64, 80n.9, 139
Allen, Judson 55
Allers, Rudolf 8-10, 22n.27
Altar 33-35
   equated with heart 146
   equated with navel 149
   symbolic compactness 17
   triptychs 67
   two main altars 42
Altar vessels 6, 28, 43-45, 74
   and *Pearl* 104
Ambrose 113, 134, 139
Anderson, J. J. 95, 174
Andrew, Malcolm 173
Anselm 140
Apse, in Gothic design 42
   and corona 107
Aquinas, Thomas 8, 11, 19, 147
Aristotle 10
Arnheim, Rudolf 62n.28
Auerbach, Erich 13, 58-59
Augustine 9, 12, 16, 19, 58, 78, 87, 111, 119, 137, 138, 140, 146, 147

Bachelard, Gaston 2, 55, 105-06, 116, 128nn.70-71, 174
Bainvel, Jean V. 140
Baltrusaitis, J. 39
Barney, Stephen 73

Bauer, Gerhard 141
Baybak, Michael 77
Bea, Augustinus 150n.1
Beer, Ellen 36-37, 48n.57
Beowulf 67
Bernardus Silvestris 8
"Bird with Four Feathers, The" 67-68
Billyng, William 151n.23
Bishop, Ian 39, 103-04, 106, 118, 128n.64
Bloomer, Kent 2
Bloomfield, Morton 165
Body politic 6, 8-9
   in *Sir Gawain and the Green Knight* 166
Boethius 11, 75-76, 94
Bonaventure 11, 93-94, 180n.7
Book of Nature 10, 52, 54
Borroff, Marie 88, 97n.8, 98n.16
Boss, in Gothic design 41
Braun, Joseph 33, 45
Bronfen, Elisabeth 62n.43
Brown, Norman O. 122
Brun von Schoenbeck 135-36
Burrow, John 111, 160

Caelius Sedulius 141
Cassiodorus 141
Chain 6
   and Gothic bosses 41
   and Gothic labyrinths 39
   and the heart 141
   in *Troilus* 75

in *Sir Gawain and the Green Knight* 160
Chalcidius 8, 11
Chartres Cathedral 38, 112
Chaucer, Geoffrey 8, 55, 70-75, 134, 141, 163, 164
Ciborium 43
Cicero, Marcus Tullius 145
Clark, S. L. 158, 172, 177
Cleanness 157-58
Clement of Alexandria 130n.98
Conger, G. P. 8, 10, 112
Corona 38-39, 41, 103, 106-08
Corpus Christi cycles 68-70
Cowen, Painton 35
Crane, John K. 152n.36
Cullmann, Oscar 88-89, 168n.27
Curtius, Ernst Robert 53
Cyprian 141, 155n.103

Dante 9, 12, 67, 76, 90, 94, 117-18, 142, 159, 176
De Bruyne, Edgar 19, 148, 159
De Lubac, Henri 52, 56
Delany, Paul 77
Di Giorgio, Francesco 31
Dolan, Gilbert 142
Durandus 103, 111, 146
Durling, Robert 76, 94

Eldredge, Laurence 171, 172
Eliade, Mircea 1, 13, 16, 20n.3, 22n.24, 33, 34
Eucharist
    and Gothic form 28
    and iconography 89
    and *plenitudo temporis* 89
    as symbolic *summa* 17
    equated with heart 134
    equated with pearl 90, 134
    equated with penny 88-89, 135
    in *Pearl* 84
Eucherius of Lyon 52

Façade 35-36, 118, 181n.11
Fichtner, Edward 66
Filograssi, Josephus 138
Finkelstein, Dorothee 135
Fowler, Alastair 78-79
Frank, Joseph 2
Freckmann, K. 32
Freud, Sigmund 1, 2, 57, 149
Friedman, John B. 99n.48, 172, 173, 175
Frye, Northrop 13, 15, 19, 53, 58, 112, 121, 123, 162

Gadamer, Hans-Georg 57
Garrett, Robert 84
Gatta, John 87, 88
Geoffrey of St. Victor 8
Geoffrey of Vinsauf 54, 148
Gilligan, Janet 22n.27, 180n.1
Gilson, Étienne 96
Gordon, E. V. 93, 148
Gray, D. 142
Green mound 129n.86
Gregory the Great 52, 87, 134, 140, 146, 172

Hall, Edward T. 5, 17, 26n.113, 54
Hart, Thomas Elwood 67
Haubrichs, Wolfgang 64, 65, 87, 91, 105, 113, 124, 146, 150, 161, 162, 164
Heart
    and central breast pearl 131, 141, 144
    and doctrine of plenitude 135, 136, 161
    and pentangle 160

and recapitulation 138
as monad 138
as stomach 181
as *summa* 132, 138
Christ's birth from 135, 137, 139, 147
equated with altar 35, 135
equated with garden 18, 135
equated with pearl 133-34
in Chaucer 70-75
in hell 76, 173, 180n.7
in *Patience* 171-82
nuptial chamber of 144-45
of Mary 136, 144
site of birthgiving 18, 64-65
Heraclitus 9
Hieatt, A. Kent 67, 77
Hieatt, Constance 67
Hilary 139
Hildebert of Lavardin 53, 147
Hildegard of Bingen 10, 12, 18, 25n.80, 44
Hillmann, Sister Mary Vincent 92, 95, 148
Holböck, Ferdinand 111
Honorius Augustodunensis 111, 128n.58
Hopkins, Gerard Manley 16
Howard, Donald 162
Hrabanus Maurus 52
Hugh of St. Victor 8, 12, 132
Huisman, J. A. 66
Husserl, Edmund 1

Idiart, P. 19, 46n.10
Innocent III 87
Irenaeus 59
Isidore of Seville 8, 103, 162

Jeffrey, David L. 7, 13, 59
Jerome 52, 139, 172

Johannes Scotus 8
John Chrysostomus 140
John of Hanville 53
John of Salisbury 8
Johnson, Lynn Staley 123, 135
Jordan, Robert 73
Joseph Ibn Zaddik 8
Jung, C. G. 1, 60
Jung, Emma 105, 140, 151n.12
Justinian 53, 149

Kamper, Dietmar 1, 7, 20n.6
Kanters, Ch. G. 133, 141
Kantorowicz, Ernst H. 107-08, 115
Kaske, Carol 129n.83
Kaske, R. E. 61n.8, 99n.52, 168n.23
Kean, P. M. 92, 118
Kermode, Frank 58
Kolve, V. A. 69

Labyrinth 37-38
Ladner, Gerhart B. 7
Langland, William 87, 111, 138
Lass, Roger 159, 161
Leeming, Bernard 138
Lesser, George 28, 32
Lewis, C. S. 110
Leyerle, John 70, 158, 160
Liber XXIV Philosophorum 17, 94
Logos Child 139, 143
Lorenz, S. 97n.10
Lotman, Jurij 54
Löwith, Karl 53

Macrobius 8, 78
Madaleva, Sister Mary 101
Mahnke, Dietrich 17, 23n.51, 36
Maimonides 152n.53
Mandorla 39

Margeson, Robert 165
Marsilius of Padua 8
Marx, Karl 1
Mazzotta, Giuseppe 150n.1
McCarthy, Mary F. 65
McLuhan, Marshall 7, 16, 125n.18
Mechthild von Magdeburg, St. 135-36
Meister Eckhart 11, 134
Mendillo, Louise 87-88
Mersch, Émile 7, 9, 14, 22n.22, 56
Meyer, Adolf 8, 10, 22n.27
Mitchell, W. J. T. 51
Moessel, Ernst 30, 34, 41, 161
Monstrance 43, 45
    relation to rose window 35-36
Moore, Charles 2
Morse, Charlotte 157-58
Mount Sinai 12
Mount Zion 12, 119, 149
Mystical body 6-7, 13-14
    and symbolism of ring 107-08
    children in 103
    in *Pearl*'s Vineyard 90, 92

Navel
    as bodily center 19
    as Jerusalem 122
    equated with altar 149
    in *Patience* 174-75
    in *Pearl* 147-49
    of dream 57, 102, 149
    of texts 149
Nelson, Cary 84, 88, 104
New song 130n.98
Nibelungenlied 65-66, 92
Nicolas of Cusa 8, 9, 11

Ohly, Friedrich 29, 32, 105
Origen 19, 52, 111, 113, 133, 141

Otfrid von Weißenburg 64-65, 112-13, 124, 159, 161-62
Ovid 142

Padolsky, Enoch 172
Panofsky, Erwin 66
Paré, Gerard 19, 123
Parzival 169n.41
Peck, Russell A. 69-70, 136-37
Peter Damian 142
Peter Lombard 139
Peter the Venerable 53
Petroff, Elizabeth 87, 117-121
Petrus Cellensis 134
Phenomenology 2
Philo of Alexandria 9
Piehler, Paul 101, 118, 120
Pier, in Gothic design 39
Plato 8, 9, 10, 32, 78
Plenitude 5, 12-14
    and Gothic form 29
    in *Patience* 178
Plenitudo temporis 17-19, 29-30, 65, 69-70, 76, 87-88, 91, 94, 105, 107, 136-37
Pliny 145
Point, geometry of
    in *Patience* 171-72
    in *Pearl* 94-96, 102
Poulet, Georges 94
Prudentius 53
Ps.-Ambrosius 34
Ps.-Aristotle 123
Ps.-Rabanus Maurus 10
Ps.-Chrysostom 106

Rabanus Maurus 90, 146
Rahner, Hugo 6, 133, 137
Randall, Dale 164
Recapitulation 5, 13-14, 54, 59, 65, 78

Index

and conversion 103
and Gothic apse 40-41
in *erber grene* 118
in heart and womb 18-19, 138
in *Patience* 174, 179, 180n.11
in *Pearl*'s Vineyard 102
Richstätter, Karl 133, 140
Rolle, Richard 53
Roman de la Rose 94, 141
Rose 6, 133
Rose window 83, 169n.41
    relation to eucharist 35-36
    relation to heart 74
    relation to labyrinths 38
Rupert of Deutz 111
Rupp, Henry 125n.6

Sacramental symbolism 84
Salter, Elizabeth 13
Sanchis, Dominique 104
Sauer, Joseph 6, 28, 34, 35, 46n.9
Savage, Henry L. 163
Scarry, Elaine 1, 34, 54, 75-76, 90
Scharl, Emmeran 14, 54, 103
Sedlmayr, Hans 41-42, 55, 66, 106, 112
Settings for pearl
    clothing 109-14
    coffer 114-16
    crown 106-08
    landscapes 117-23
    ring 108-09
    shell 105-06
Shoaf, R. A. 165
Singleton, Charles 76
Spearing, A. C. 85, 99n.52, 177
Speculative grammar 52, 54
Spenser, Edmund 77-79, 118
Spitz, Hans Jörg 52, 55, 128n.59
Spraycar, Rudy 76
St.-Jacques, Raymond 111
Suger of Denis 112

Synecdoche 56-57
    and the heart 140
    in *Pearl*'s Vineyard 92

Taylor, Jerome 69
Tertullian 138

Upside-down structure
    in *Book of the Duchess* 72
    in Dante 90, 181n.16
    in *Patience* 176
    in *Pearl*'s Vineyard 90

Vantuono, William 178
Venantius Fortunatus 136
Vessel, theology of 104-05, 157
Vincent of Beauvais 55
Virgil 142
Von Ertzdorff, Xenja 142, 154n.95
Von Simson, Otto 30, 31

Walther von der Vogelweide 66, 146
Wasserman, J. N. 158, 172, 177
Watts, Alan 1
Wetherbee, W. 73
Wheel of Fortune 6
    and the heart 141
    in Boethius 76
    relation to rose windows 36, 169n.41
White, Hayden 56, 140
Wilson, Edward 135
Wittkower, Rudolf 47n.21
Womb
    and doctrine of plenitude 136
    and nuptial chamber of the heart 145
    as bodily center 18

    of hell 18, 174
    of Mary 11, 104
Wounds 16
    and birth of church 132
    and manuscript rubrication 53
    and pentangle 161
    in iconography 142-43
    inside out structure of 103

STUDIES IN MEDIAEVAL LITERATURE

1. J. Elizabeth Jeffrey, **Blickling Spirituality and the Old English Vernacular Homily**
2. Ronald Pepin, **Literature of Satire in the Twelfth Century:** *A Neglected Mediaeval Genre*
3. Aileen Ann Macdonald, **The Figure of Merlin in Thirteenth-Century French Romance**
4. Jillian M. Hill, **Medieval Debate on Jean De Meung's** *Roman de la Rose*
5. Ronald G. Koss, **Family, Lineage and Kinship in the** *Cycle de Guillaume d'Orange*
6. George Bond, **The** *Pearl* **Poem: An Introduction and Interpretation**
7. Richard of St. Victor, **Richard Of St. Victor's** *Treatise Of The Study Of Wisdom That Men Call Benjamin*: **As Adapted In Middle English By The Author of** *The Cloud Of Unknowing* **Together with** *Treatise on Discretion of Spirits* **and** *Epistle on Discretion of Stirrings*, Dick Barnes (trans.)
8. Sandra McEntire, **The Doctrine of Compunction in Medieval England:** *Holy Tears*
9. Dennis P. Donahue, **Lawman's** *Brut*, **An Early Arthurian Poem: A Study in Middle English Formulaic Composition.**
10. Neil Thomas, **Tristan in the Underworld: A Study of Gottfried von Strassburg's** *Tristan* **together with the** *Tristran* **of Thomas**
11. R. E. Stratton, **A Critical Edition of** *Cheuelere Assigne*: **Text, Glossary, and Critical Analyses.**
12. Kevin Marti, **Body, Heart, and Text in the** *Pearl*-**Poet**